story CHUCK AUSTEN
art RON GARNEY & MARK MORALES
SEAN PHILLIPS

colors HI-FI DESIGN
letters RICHARD STARKINGS &
COMICRAFT'S SAIDA & JIMMY
cover TONY HARRIS & RAY SNYDER
issue covers RON GARNEY & STEVE UY
assistant editors MIKE RAICHT & NOVA REN SUMA
editor MIKE MARTS

editor in chief JOE QUESADA
president BILL JEMAS

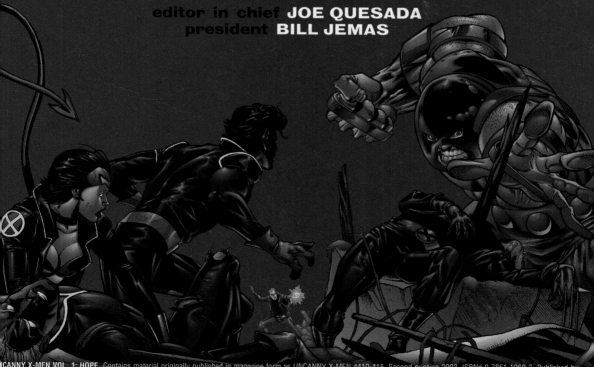

NCANNY X-MEN VOL. 1: HOPE. Contains material originally published in magazine form as UNCANNY X-MEN #410-415. Second printing 2003. ISBN# 0-7851-1060-7. Published by
ARVEL COMICS, a division of MARVEL ENTERTAINMENT GROUP, INC. OFFICE OF PUBLICATION: 10 East 40th Street, New York, NY 10016. Copyright © 2002 and 2003 Marvel
aracters, Inc. All rights reserved. $12.99 per copy in the U.S. and $21.00 in Canada (GST #R127032852); Canadian Agreement #40668537. All characters featured in this issue and the
tinctive names and likenesses thereof, and all related indicia are trademarks of Marvel Characters, Inc. No similarity between any of the names, characters, persons, and/or institutions
his magazine with those of any living or dead person or institution is intended, and any such similarity which may exist is purely coincidental. **Printed in Canada.** STAN LEE, Chairman
eritus. For information regarding advertising in Marvel Comics or on Marvel.com, please contact Russell Brown, Executive Vice President, Consumer Products, Promotions and Media
es at 212-576-8561 or rbrown@marvel.com

9 8 7 6 5 4 3 2

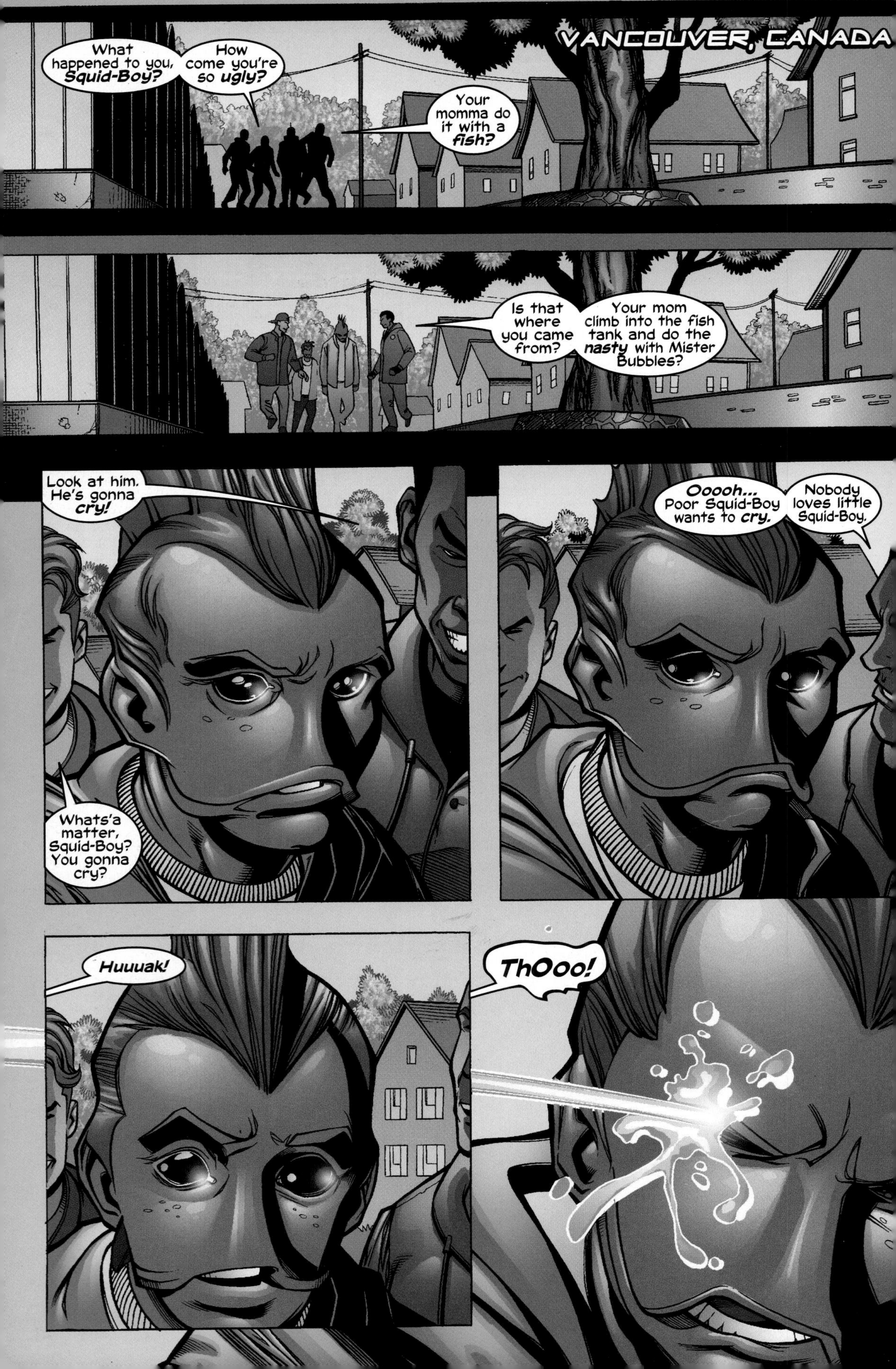

VANCOUVER, CANADA
What happened to you, Squid-Boy?
How come you're so ugly?
Your momma do it with a fish?
Is that where you came from?
Your mom climb into the fish tank and do the nasty with Mister Bubbles?
Look at him. He's gonna cry!
Whats'a matter, Squid-Boy? You gonna cry?
Ooooh... Poor Squid-Boy wants to cry.
Nobody loves little Squid-Boy.
Huuuak!
ThOoo!

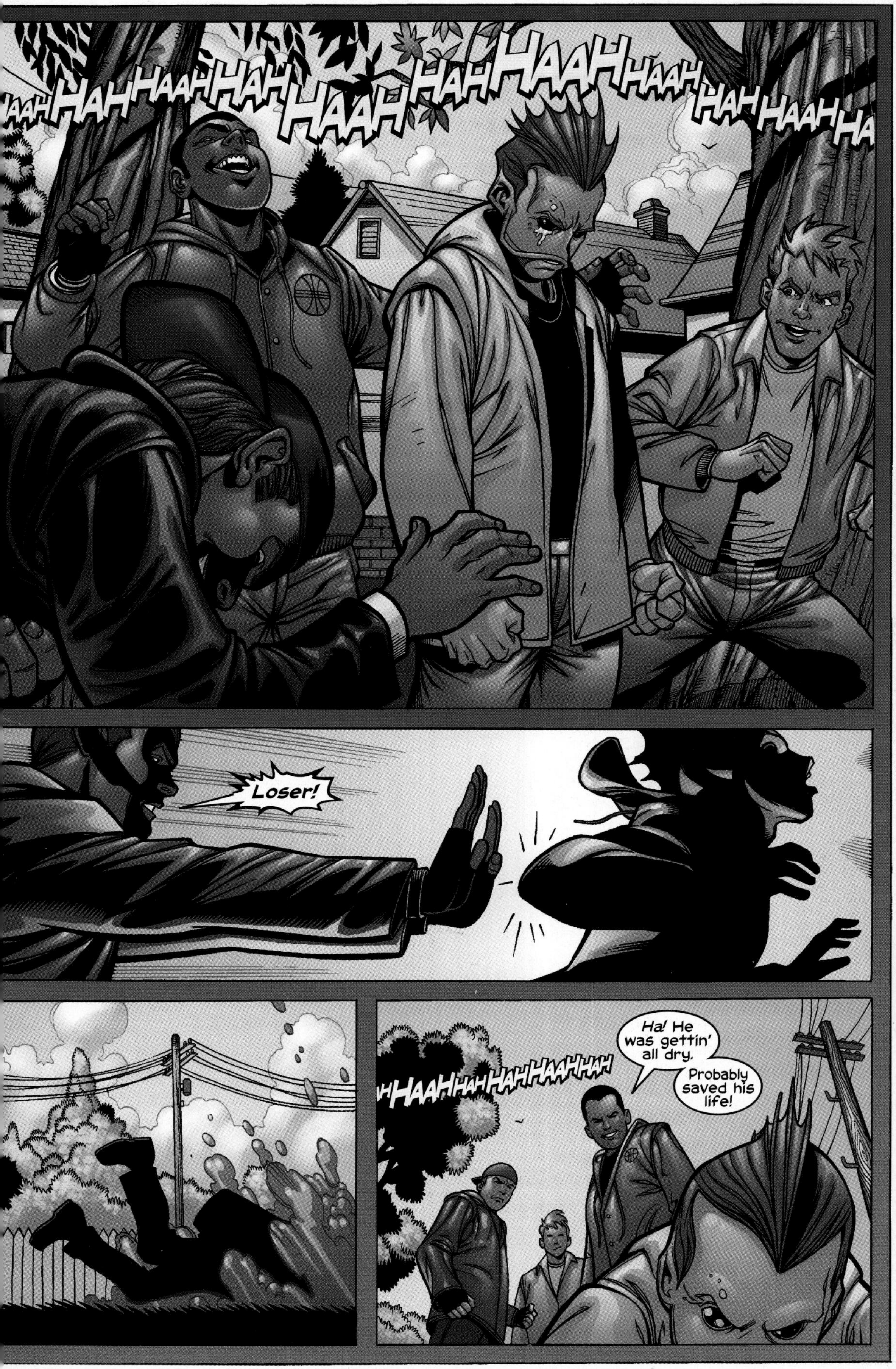
HAAH HAH HAAH HAH HAAH HAH HAAH HAAH HAH HAAH HA
Loser!
HAAH HAH HAH HAAH HAH
Ha! He was gettin' all dry.
Probably saved his life!

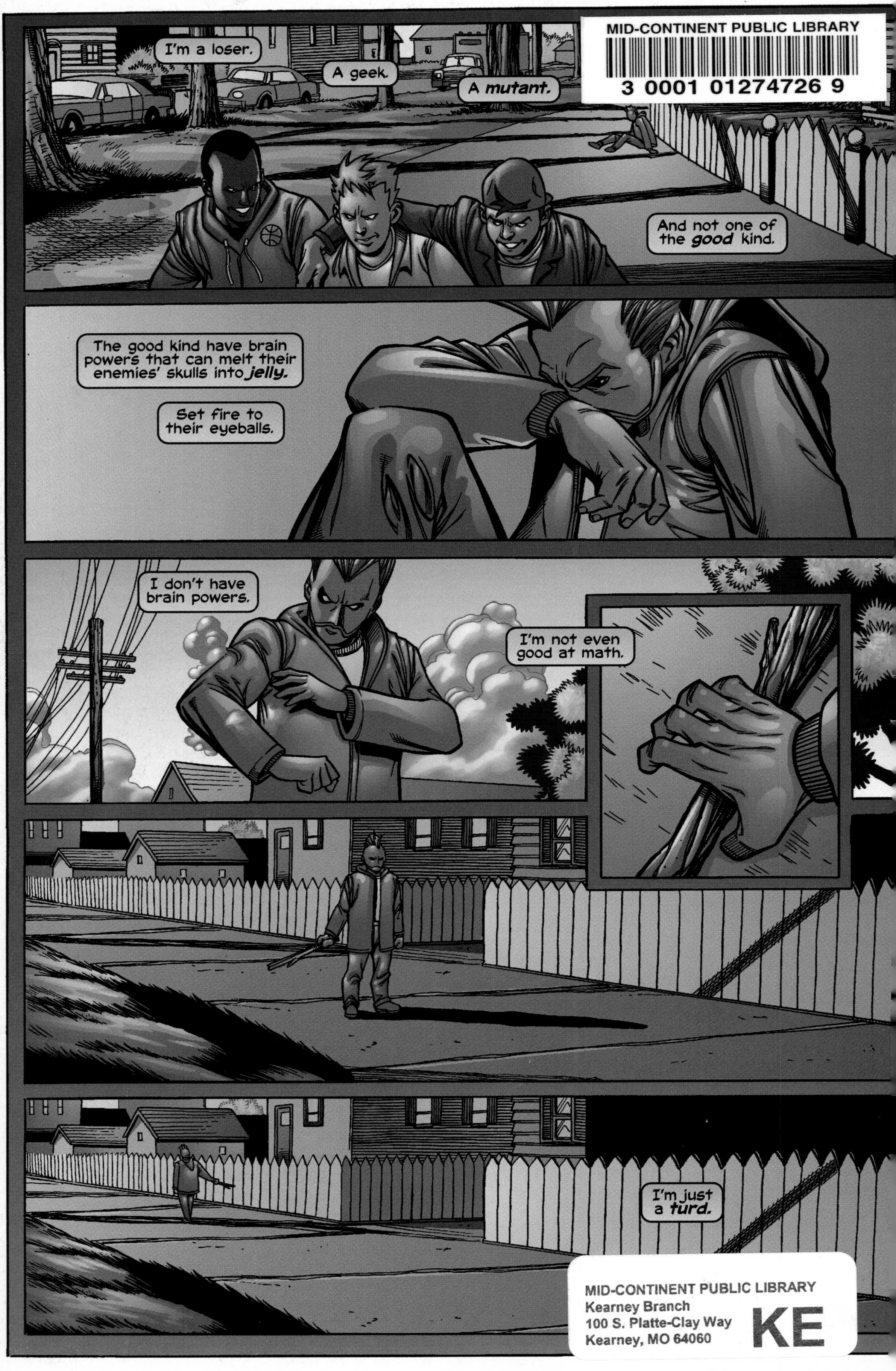

I'm a loser.
A geek.
A *mutant.*
And not one of the *good* kind.
The good kind have brain powers that can melt their enemies' skulls into *jelly.*
Set fire to their eyeballs.
I don't have brain powers.
I'm not even good at math.
I'm just a *turd.*

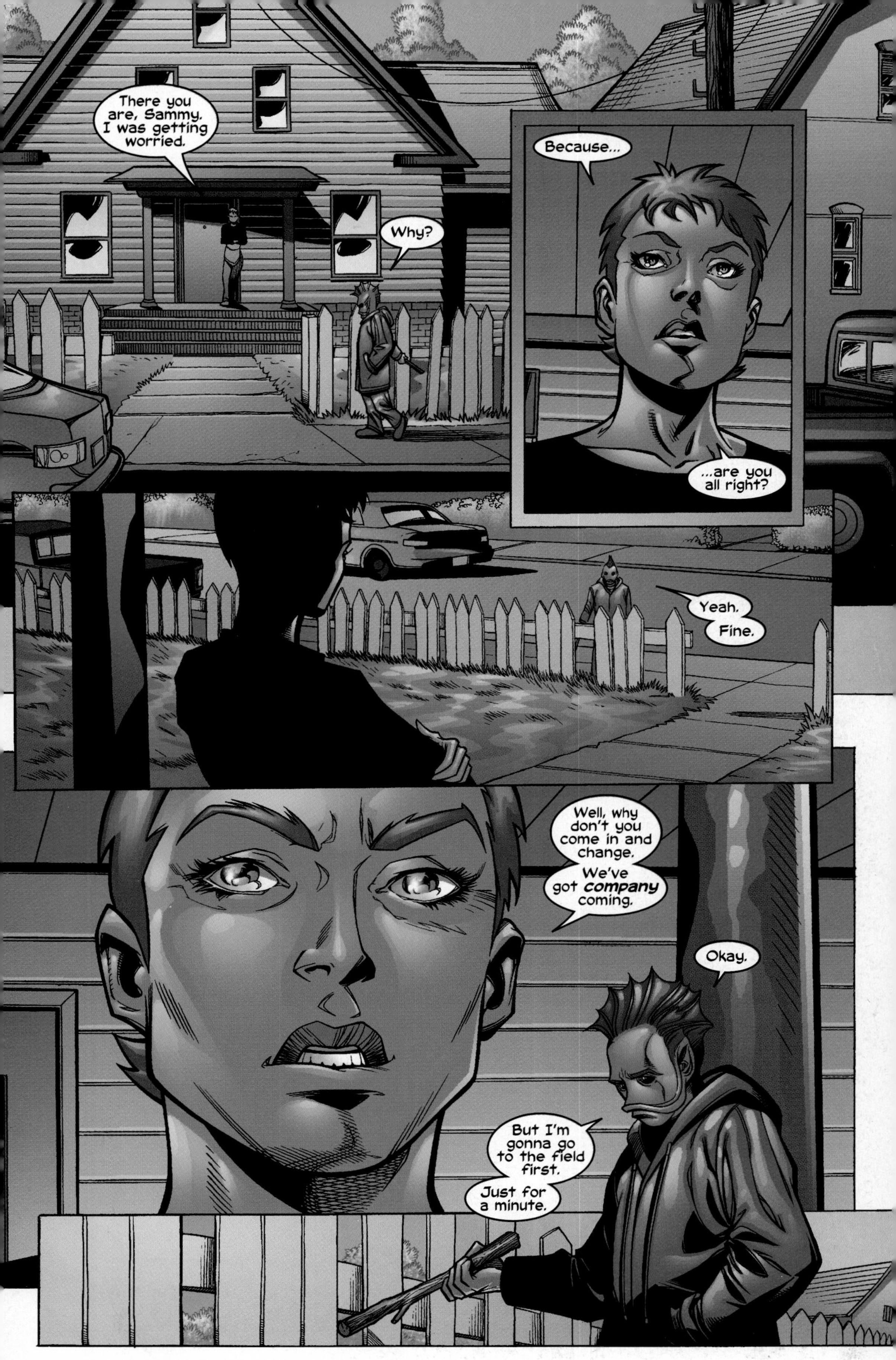
There you are, Sammy. I was getting worried.
Why?
Because...
...are you all right?
Yeah.
Fine.
Well, why don't you come in and change.
We've got *company* coming.
Okay.
But I'm gonna go to the field first.
Just for a minute.

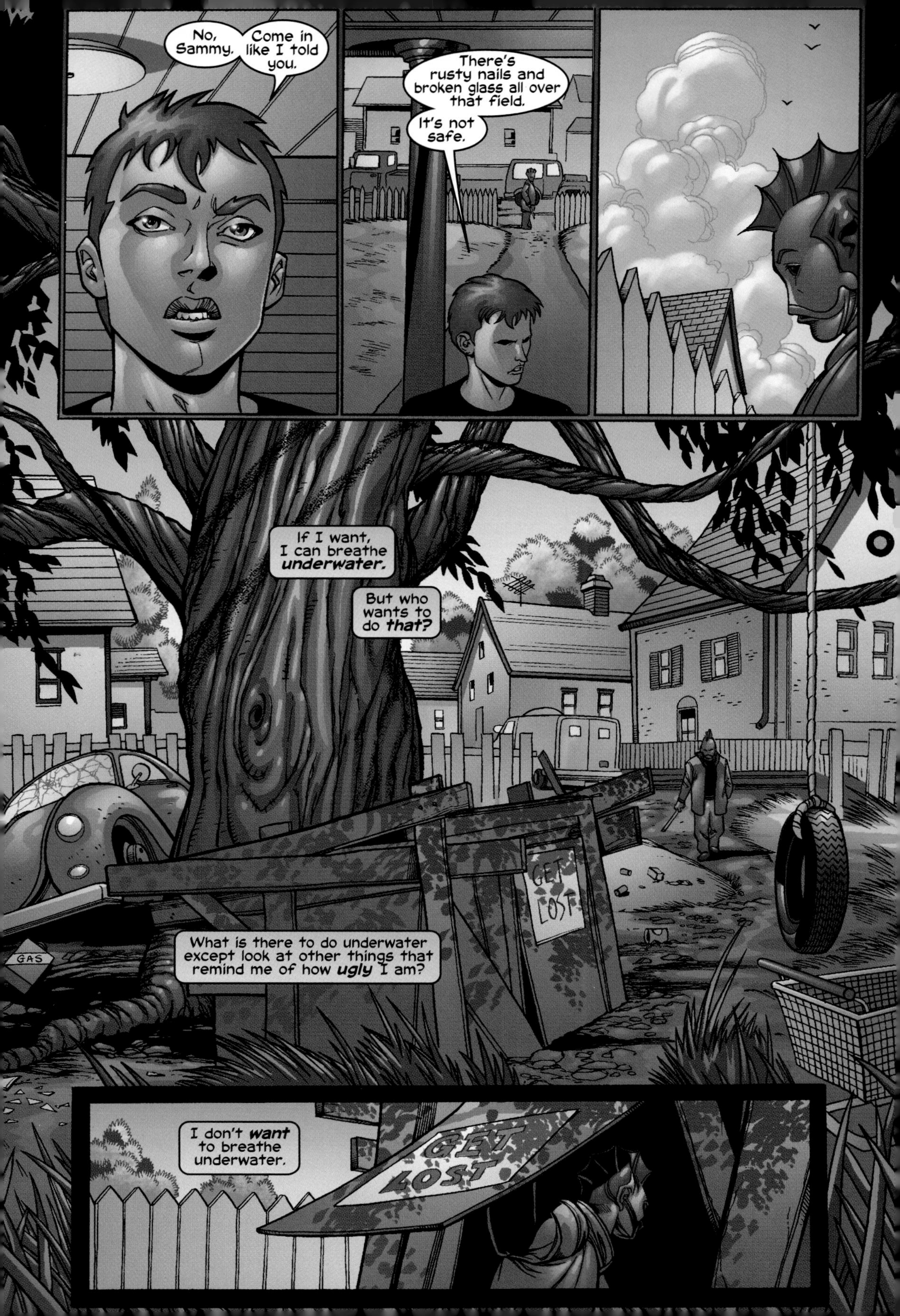

No, Sammy.
Come in like I told you.
There's rusty nails and broken glass all over that field.
It's not safe.
If I want, I can breathe underwater.
But who wants to do that?
GET LOST
GAS
What is there to do underwater except look at other things that remind me of how ugly I am?
I don't want to breathe underwater.
GET LOST

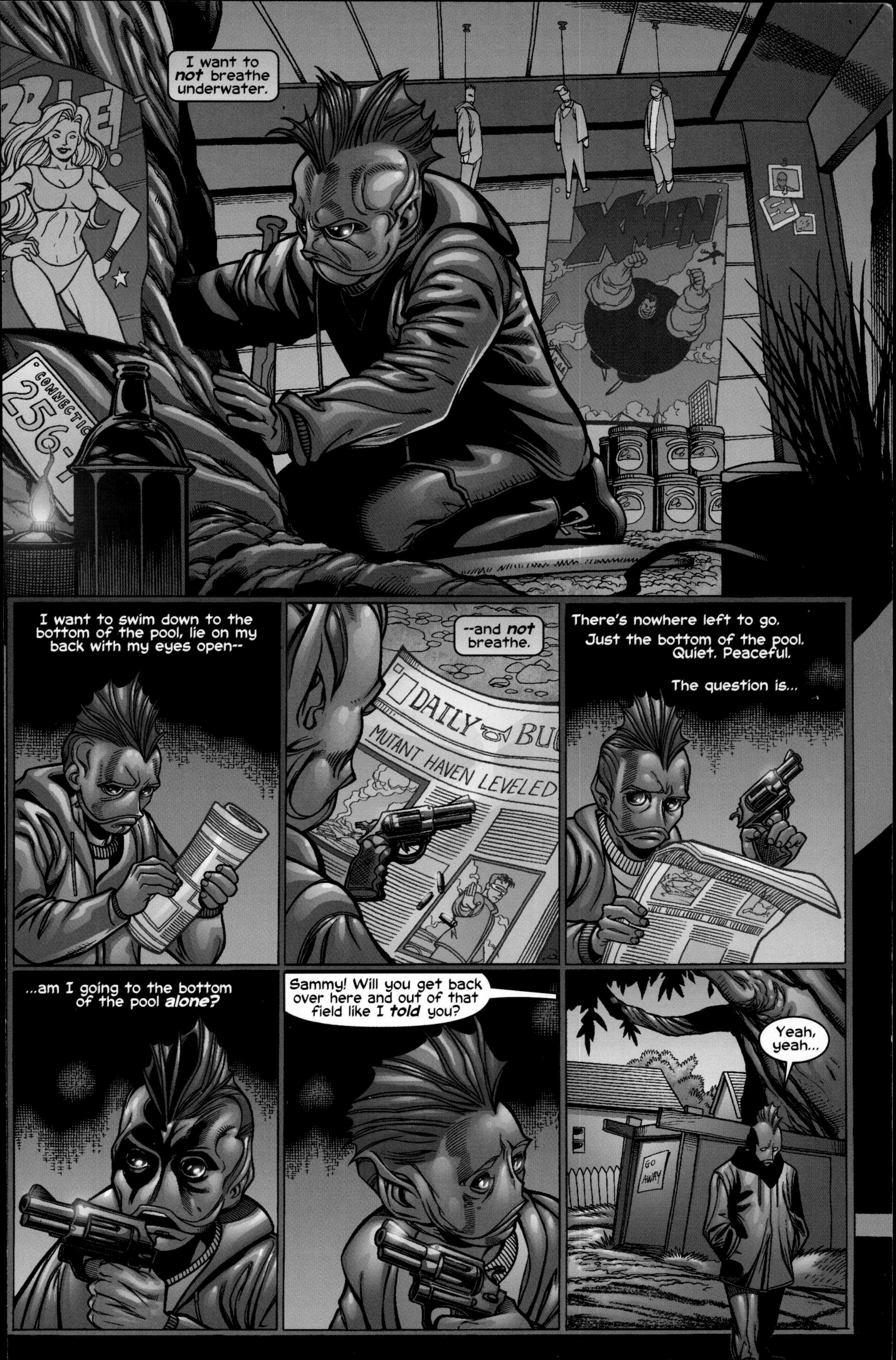
I want to *not* breathe underwater.
CONNECTICUT
256-
X-MEN
I want to swim down to the bottom of the pool, lie on my back with my eyes open--
--and *not* breathe.
DAILY BU
MUTANT HAVEN LEVELED
There's nowhere left to go.
Just the bottom of the pool.
Quiet. Peaceful.
The question is...
...am I going to the bottom of the pool *alone?*
Sammy! Will you get back over here and out of that field like I *told* you?
Yeah, yeah...
GO AWAY

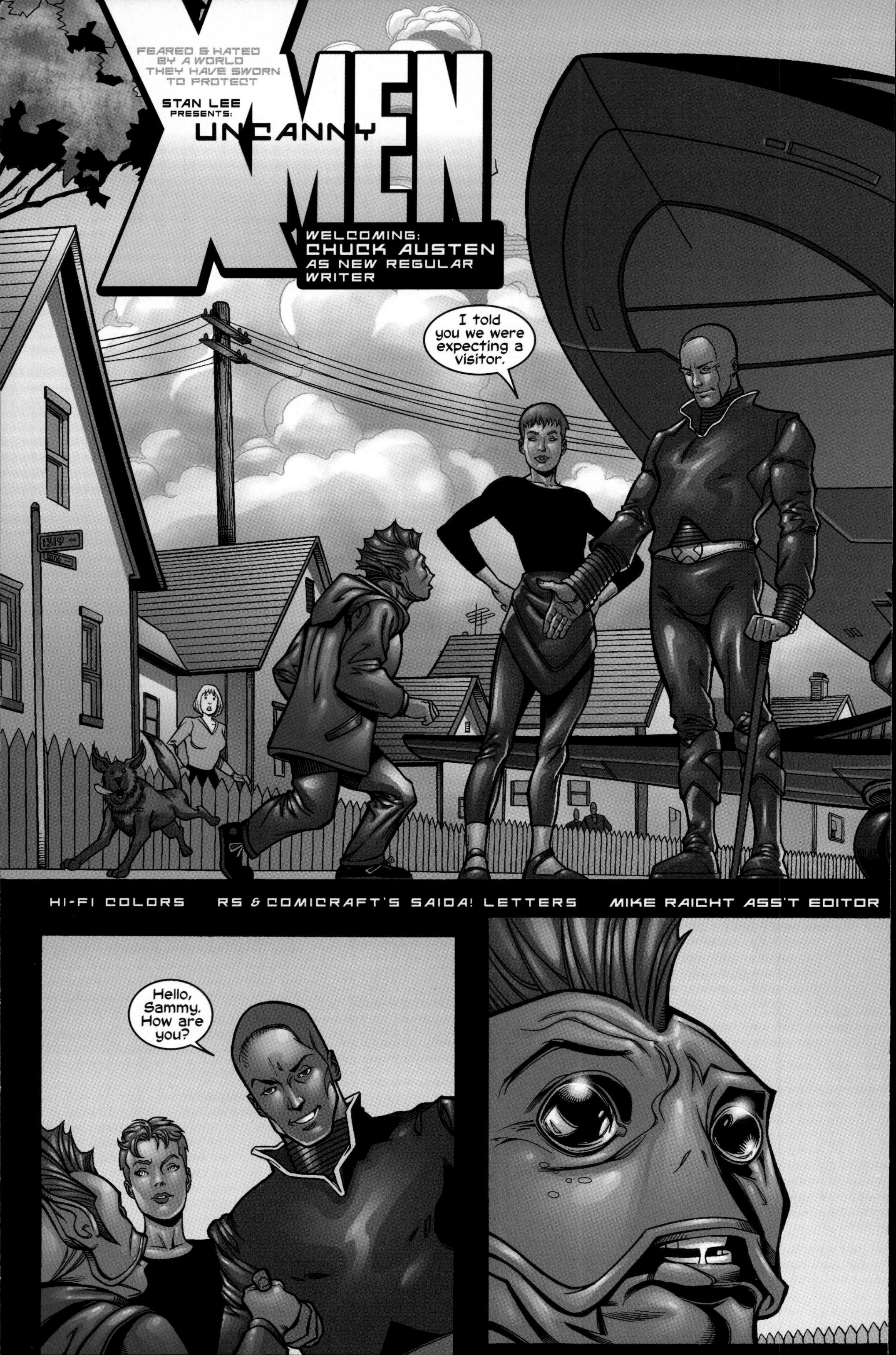
FEARED & HATED BY A WORLD THEY HAVE SWORN TO PROTECT
STAN LEE PRESENTS:
UNCANNY X-MEN
WELCOMING: CHUCK AUSTEN AS NEW REGULAR WRITER
I told you we were expecting a visitor.
1319
HI-FI COLORS
RS & COMICRAFT'S SAIDA! LETTERS
MIKE RAICHT ASS'T EDITOR
Hello, Sammy. How are you?

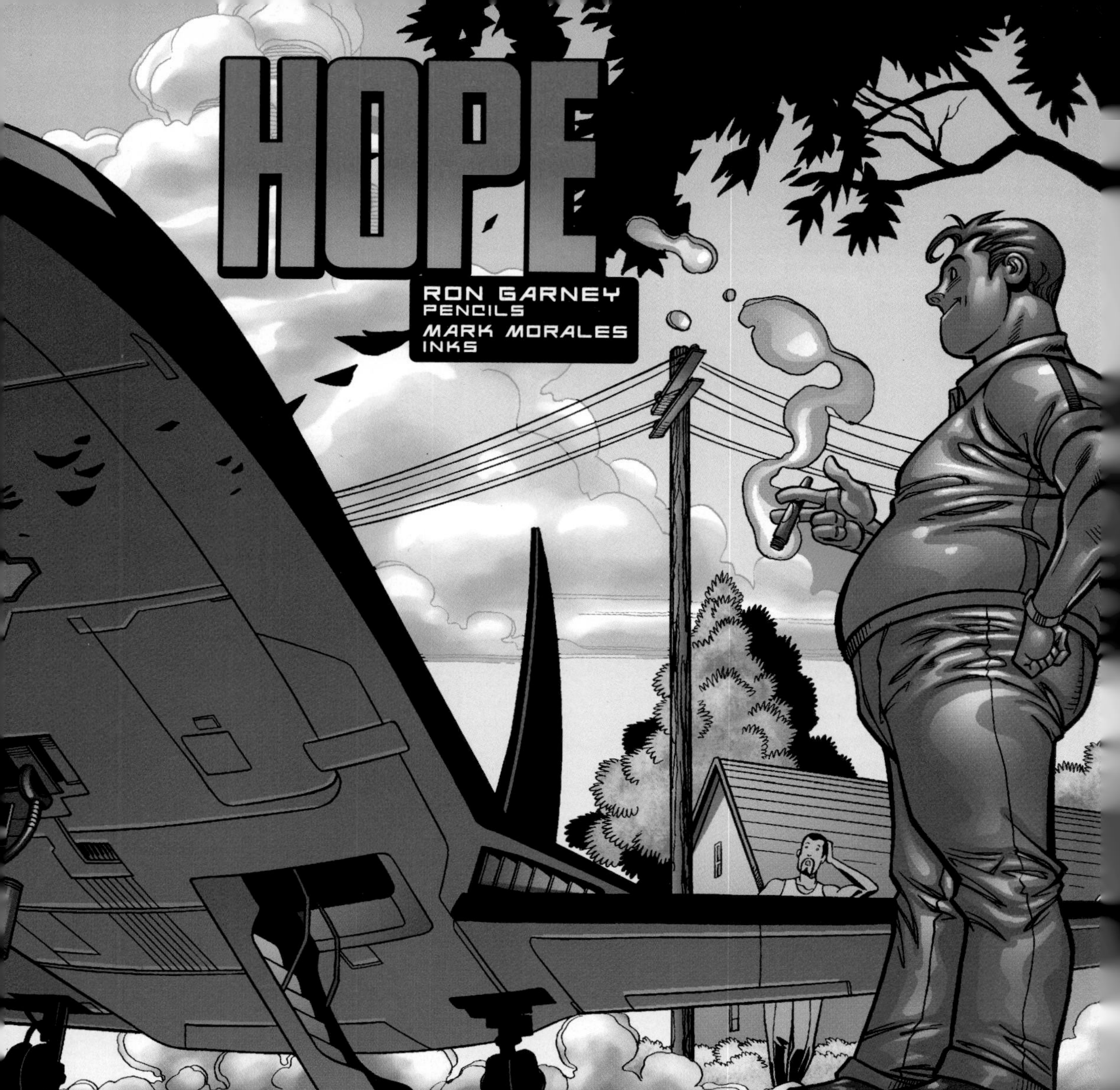
HOPE
RON GARNEY
PENCILS
MARK MORALES
INKS

MIKE MARTS EDITOR JOE QUESADA CHIEF BILL JEMAS PRESIDENT

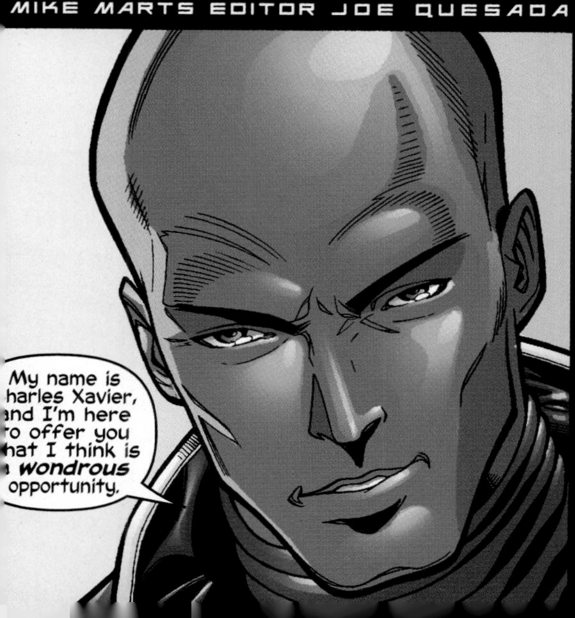
My name is harles Xavier, and I'm here o offer you hat I think is a ***wondrous*** opportunity.

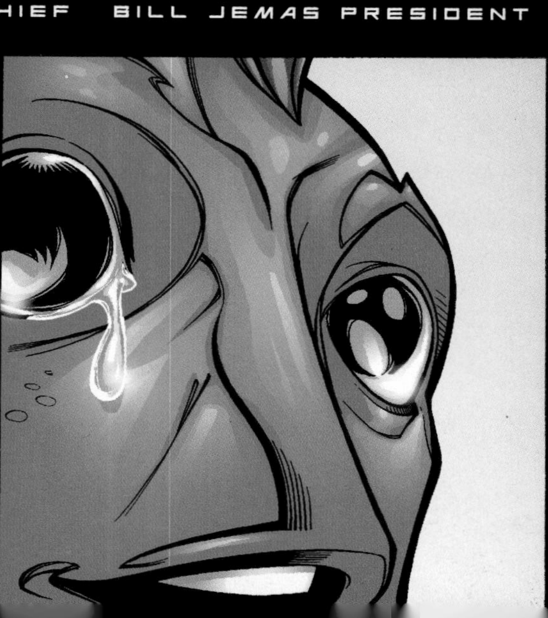

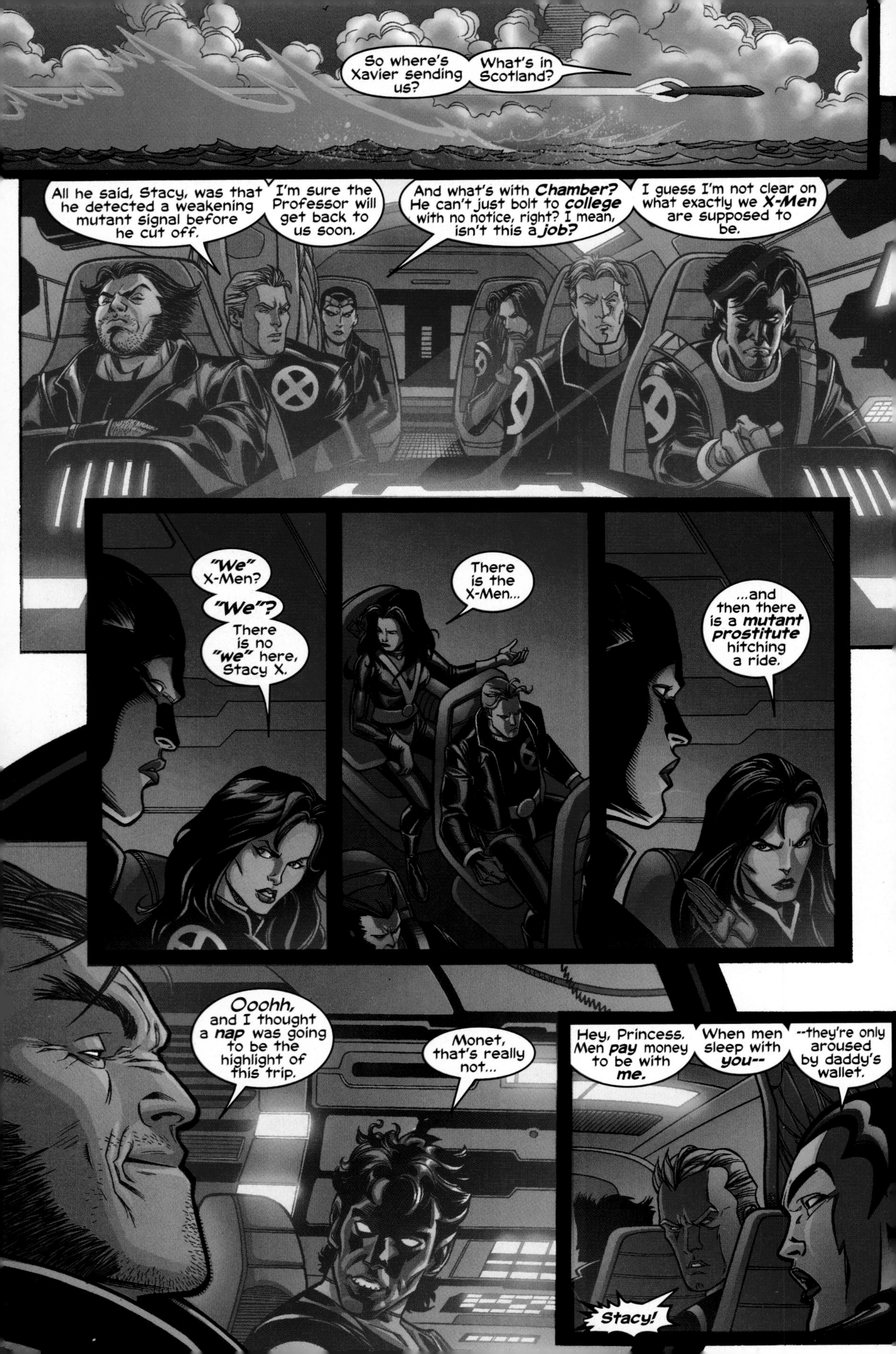
So where's Xavier sending us?
What's in Scotland?
All he said, Stacy, was that he detected a weakening mutant signal before he cut off.
I'm sure the Professor will get back to us soon.
And what's with Chamber? He can't just bolt to college with no notice, right? I mean, isn't this a job?
I guess I'm not clear on what exactly we X-Men are supposed to be.
"We" X-Men?
"We"?
There is no "we" here, Stacy X.
There is the X-Men...
...and then there is a mutant prostitute hitching a ride.
Ooohh, and I thought a nap was going to be the highlight of this trip.
Monet, that's really not...
Hey, Princess. Men pay money to be with me.
When men sleep with you--
--they're only aroused by daddy's wallet.
Stacy!

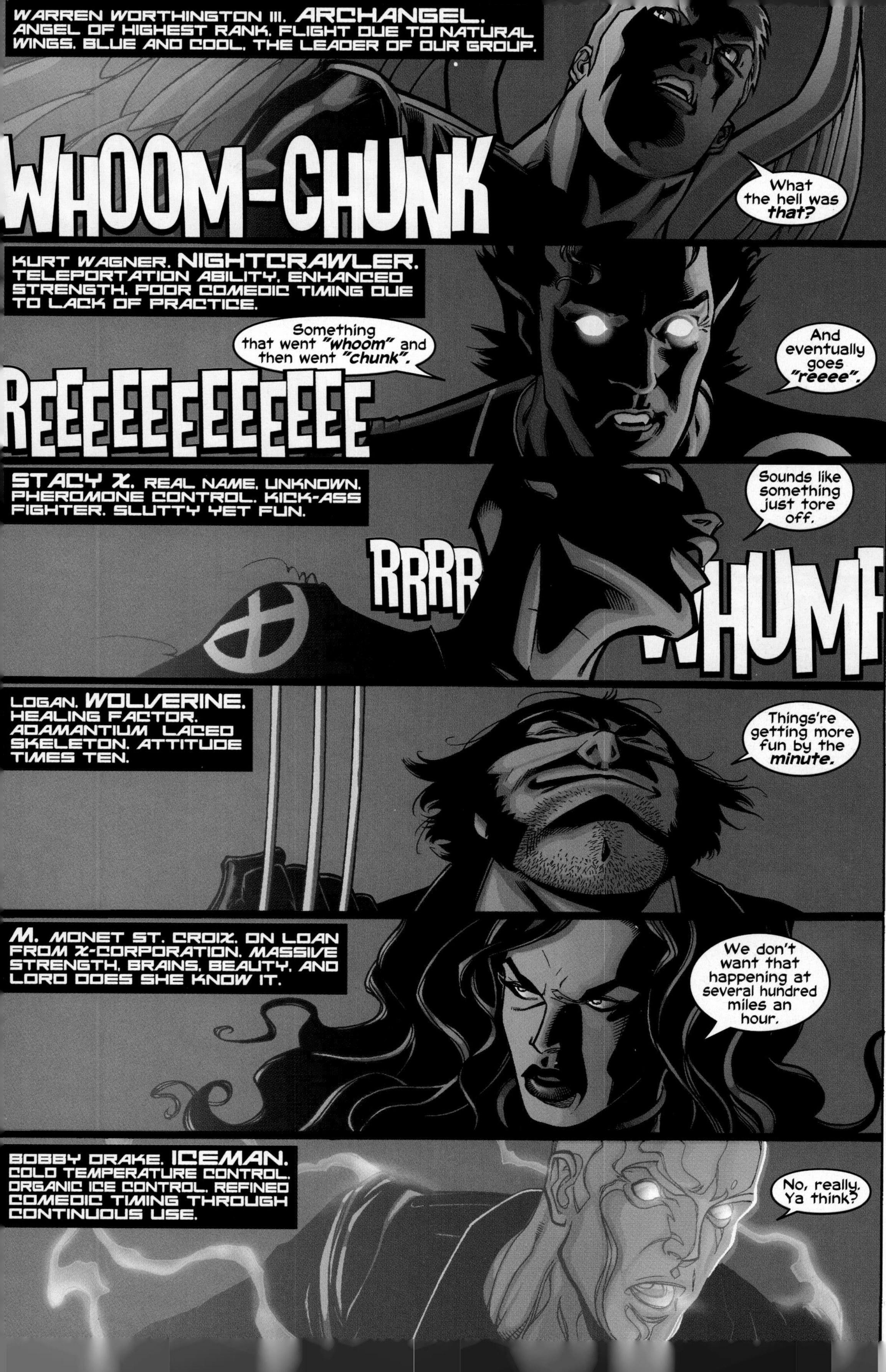

WARREN WORTHINGTON III. ARCHANGEL. ANGEL OF HIGHEST RANK. FLIGHT DUE TO NATURAL WINGS. BLUE AND COOL. THE LEADER OF OUR GROUP.
WHOOM-CHUNK
What the hell was that?
KURT WAGNER. NIGHTCRAWLER. TELEPORTATION ABILITY. ENHANCED STRENGTH. POOR COMEDIC TIMING DUE TO LACK OF PRACTICE.
Something that went "whoom" and then went "chunk".
And eventually goes "reeee".
REEEEEEEEEEEE
STACY X. REAL NAME. UNKNOWN. PHEROMONE CONTROL. KICK-ASS FIGHTER. SLUTTY YET FUN.
Sounds like something just tore off.
RRRR
HUMF
LOGAN. WOLVERINE. HEALING FACTOR. ADAMANTIUM LACED SKELETON. ATTITUDE TIMES TEN.
Things're getting more fun by the minute.
M. MONET ST. CROIX. ON LOAN FROM X-CORPORATION. MASSIVE STRENGTH. BRAINS. BEAUTY. AND LORD DOES SHE KNOW IT.
We don't want that happening at several hundred miles an hour.
BOBBY DRAKE. ICEMAN. COLD TEMPERATURE CONTROL. ORGANIC ICE CONTROL. REFINED COMEDIC TIMING THROUGH CONTINUOUS USE.
No, really. Ya think?

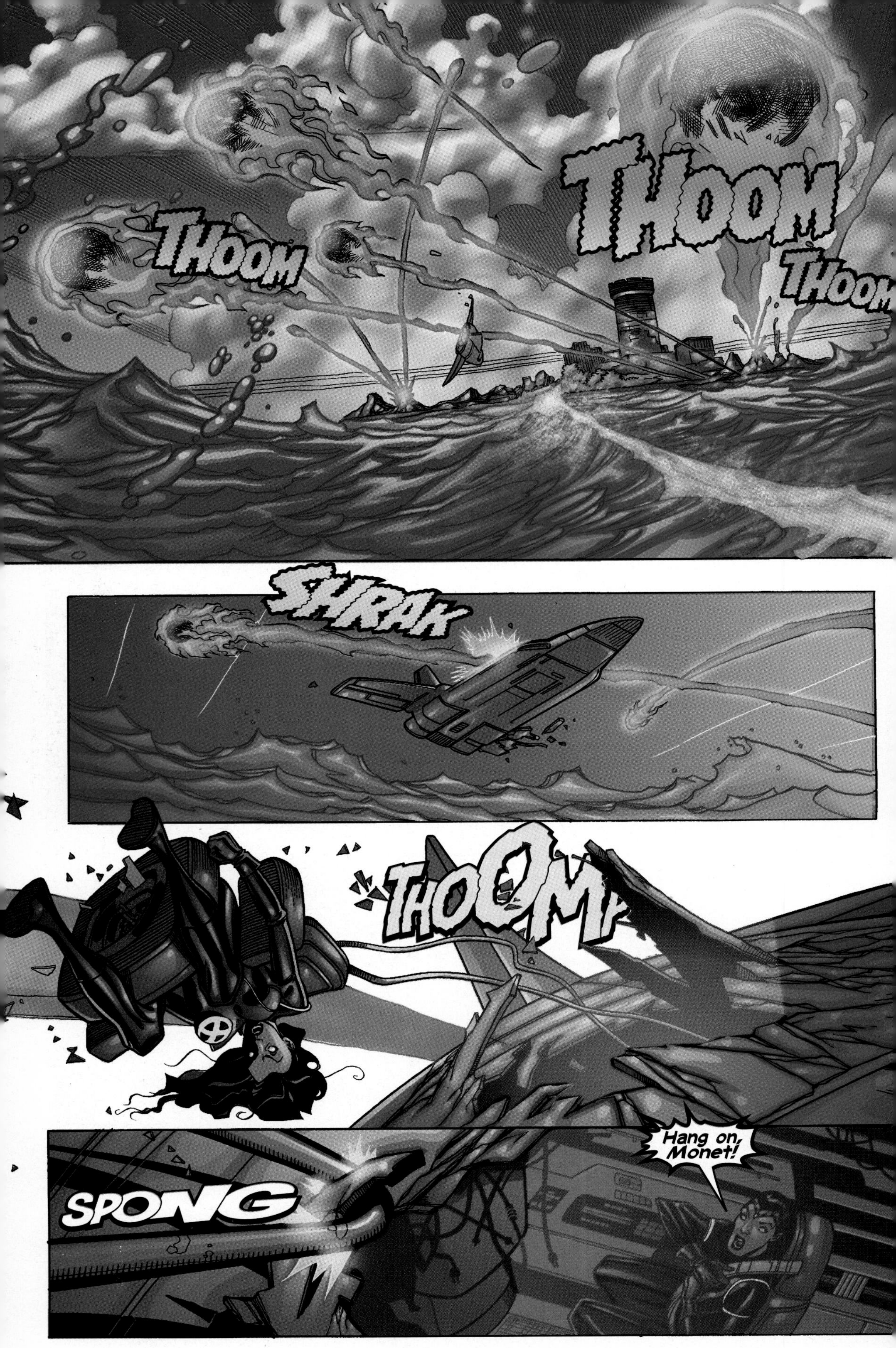
THOOM
THOOM
THOOM
SHRAK
THOOM
SPONG
Hang on, Monet!

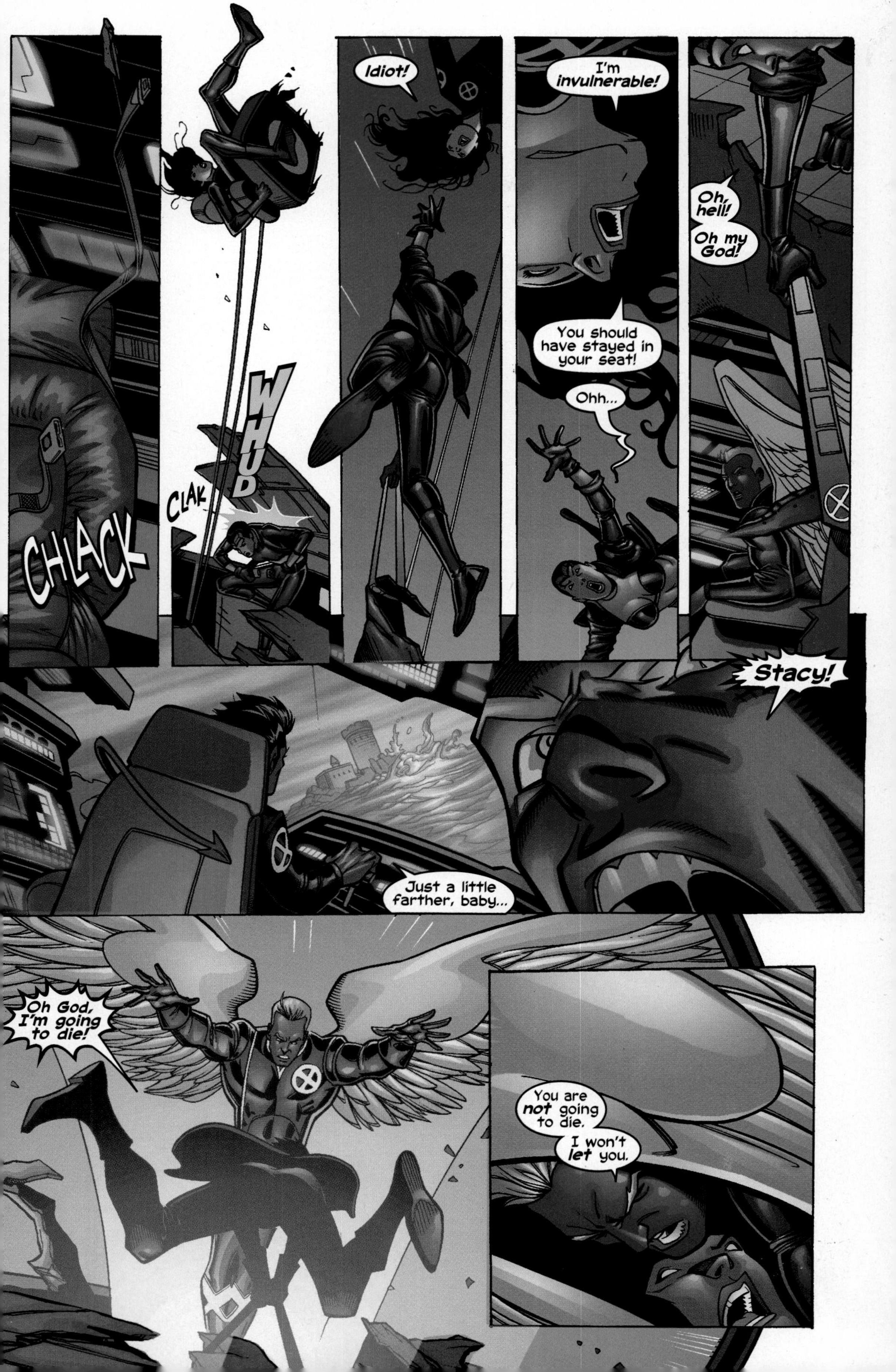
CHLACK
CLAK
WHUD
Idiot!
I'm invulnerable!
You should have stayed in your seat!
Ohh...
Oh, hell!
Oh my God!
Stacy!
Just a little farther, baby...
Oh God, I'm going to die!
You are not going to die.
I won't let you.

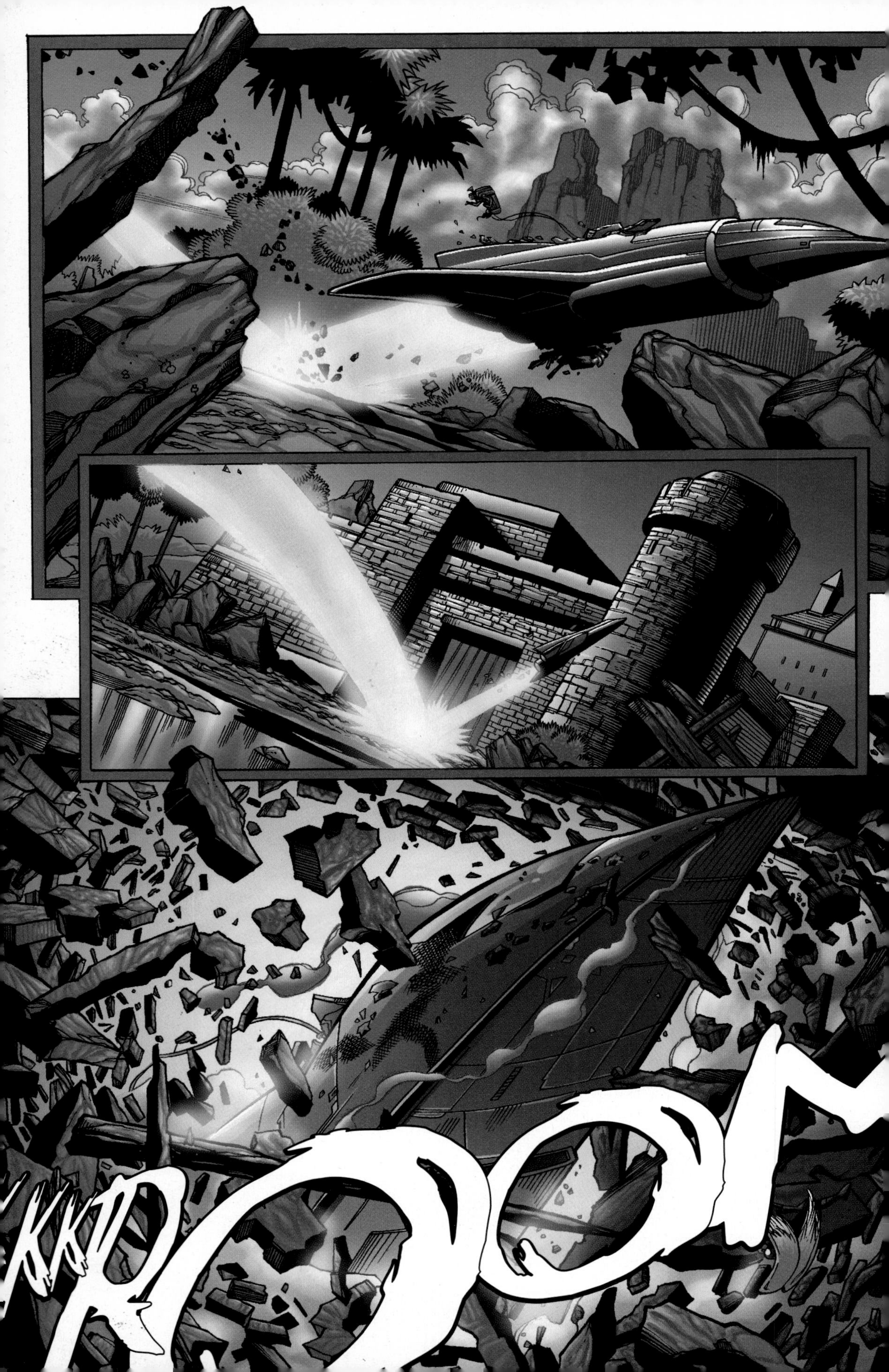
KKTHROOOM

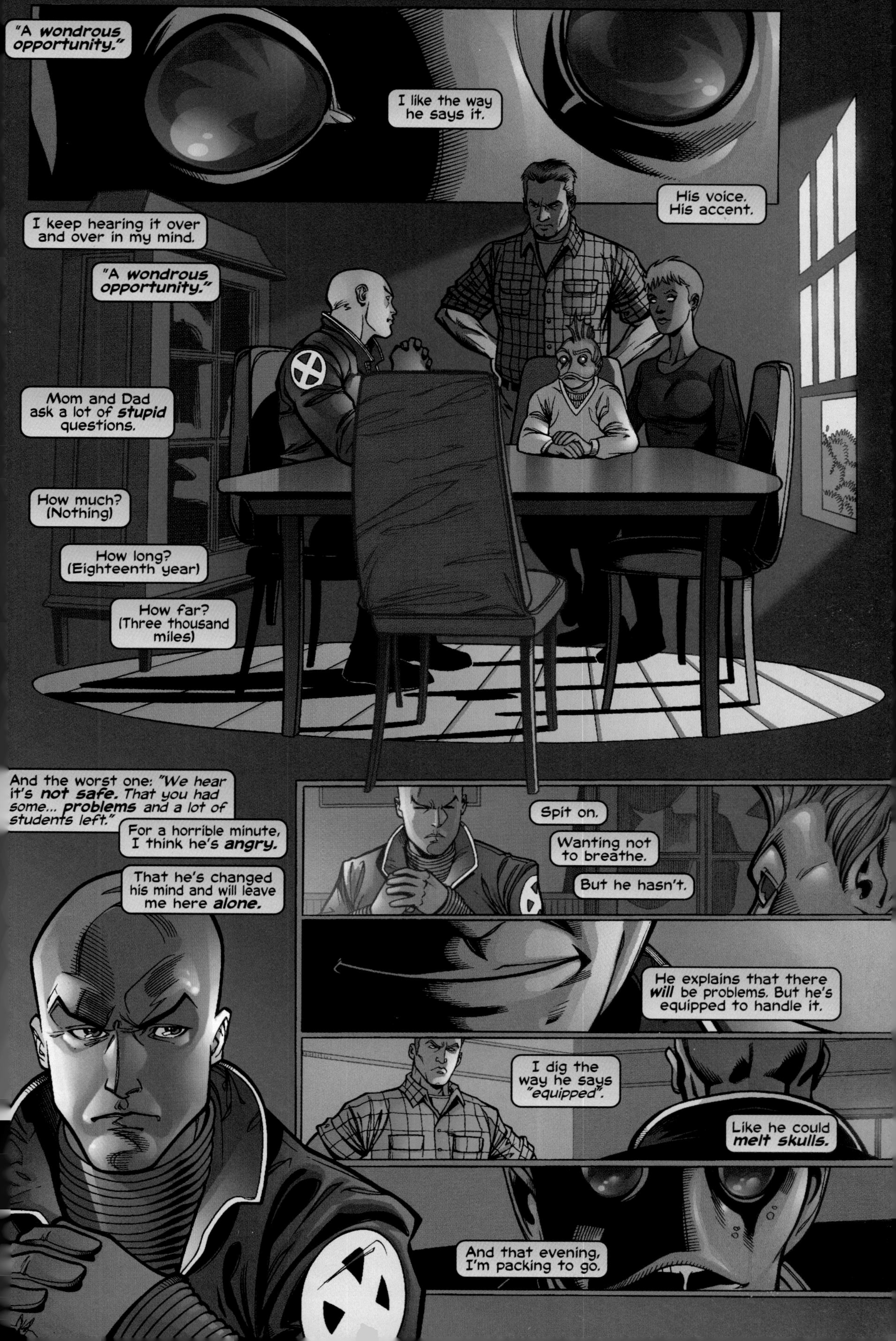
"A wondrous opportunity."
I like the way he says it.
His voice. His accent.
I keep hearing it over and over in my mind.
"A wondrous opportunity."
Mom and Dad ask a lot of stupid questions.
How much? (Nothing)
How long? (Eighteenth year)
How far? (Three thousand miles)
And the worst one: "We hear it's not safe. That you had some... problems and a lot of students left."
For a horrible minute, I think he's angry.
That he's changed his mind and will leave me here alone.
Spit on.
Wanting not to breathe.
But he hasn't.
He explains that there will be problems. But he's equipped to handle it.
I dig the way he says "equipped".
Like he could melt skulls.
And that evening, I'm packing to go.

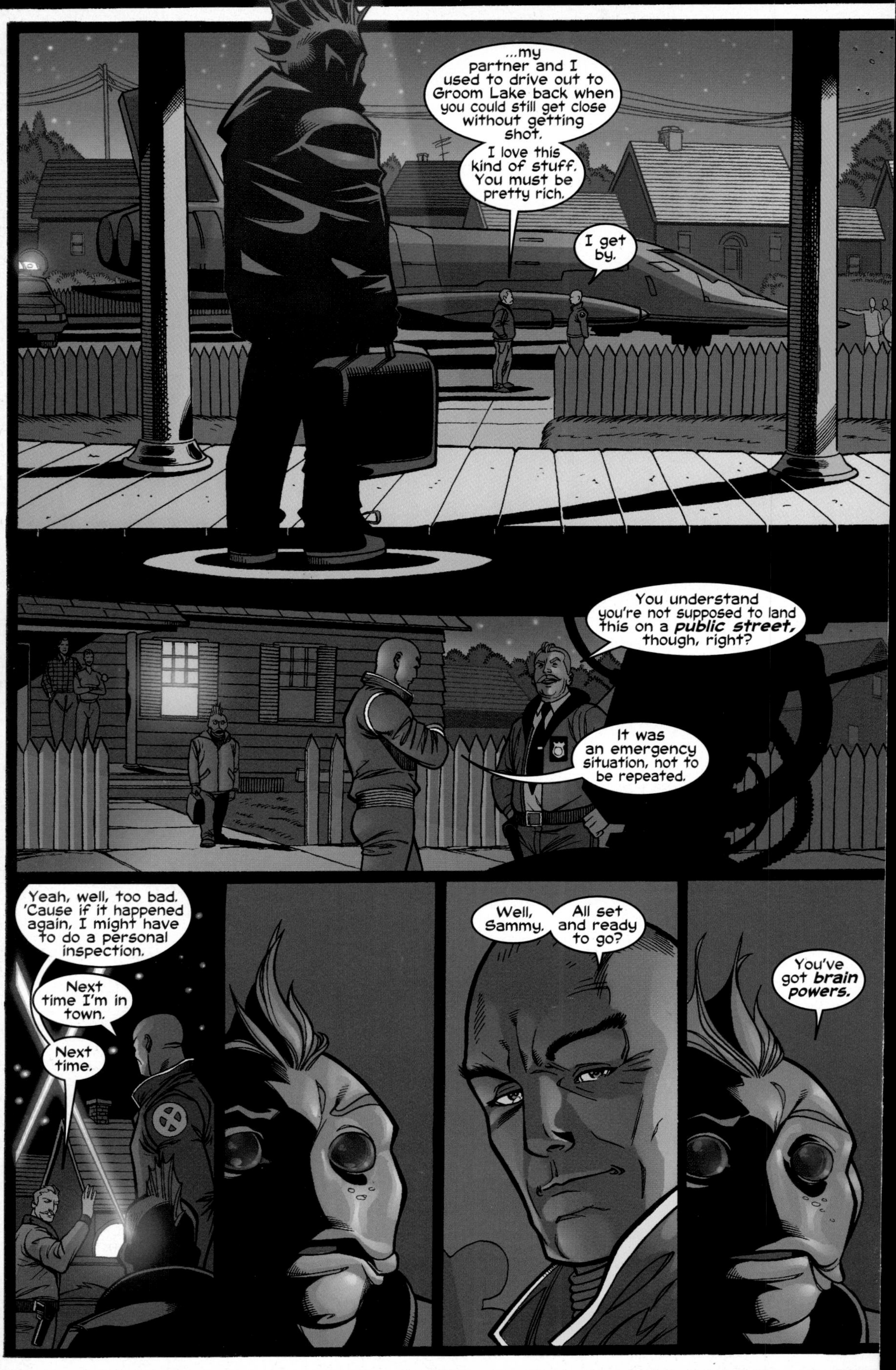
...my partner and I used to drive out to Groom Lake back when you could still get close without getting shot.
I love this kind of stuff. You must be pretty rich.
I get by.
You understand you're not supposed to land this on a *public street,* though, right?
It was an emergency situation, not to be repeated.
Yeah, well, too bad. 'Cause if it happened again, I might have to do a personal inspection.
Next time I'm in town.
Next time.
Well, Sammy.
All set and ready to go?
You've got *brain powers.*

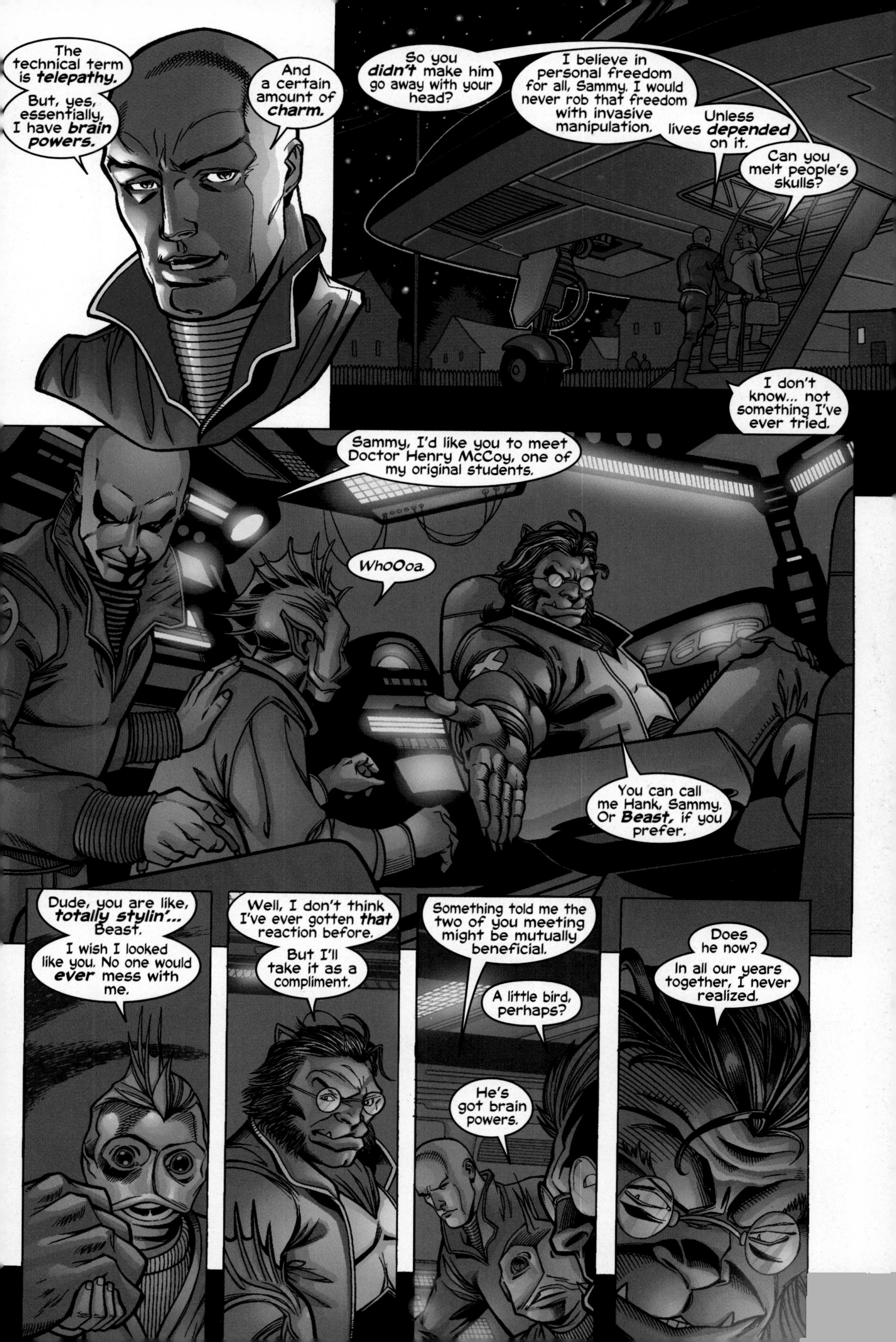
The technical term is telepathy.
But, yes, essentially, I have brain powers.
And a certain amount of charm.
So you didn't make him go away with your head?
I believe in personal freedom for all, Sammy. I would never rob that freedom with invasive manipulation.
Unless lives depended on it.
Can you melt people's skulls?
I don't know... not something I've ever tried.
Sammy, I'd like you to meet Doctor Henry McCoy, one of my original students.
WhoOoa.
You can call me Hank, Sammy. Or Beast, if you prefer.
Dude, you are like, totally stylin'... Beast.
I wish I looked like you. No one would ever mess with me.
Well, I don't think I've ever gotten that reaction before.
But I'll take it as a compliment.
Something told me the two of you meeting might be mutually beneficial.
A little bird, perhaps?
He's got brain powers.
Does he now?
In all our years together, I never realized.

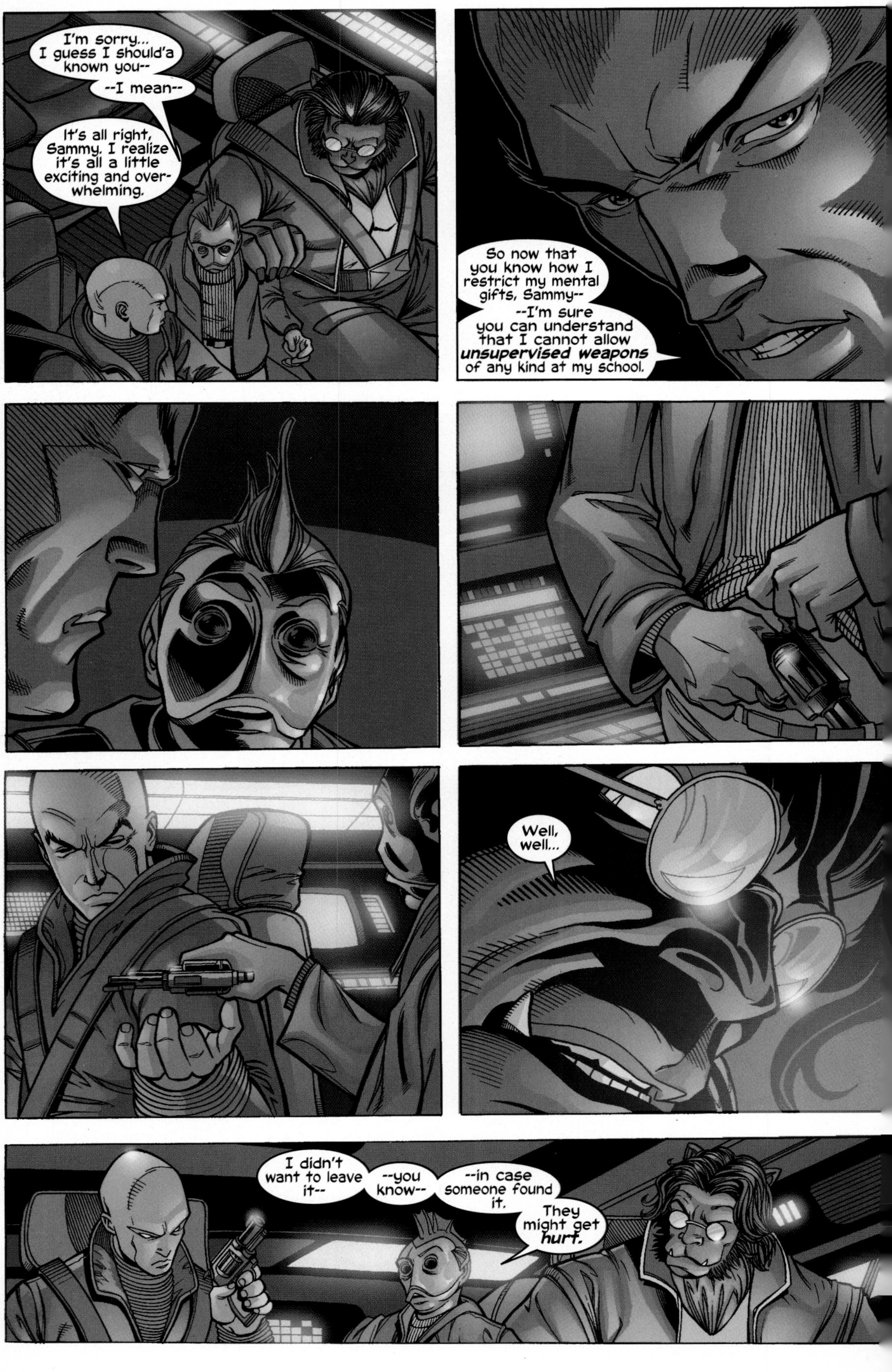
I'm sorry... I guess I should'a known you--
--I mean--
It's all right, Sammy. I realize it's all a little exciting and over-whelming.
So now that you know how I restrict my mental gifts, Sammy--
--I'm sure you can understand that I cannot allow ***unsupervised weapons*** of any kind at my school.
Well, well...
I didn't want to leave it--
--you know--
--in case someone found it.
They might get ***hurt.***

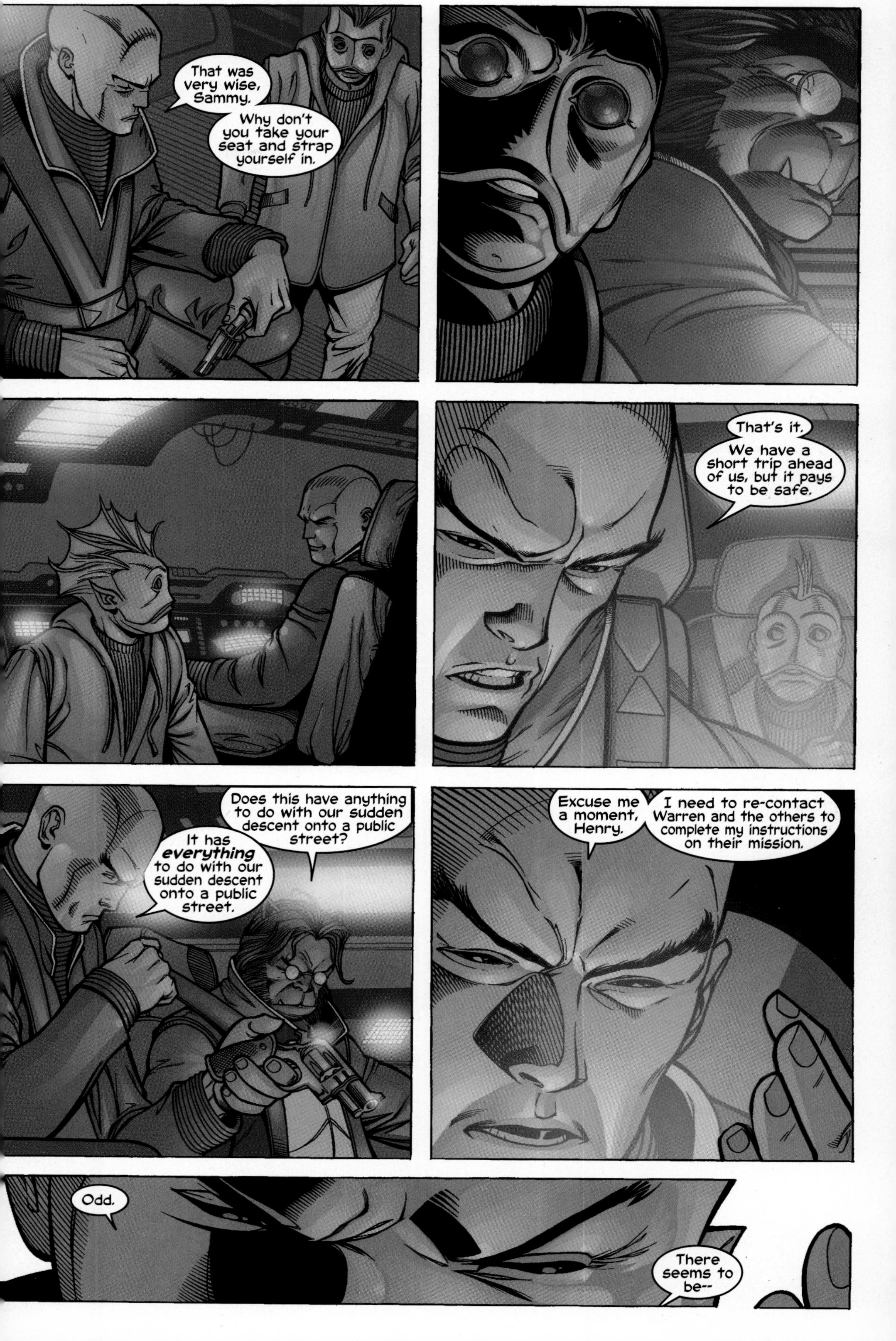

That was very wise, Sammy.
Why don't you take your seat and strap yourself in.
That's it.
We have a short trip ahead of us, but it pays to be safe.
Does this have anything to do with our sudden descent onto a public street?
It has *everything* to do with our sudden descent onto a public street.
Excuse me a moment, Henry.
I need to re-contact Warren and the others to complete my instructions on their mission.
Odd.
There seems to be--

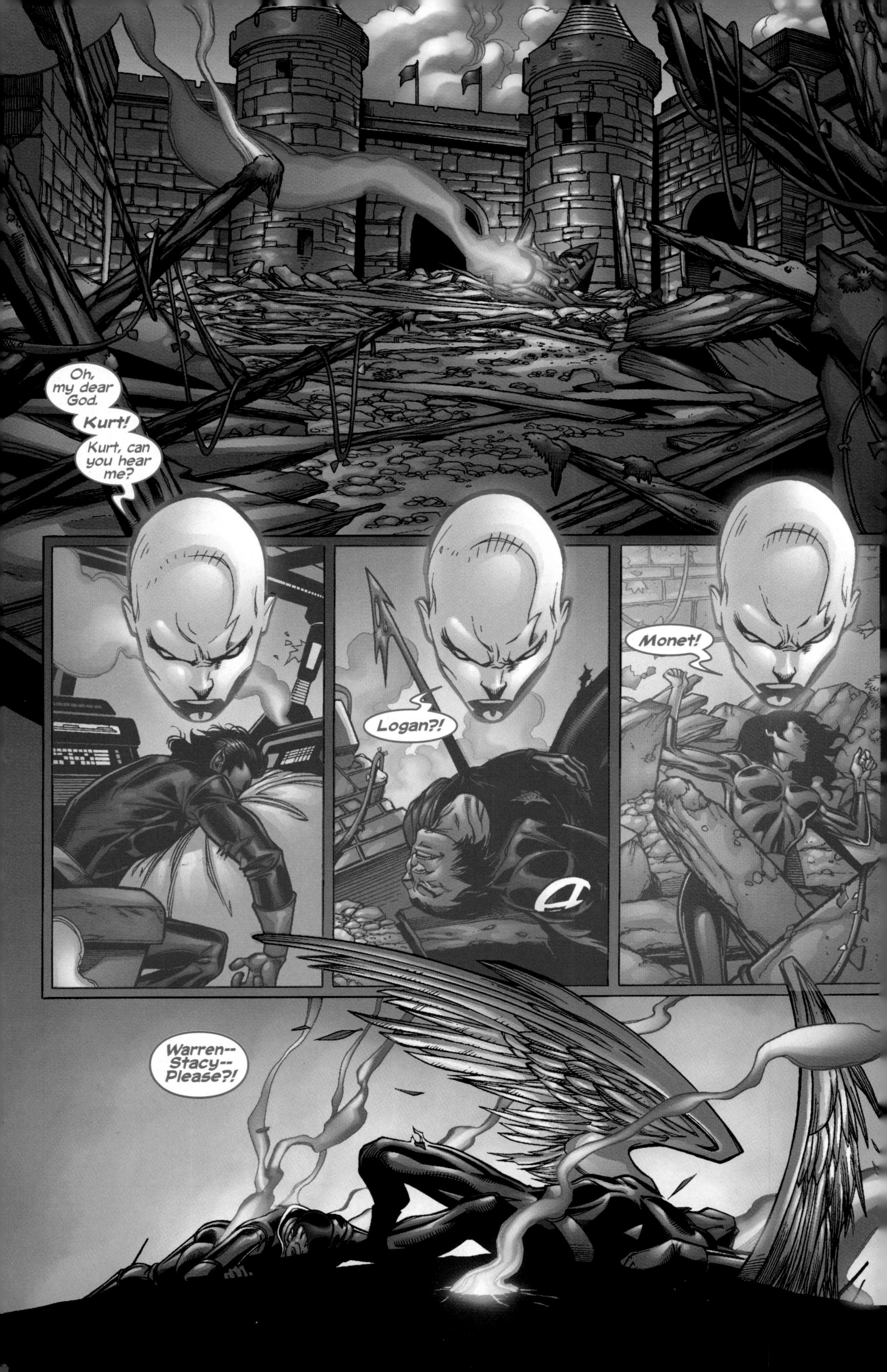
Oh, my dear God.
Kurt!
Kurt, can you hear me?
Logan?!
Monet!
Warren-- Stacy-- Please?!

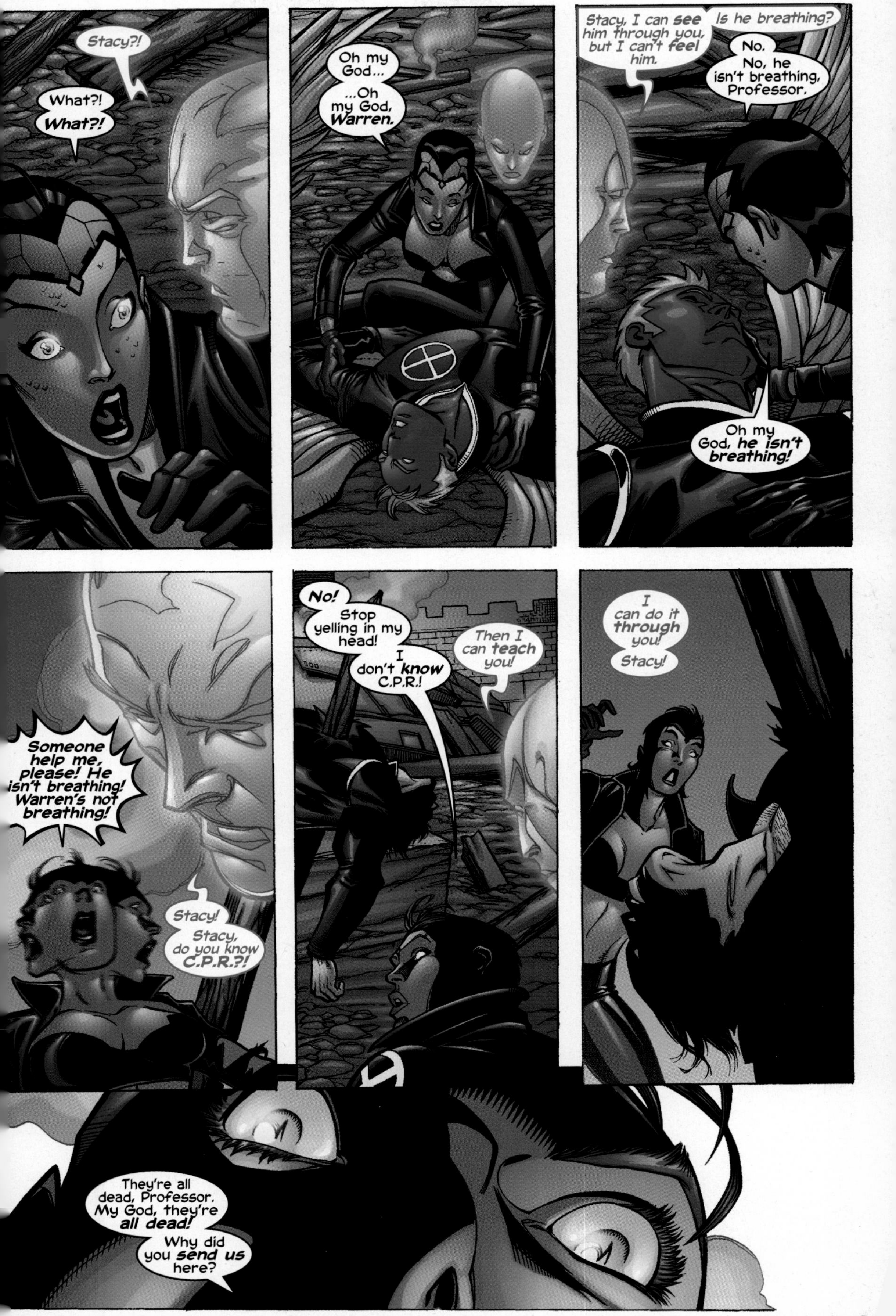
Stacy?!
What?! What?!
Oh my God...
...Oh my God, Warren.
Stacy, I can see him through you, but I can't feel him.
Is he breathing?
No.
No, he isn't breathing, Professor.
Oh my God, he isn't breathing!
Someone help me, please! He isn't breathing! Warren's not breathing!
Stacy!
Stacy, do you know C.P.R.?!
No!
Stop yelling in my head!
I don't know C.P.R.!
Then I can teach you!
I can do it through you!
Stacy!
They're all dead, Professor. My God, they're all dead!
Why did you send us here?

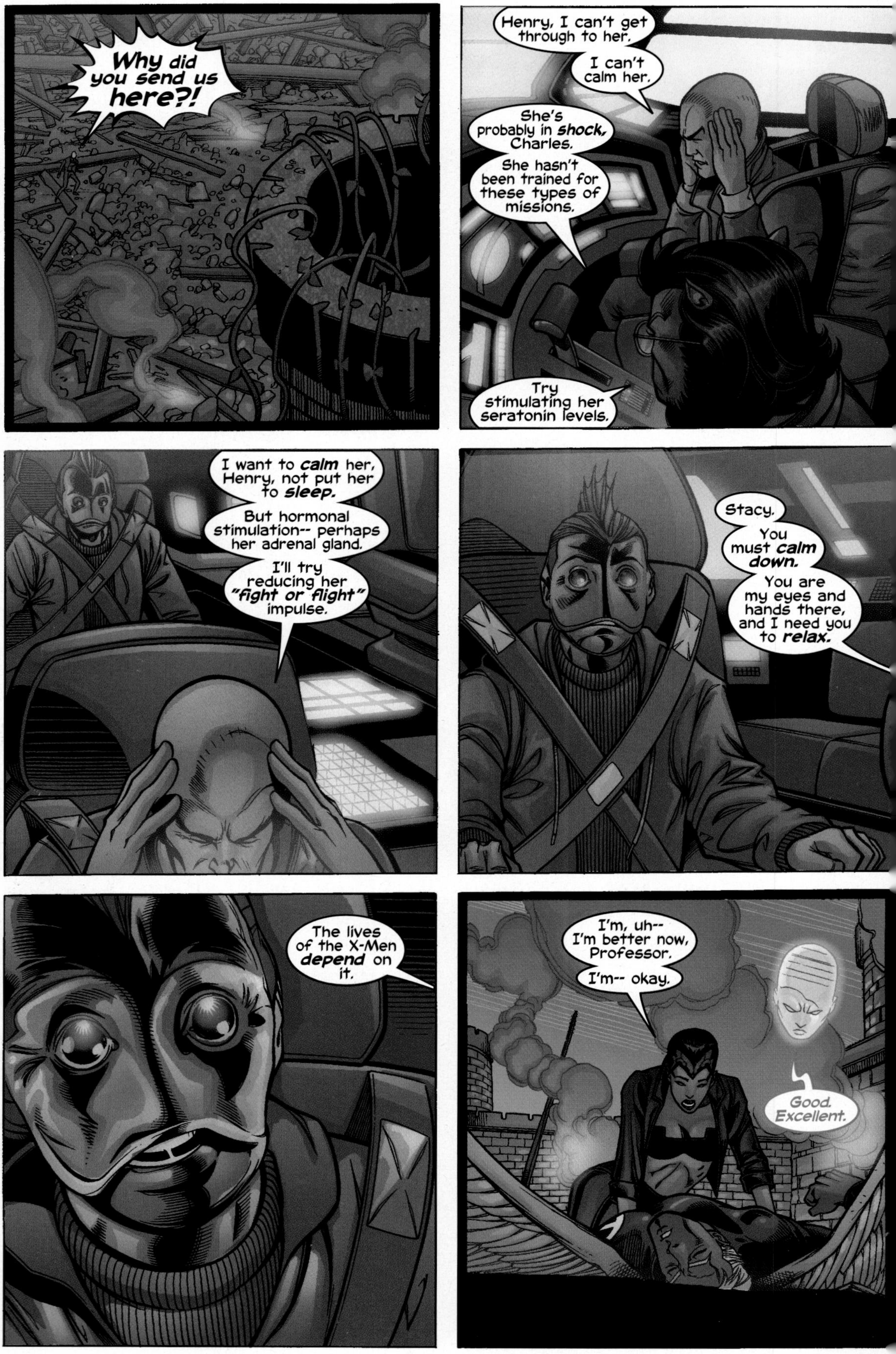
Why did you send us here?!
Henry, I can't get through to her.
I can't calm her.
She's probably in shock, Charles.
She hasn't been trained for these types of missions.
Try stimulating her seratonin levels.
I want to calm her, Henry, not put her to sleep.
But hormonal stimulation-- perhaps her adrenal gland.
I'll try reducing her "fight or flight" impulse.
Stacy.
You must calm down.
You are my eyes and hands there, and I need you to relax.
The lives of the X-Men depend on it.
I'm, uh-- I'm better now, Professor.
I'm-- okay.
Good. Excellent.

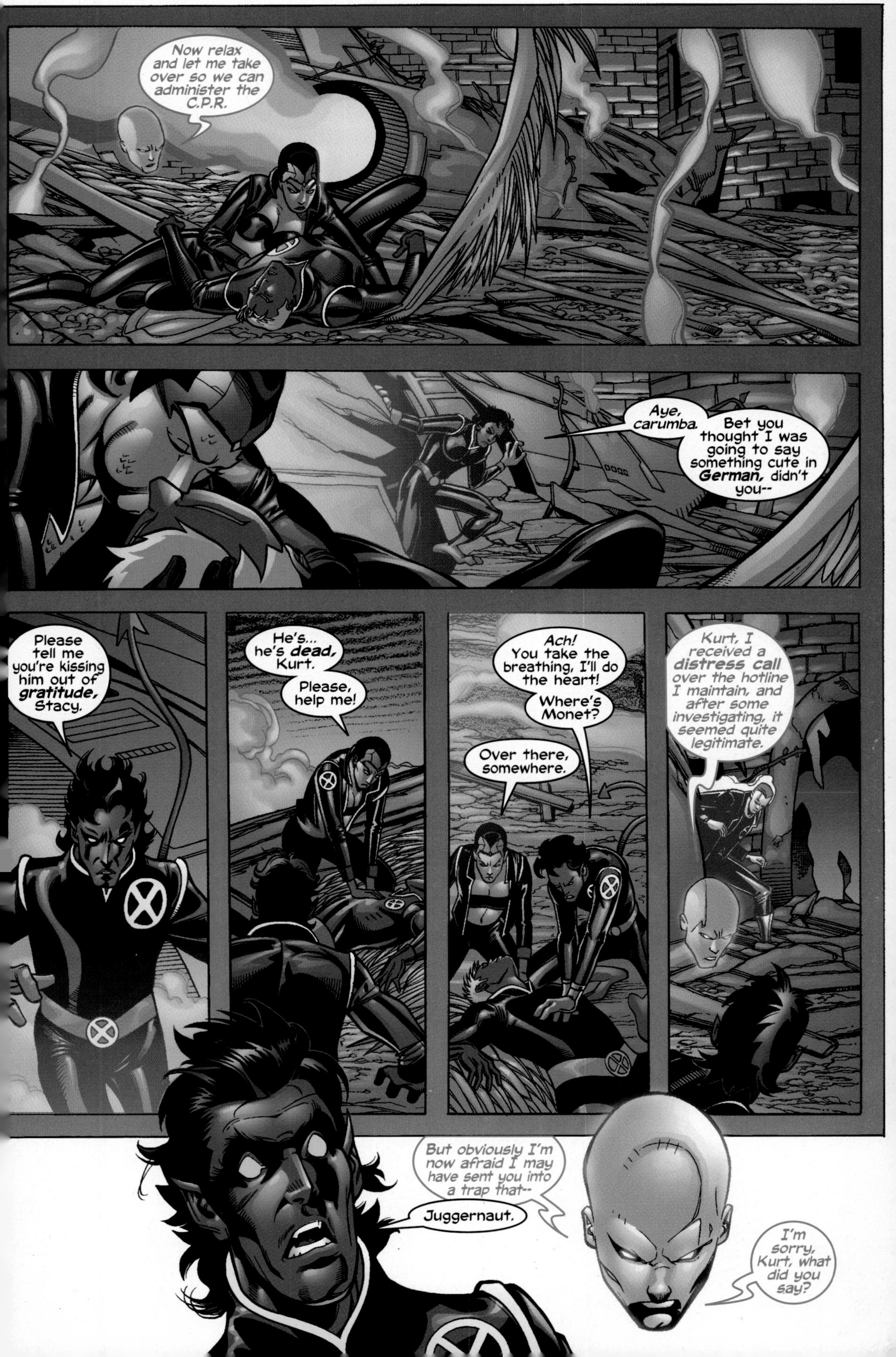
Now relax and let me take over so we can administer the C.P.R.
Aye, carumba.
Bet you thought I was going to say something cute in German, didn't you--
Please tell me you're kissing him out of gratitude, Stacy.
He's... he's dead, Kurt.
Please, help me!
Ach! You take the breathing, I'll do the heart!
Where's Monet?
Over there, somewhere.
Kurt, I received a distress call over the hotline I maintain, and after some investigating, it seemed quite legitimate.
But obviously I'm now afraid I may have sent you into a trap that--
Juggernaut.
I'm sorry, Kurt, what did you say?

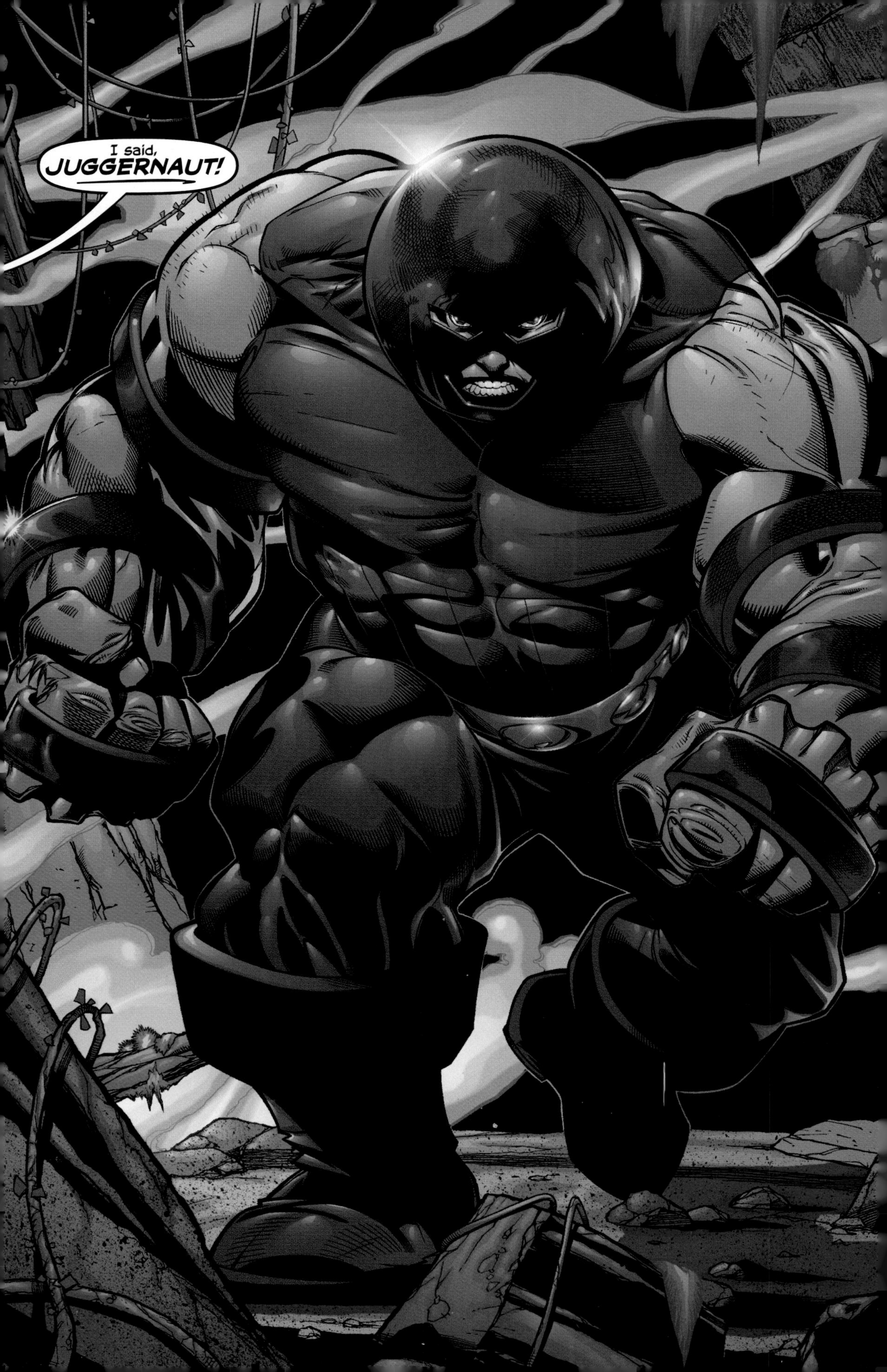
I said, JUGGERNAUT!

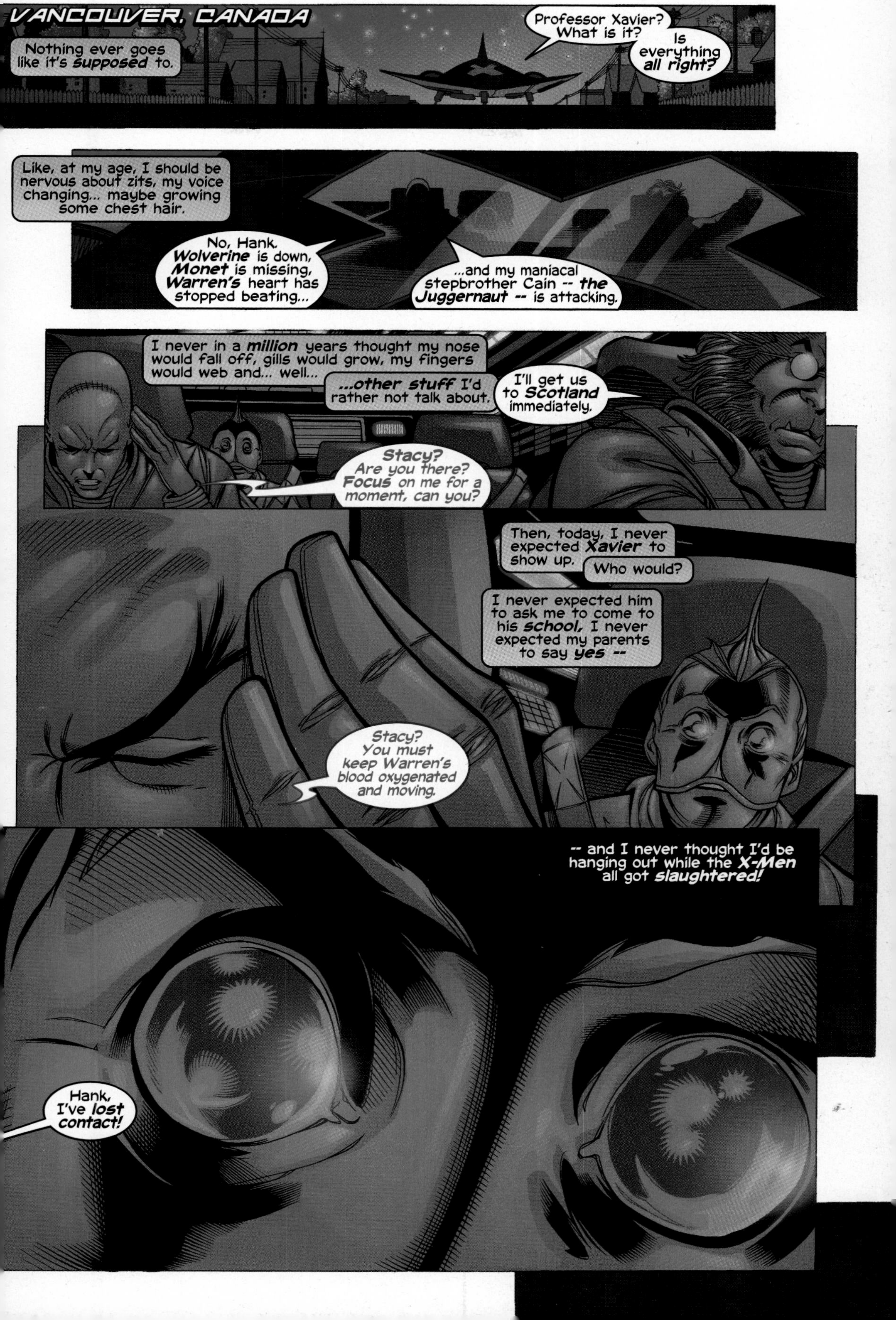
VANCOUVER, CANADA
Nothing ever goes like it's supposed to.
Professor Xavier? What is it?
Is everything all right?
Like, at my age, I should be nervous about zits, my voice changing... maybe growing some chest hair.
No, Hank. Wolverine is down, Monet is missing, Warren's heart has stopped beating...
...and my maniacal stepbrother Cain -- the Juggernaut -- is attacking.
I never in a million years thought my nose would fall off, gills would grow, my fingers would web and... well...
...other stuff I'd rather not talk about.
I'll get us to Scotland immediately.
Stacy? Are you there? Focus on me for a moment, can you?
Then, today, I never expected Xavier to show up.
Who would?
I never expected him to ask me to come to his school, I never expected my parents to say yes --
Stacy? You must keep Warren's blood oxygenated and moving.
-- and I never thought I'd be hanging out while the X-Men all got slaughtered!
Hank, I've lost contact!

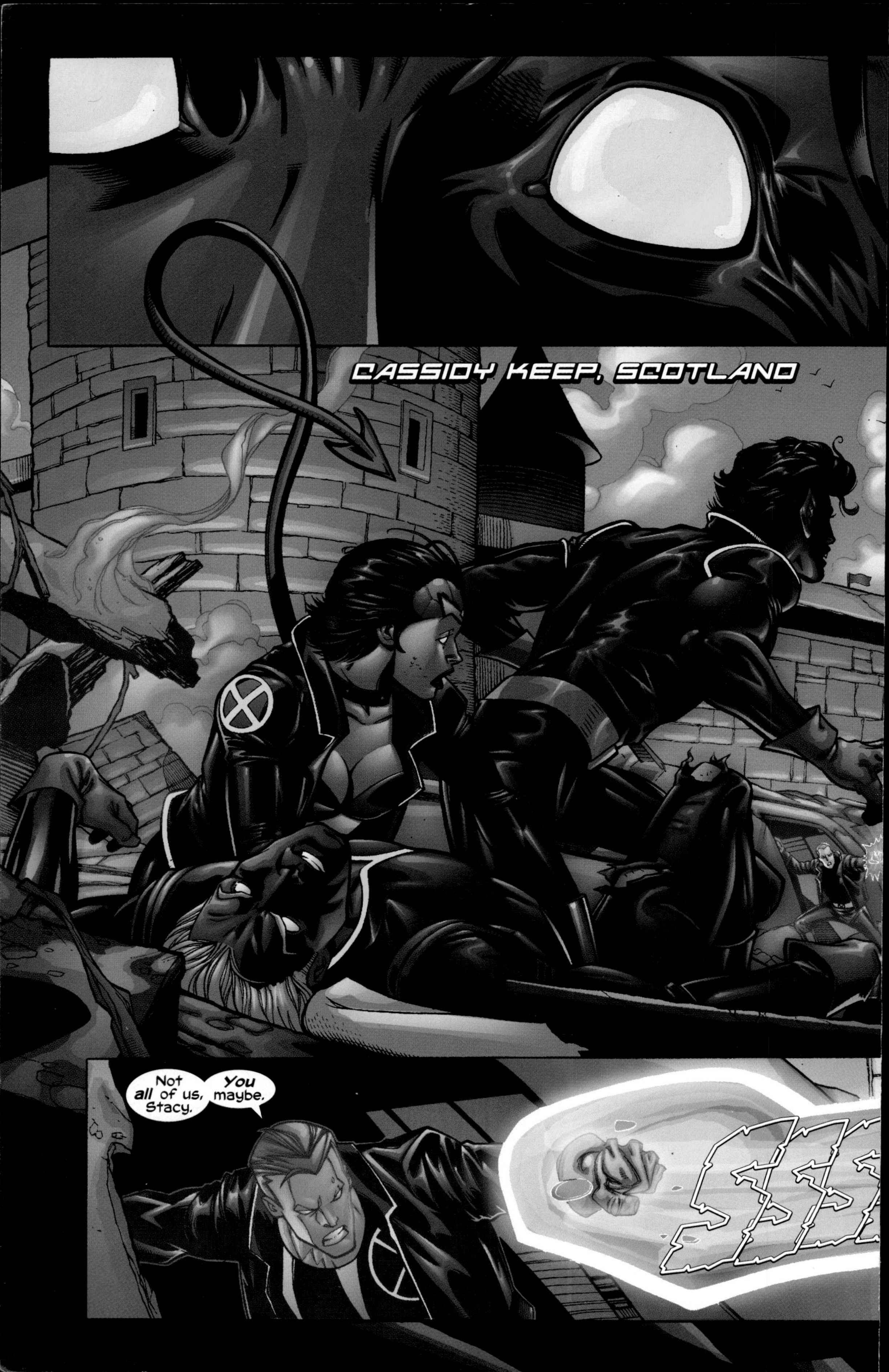
CASSIDY KEEP, SCOTLAND
Not all of us, Stacy.
You maybe.

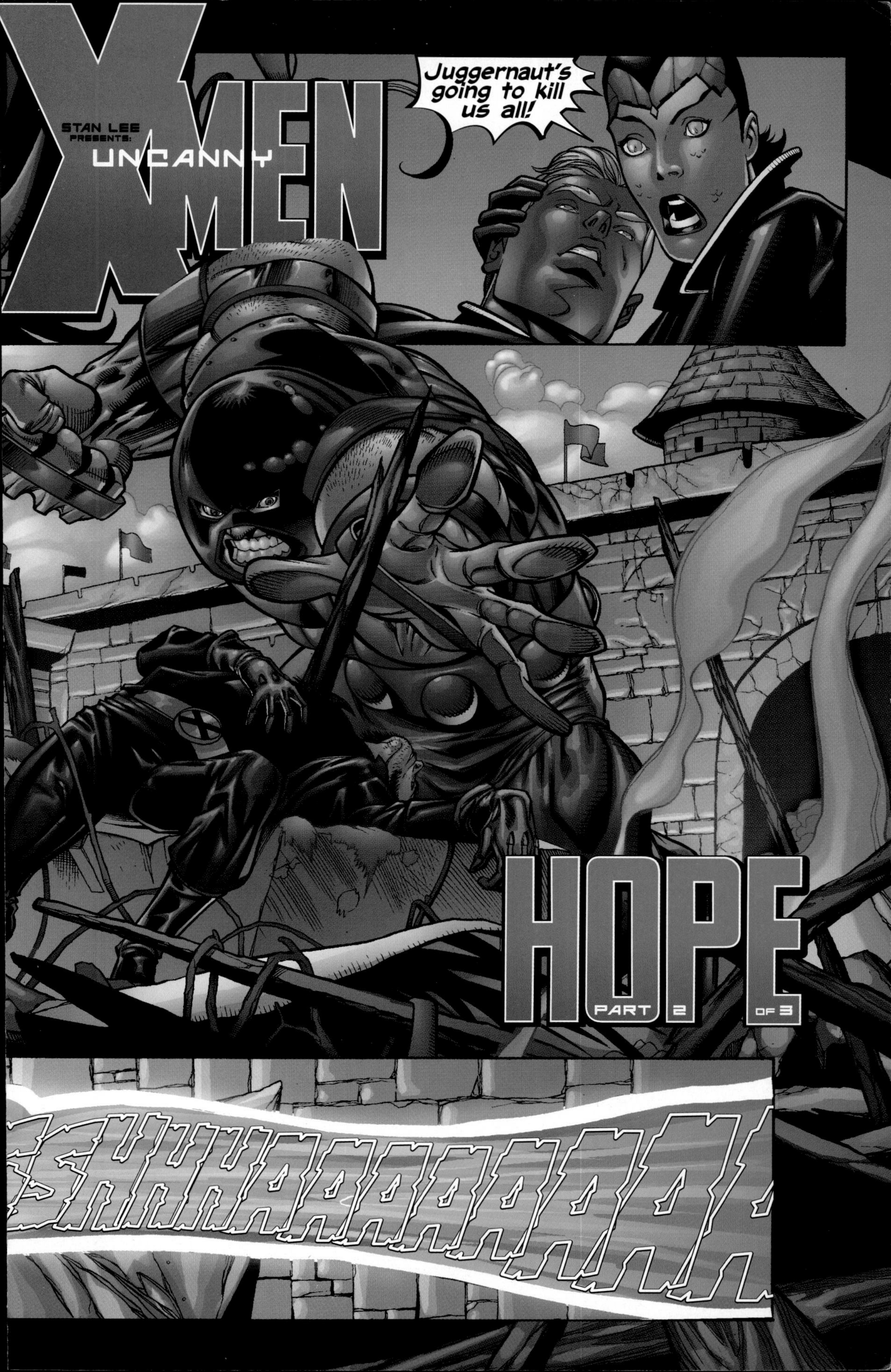
STAN LEE PRESENTS:
UNCANNY X-MEN
Juggernaut's going to kill us all!
HOPE
PART 2 OF 3
SHHHAAAAAAAAAA

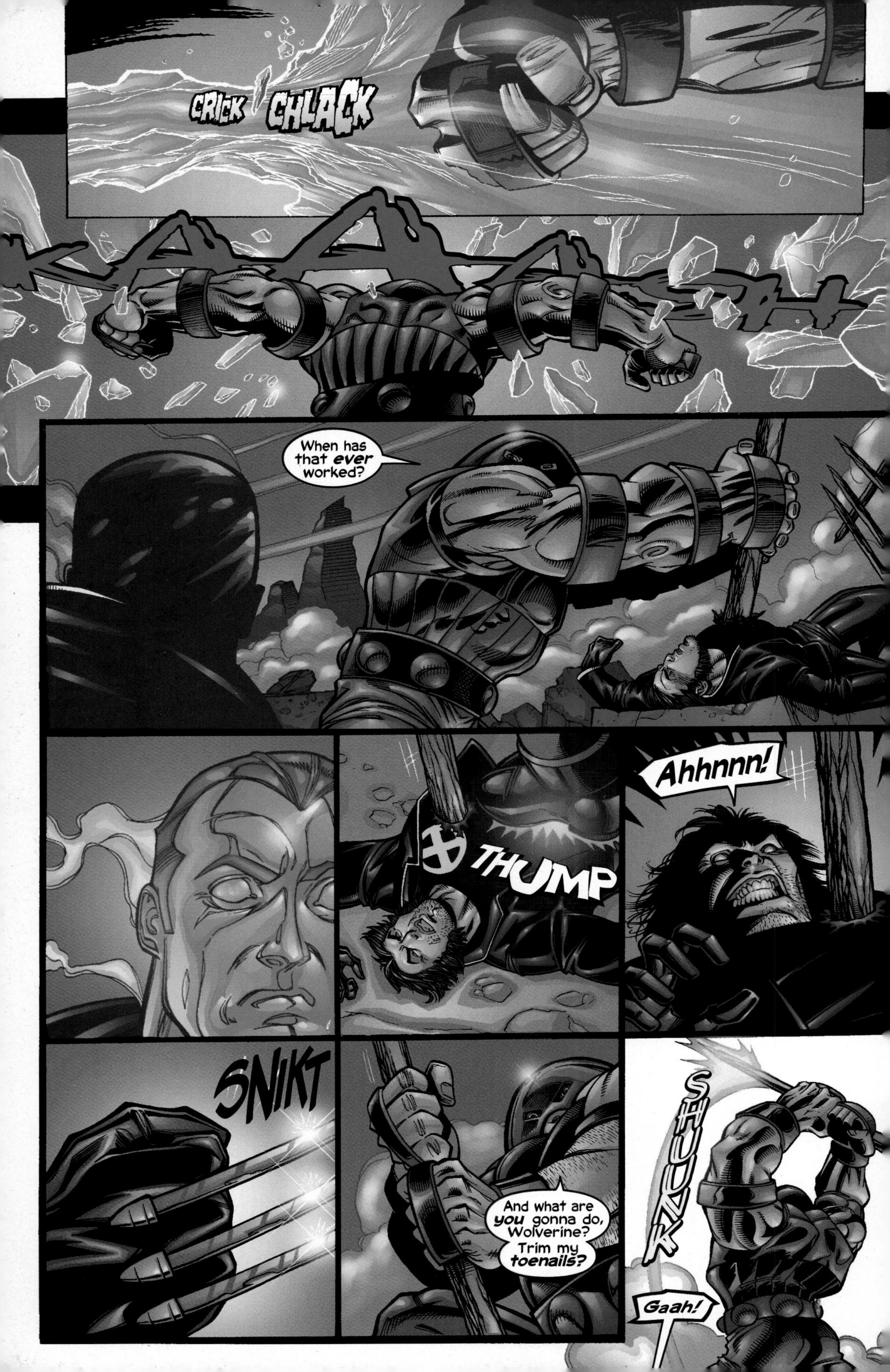
CRICK
CHLACK
When has that *ever* worked?
THUMP
Ahhnnn!
SNIKT
And what are *you* gonna do, Wolverine? Trim my *toenails?*
SHUUNK
Gaah!

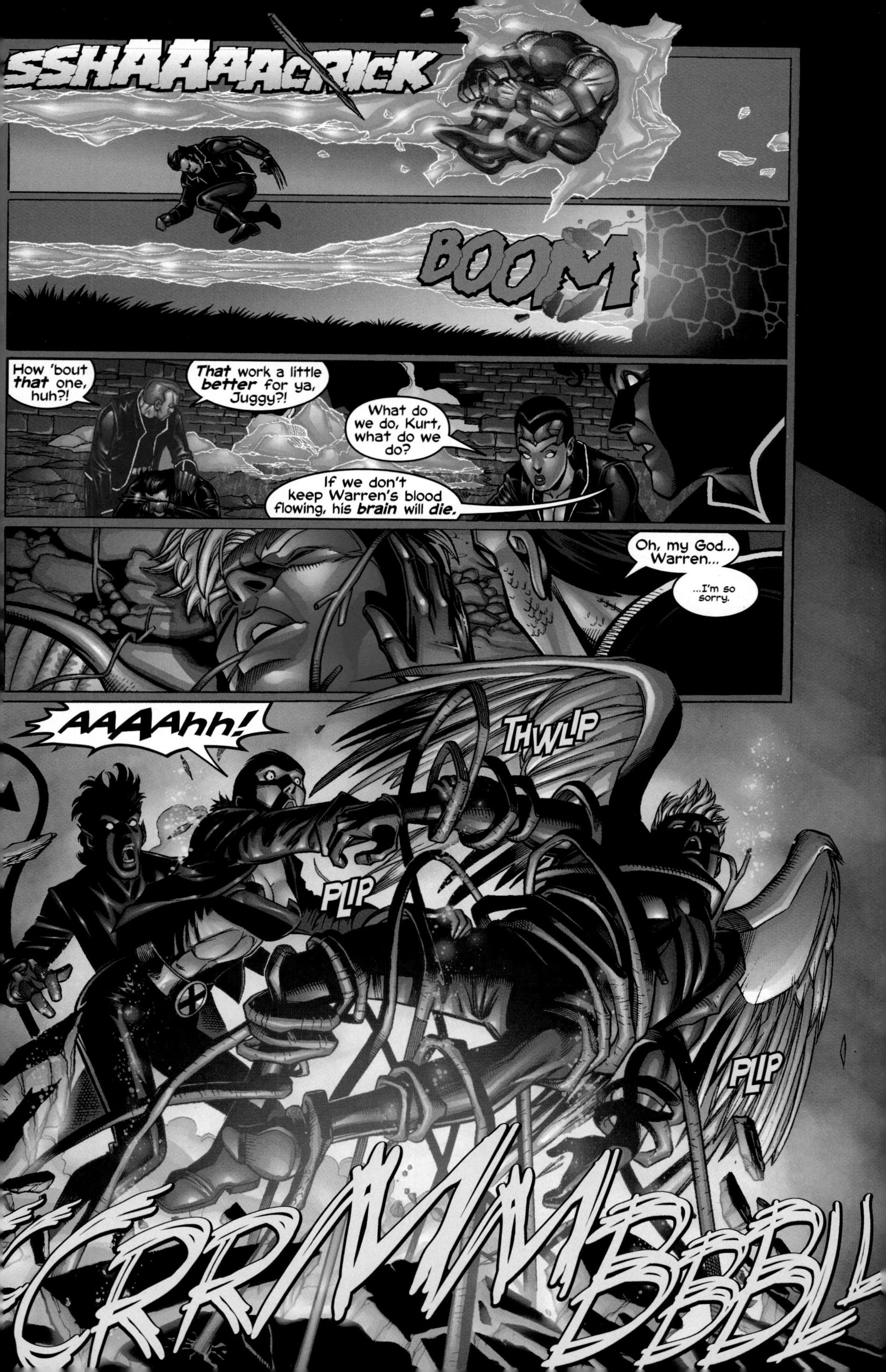
SSHAAAACRICK
BOOM
How 'bout that one, huh?!
That work a little better for ya, Juggy?!
What do we do, Kurt, what do we do?
If we don't keep Warren's blood flowing, his brain will die.
Oh, my God... Warren...
...I'm so sorry.
AAAAhh!
THWLIP
PLIP
PLIP
CRRMMBBBL

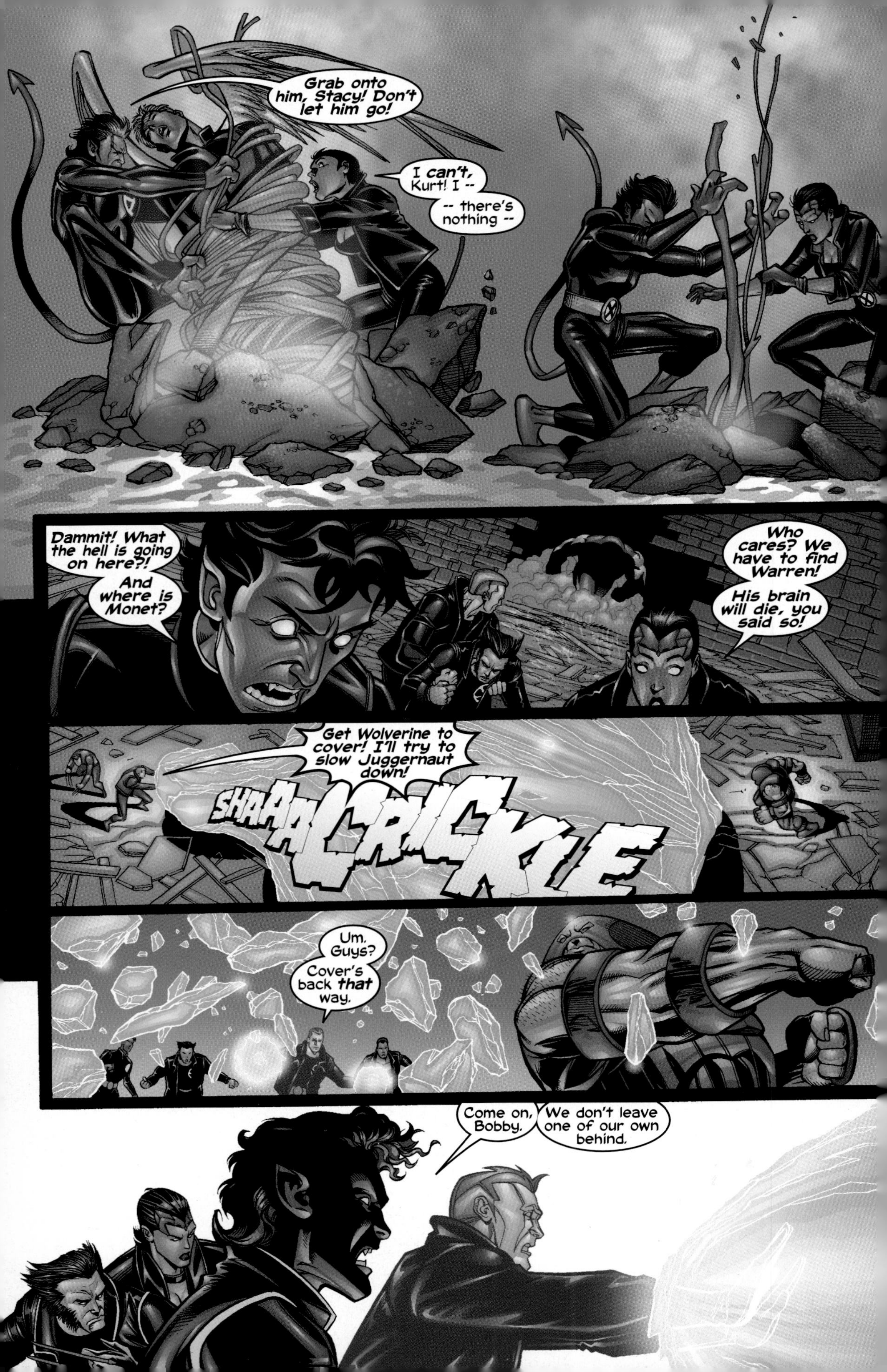
Grab onto him, Stacy! Don't let him go!
I can't, Kurt! I --
-- there's nothing --
Dammit! What the hell is going on here?!
And where is Monet?
Who cares? We have to find Warren!
His brain will die, you said so!
Get Wolverine to cover! I'll try to slow Juggernaut down!
SHAAACRICKLE
Um. Guys?
Cover's back that way.
Come on, Bobby.
We don't leave one of our own behind.

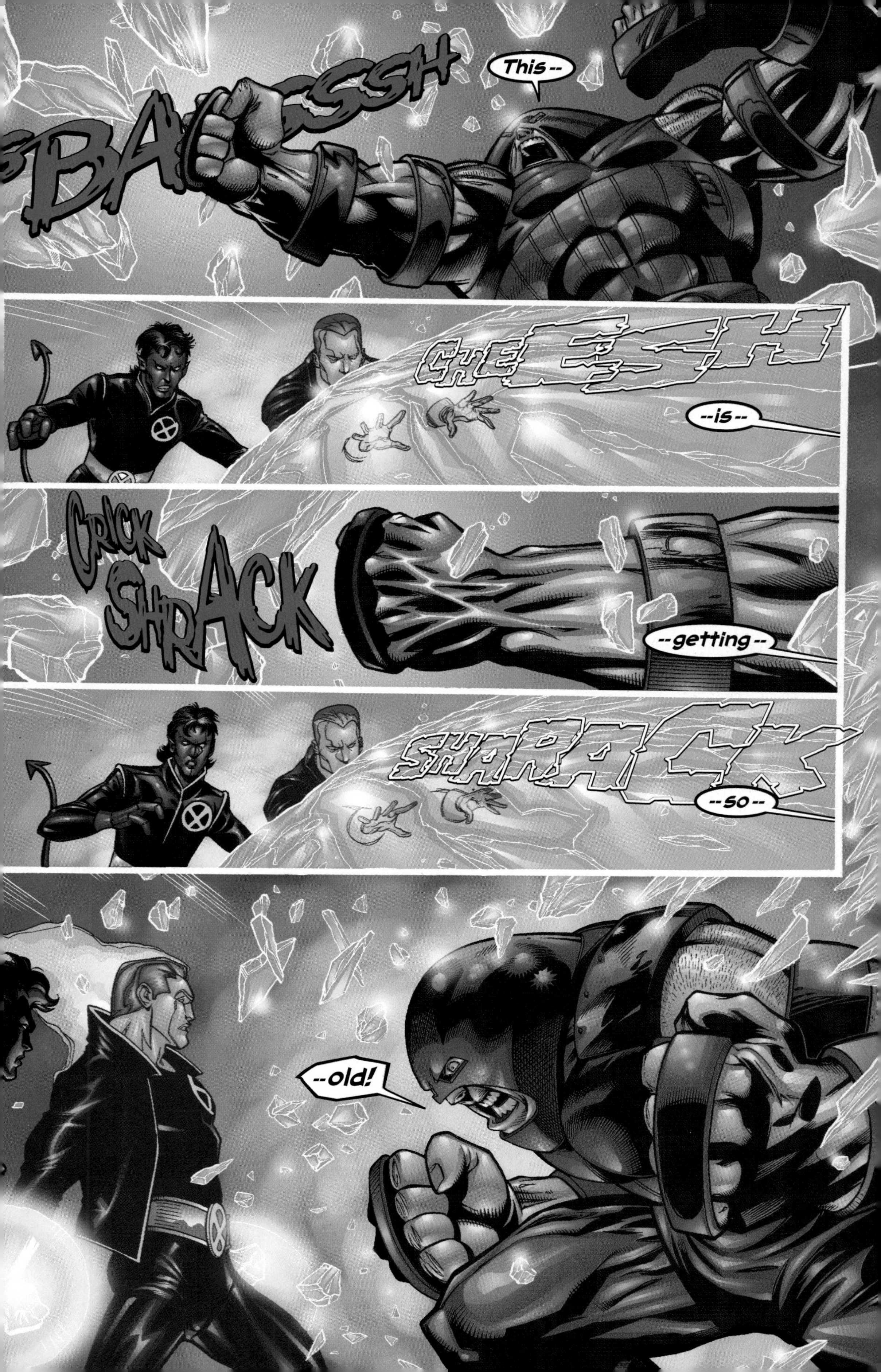

BASSSH
This--
CHEESSH
--is--
CRICK
SHRACK
--getting--
SHARACK
--so--
--old!

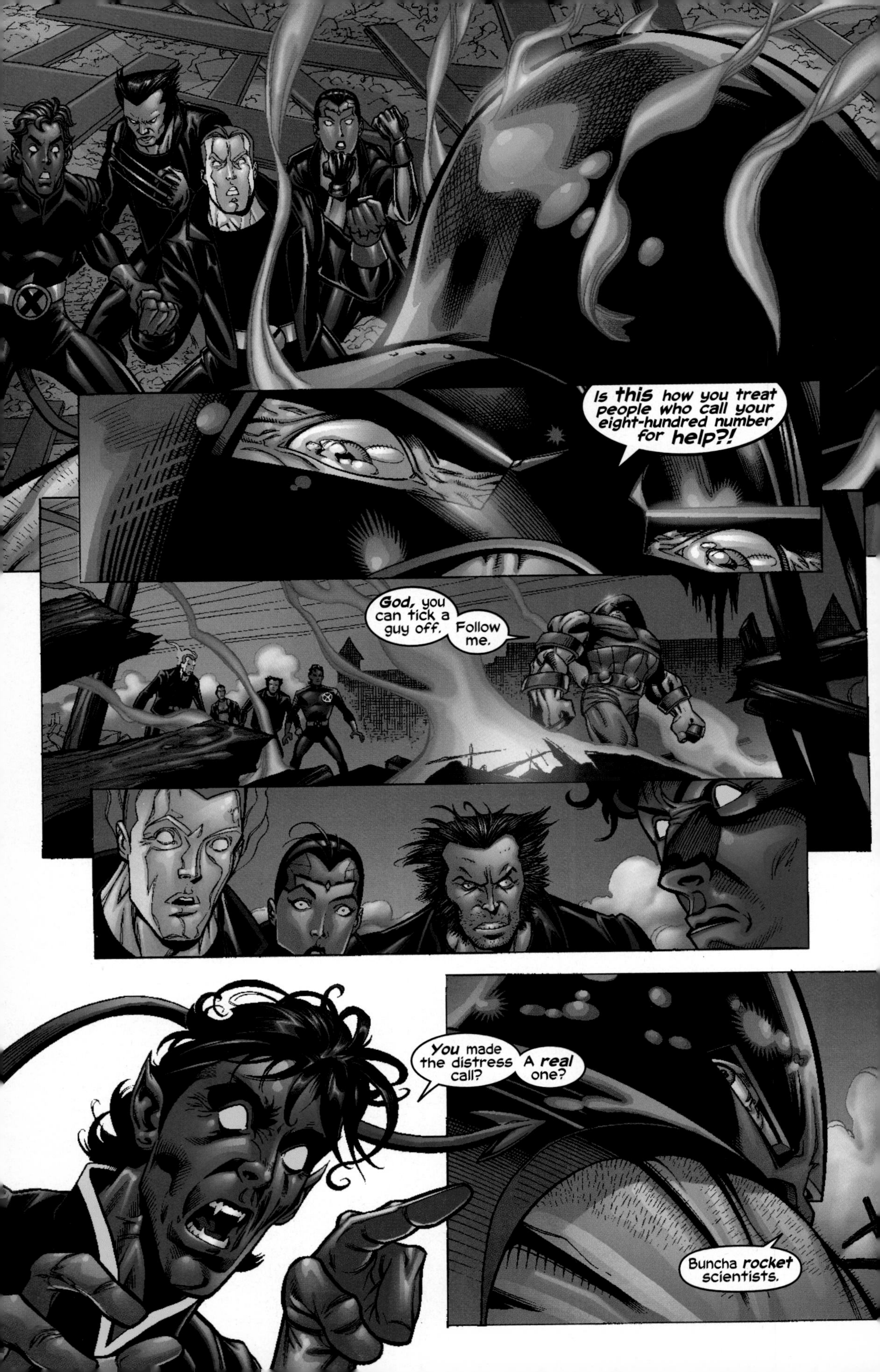
Is this how you treat people who call your eight-hundred number for help?!
God, you can tick a guy off.
Follow me.
You made the distress call?
A real one?
Buncha rocket scientists.

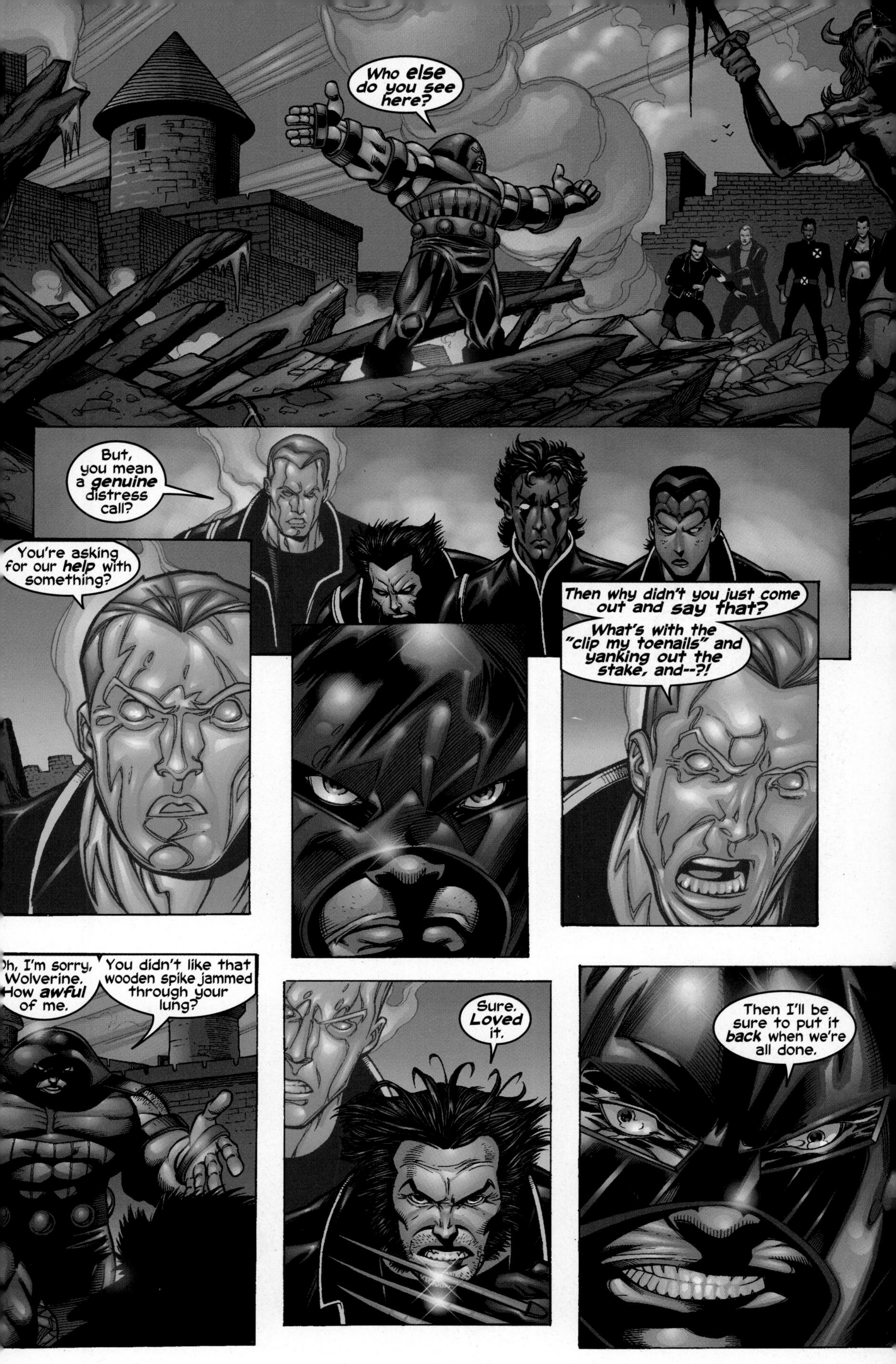

Who else do you see here?
But, you mean a genuine distress call?
You're asking for our help with something?
Then why didn't you just come out and say that?
What's with the "clip my toenails" and yanking out the stake, and--?!
h, I'm sorry, Wolverine. How awful of me.
You didn't like that wooden spike jammed through your lung?
Sure. Loved it.
Then I'll be sure to put it back when we're all done.

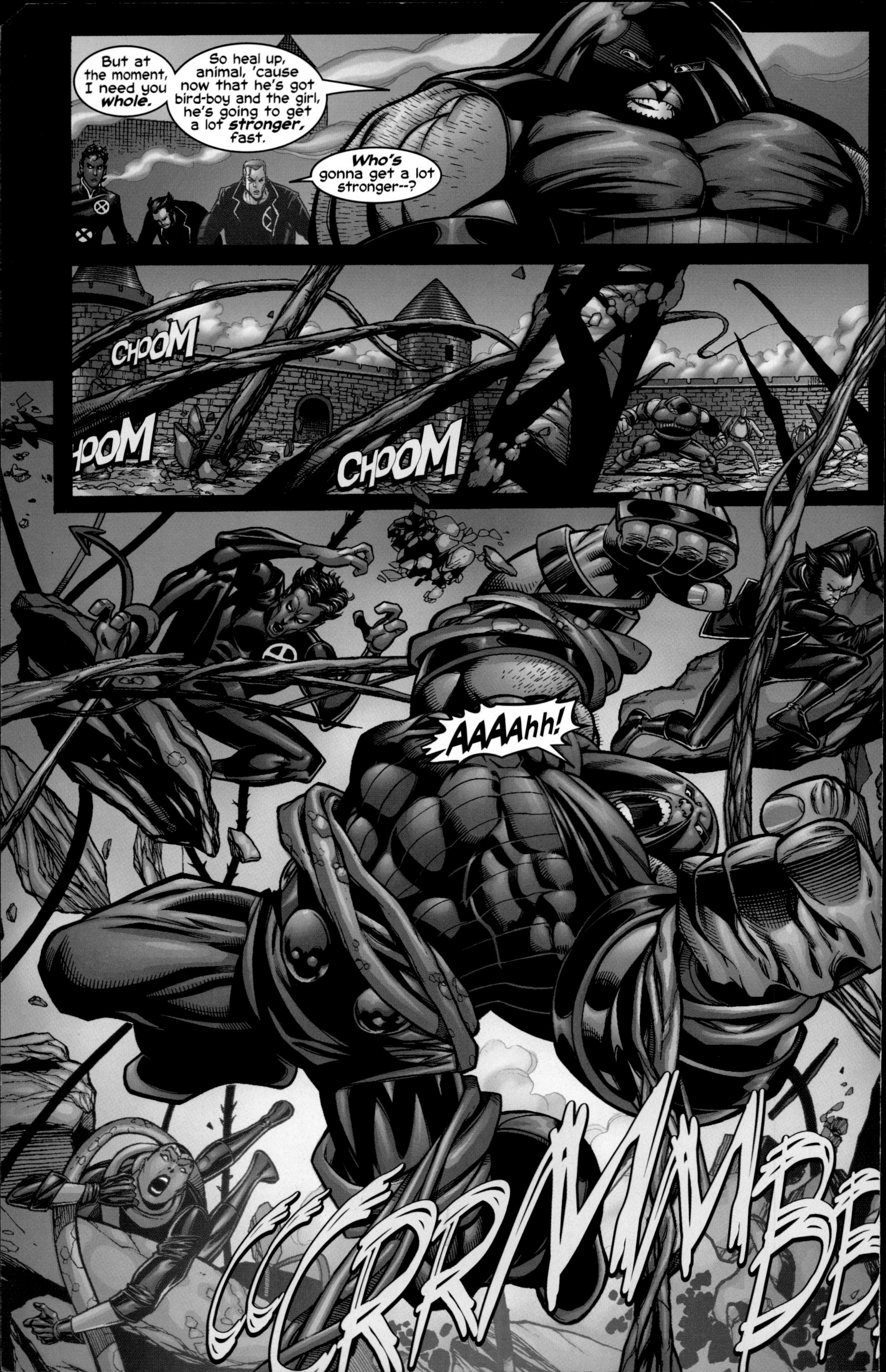

But at the moment, I need you *whole.*
So heal up, animal, 'cause now that he's got bird-boy and the girl, he's going to get a lot *stronger,* fast.
Who's gonna get a lot stronger--?
CHOOM
CHOOM
CHOOM
AAAAhh!
CCRRMMBB

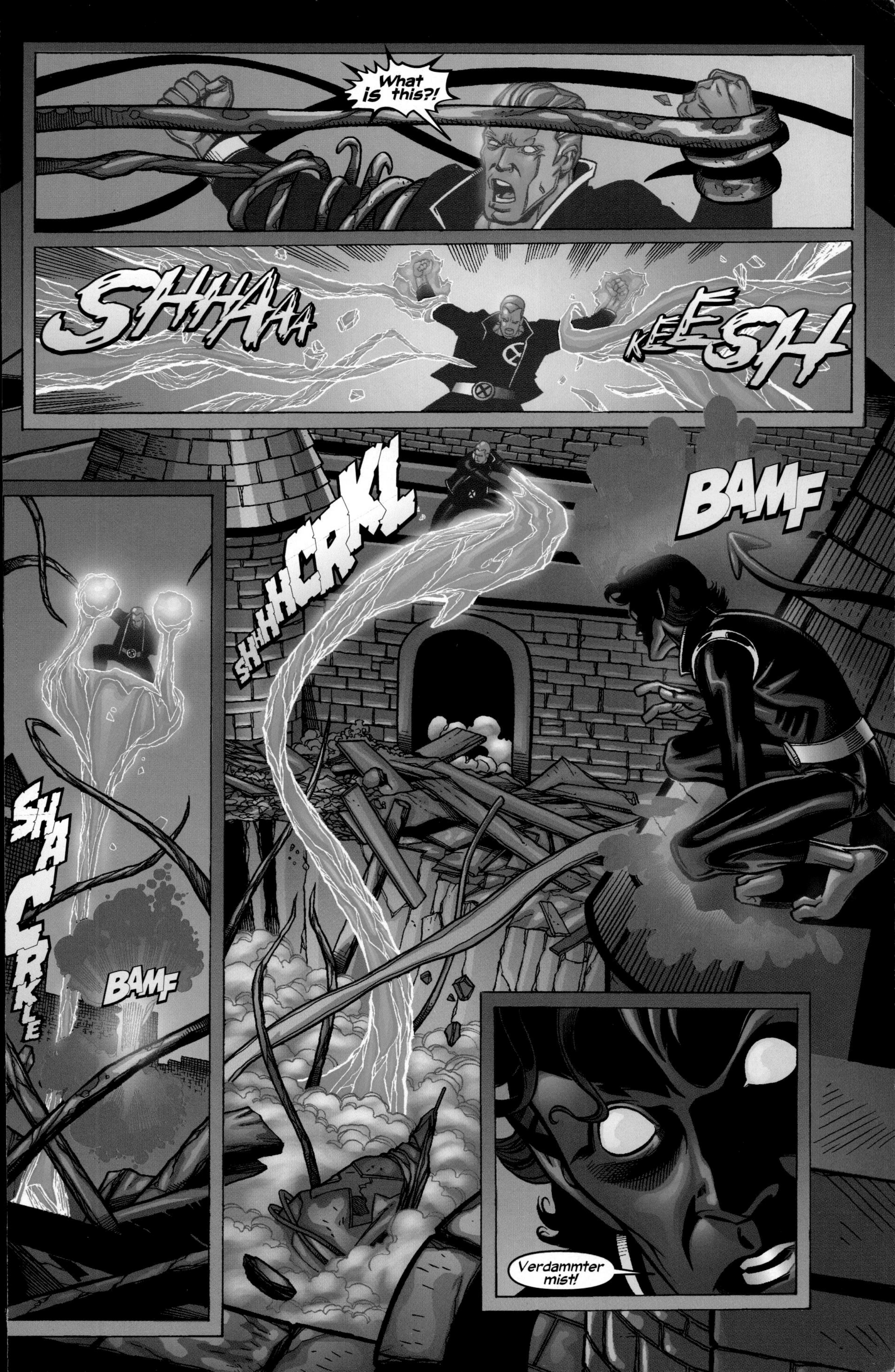

What is this?!
SHHAAAA
KEESH
SHHHHCRKL
BAMF
SHACRKLE
BAMF
Verdammter mist!

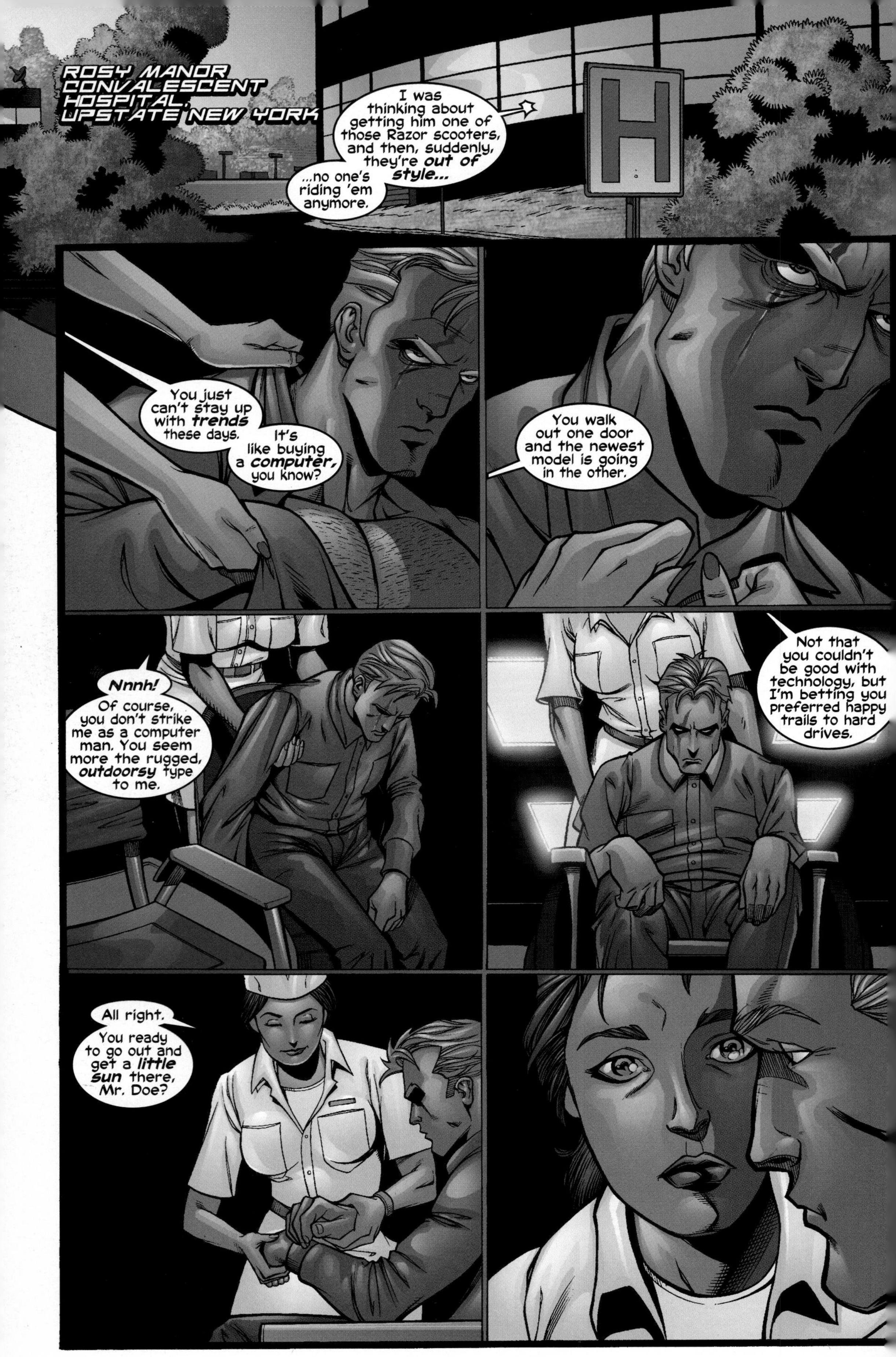
ROSY MANOR CONVALESCENT HOSPITAL, UPSTATE NEW YORK
I was thinking about getting him one of those Razor scooters, and then, suddenly, they're *out of style...*
...no one's riding 'em anymore.
You just can't stay up with *trends* these days.
It's like buying a *computer,* you know?
You walk out one door and the newest model is going in the other.
Nnnh!
Of course, you don't strike me as a computer man. You seem more the rugged, *outdoorsy* type to me.
Not that you couldn't be good with technology, but I'm betting you preferred happy trails to hard drives.
All right.
You ready to go out and get a *little sun* there, Mr. Doe?

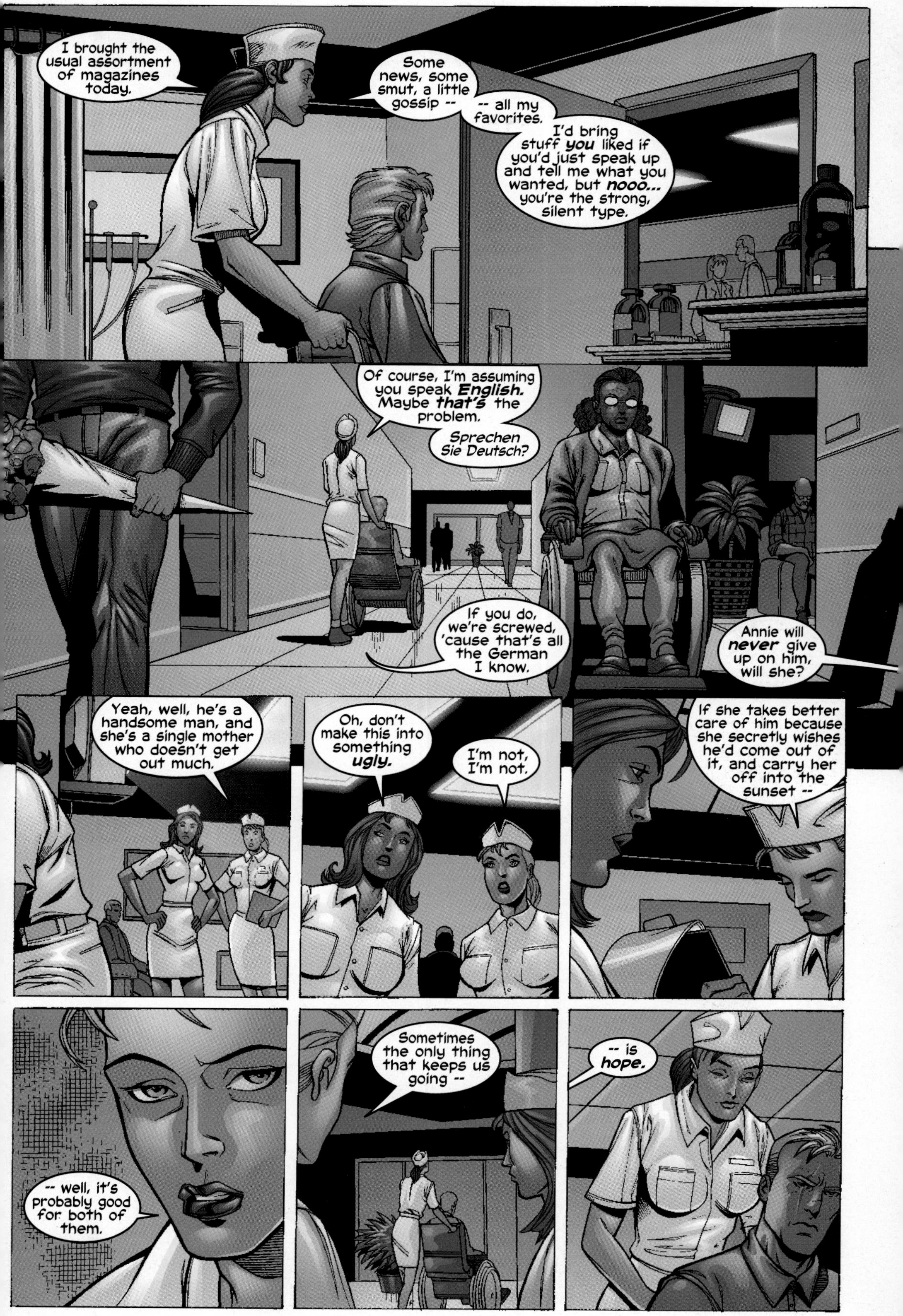
I brought the usual assortment of magazines today.
Some news, some smut, a little gossip --
-- all my favorites.
I'd bring stuff *you* liked if you'd just speak up and tell me what you wanted, but *nooo...* you're the strong, silent type.
Of course, I'm assuming you speak *English.* Maybe *that's* the problem.
Sprechen Sie Deutsch?
If you do, we're screwed, 'cause that's all the German I know.
Annie will *never* give up on him, will she?
Yeah, well, he's a handsome man, and she's a single mother who doesn't get out much.
Oh, don't make this into something *ugly.*
I'm not, I'm not.
If she takes better care of him because she secretly wishes he'd come out of it, and carry her off into the sunset --
-- well, it's probably good for both of them.
Sometimes the only thing that keeps us going --
-- is *hope.*

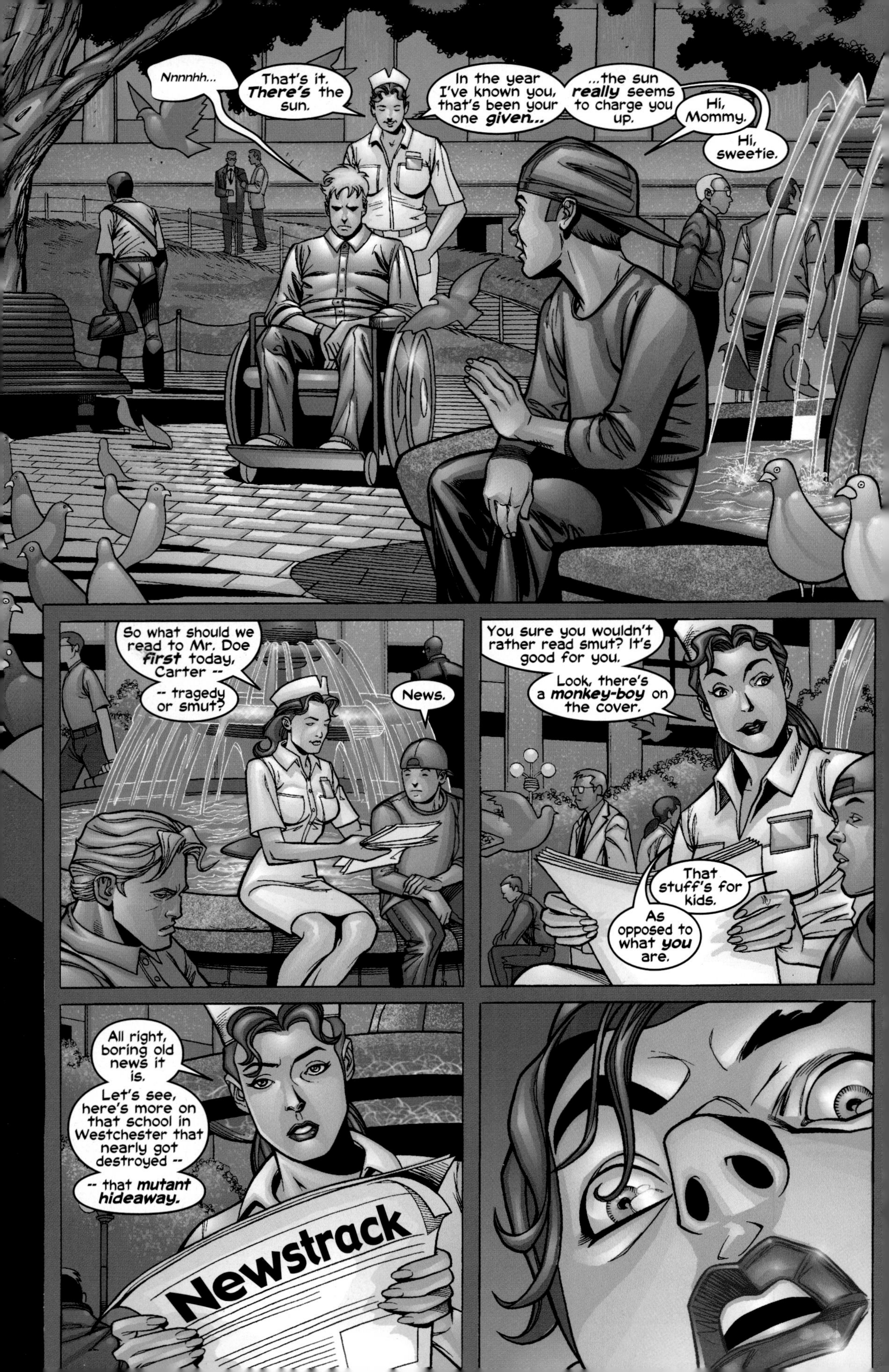
Nnnnhh...
That's it. *There's* the sun.
In the year I've known you, that's been your one *given...*
...the sun *really* seems to charge you up.
Hi, Mommy.
Hi, sweetie.
So what should we read to Mr. Doe *first* today, Carter --
-- tragedy or smut?
News.
You sure you wouldn't rather read smut? It's good for you.
Look, there's a *monkey-boy* on the cover.
That stuff's for kids.
As opposed to what *you* are.
All right, boring old news it is.
Let's see, here's more on that school in Westchester that nearly got destroyed --
-- that *mutant hideaway.*
Newstrack

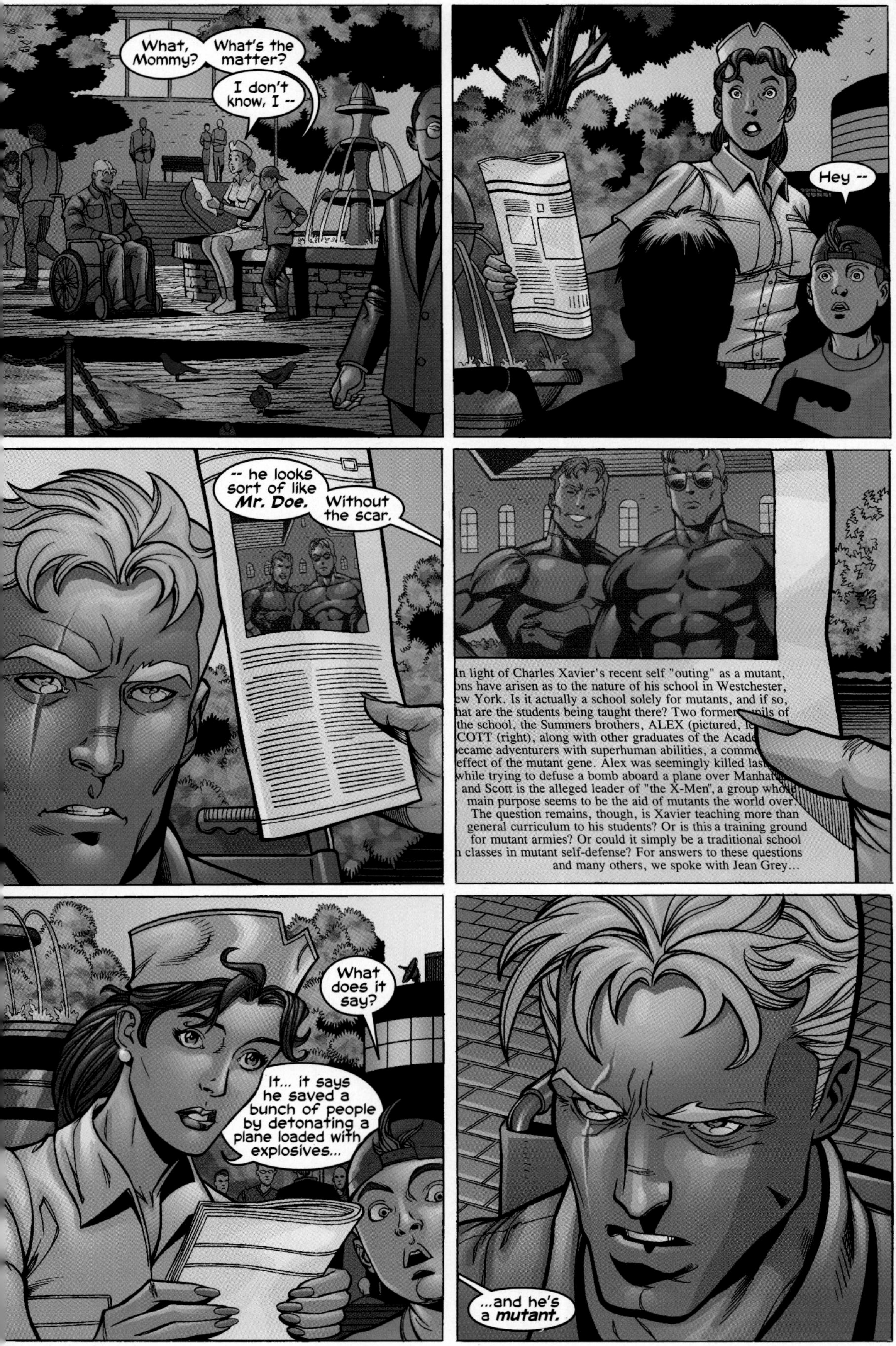
What, Mommy?
What's the matter?
I don't know, I --
Hey --
-- he looks sort of like Mr. Doe.
Without the scar.
In light of Charles Xavier's recent self "outing" as a mutant, ons have arisen as to the nature of his school in Westchester, ew York. Is it actually a school solely for mutants, and if so, hat are the students being taught there? Two former upils of the school, the Summers brothers, ALEX (pictured, le COTT (right), along with other graduates of the Acade ecame adventurers with superhuman abilities, a commo effect of the mutant gene. Alex was seemingly killed las while trying to defuse a bomb aboard a plane over Manhat and Scott is the alleged leader of "the X-Men", a group whose main purpose seems to be the aid of mutants the world over. The question remains, though, is Xavier teaching more than general curriculum to his students? Or is this a training ground for mutant armies? Or could it simply be a traditional school n classes in mutant self-defense? For answers to these questions and many others, we spoke with Jean Grey...
What does it say?
It... it says he saved a bunch of people by detonating a plane loaded with explosives...
...and he's a mutant.

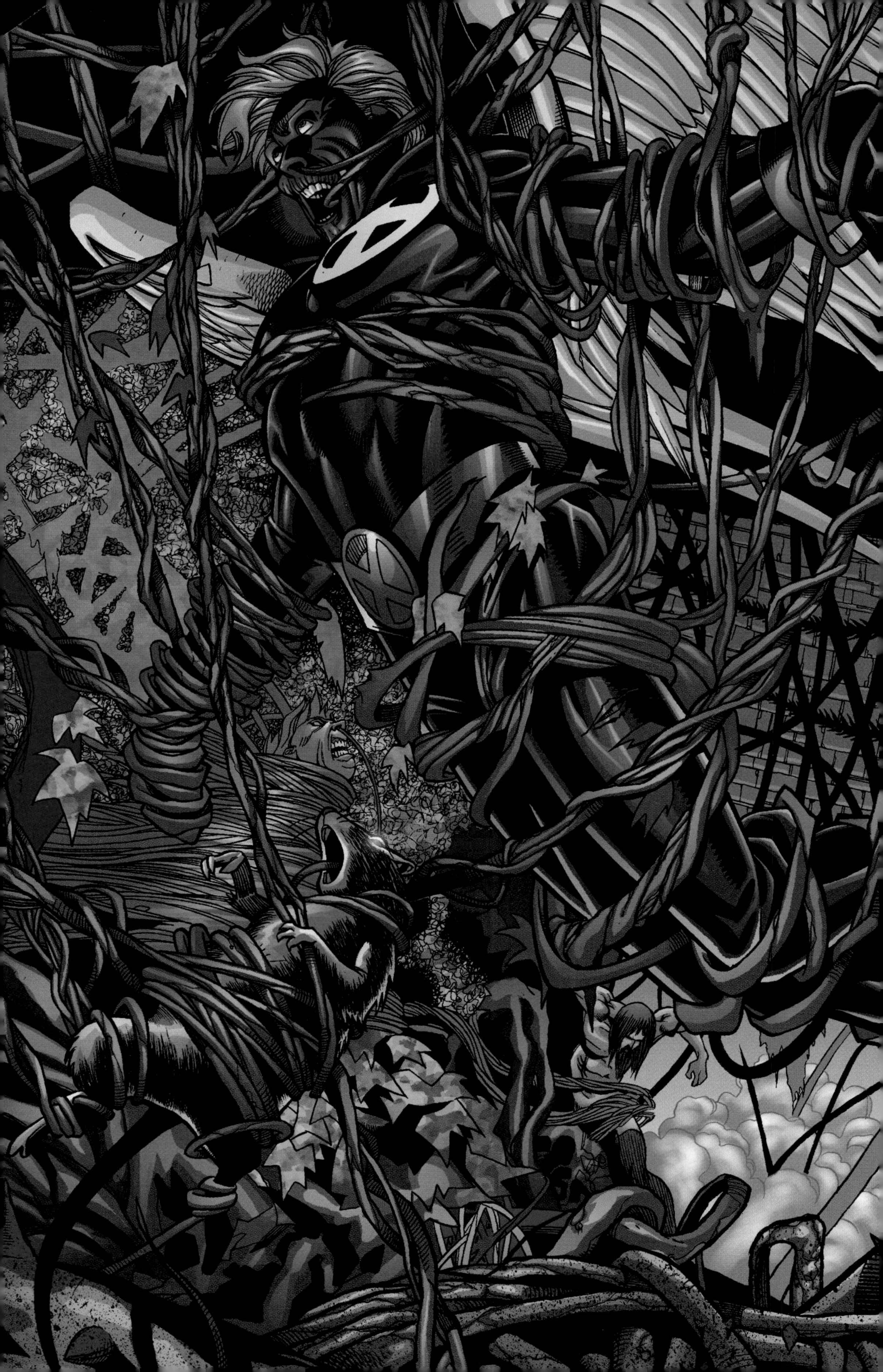

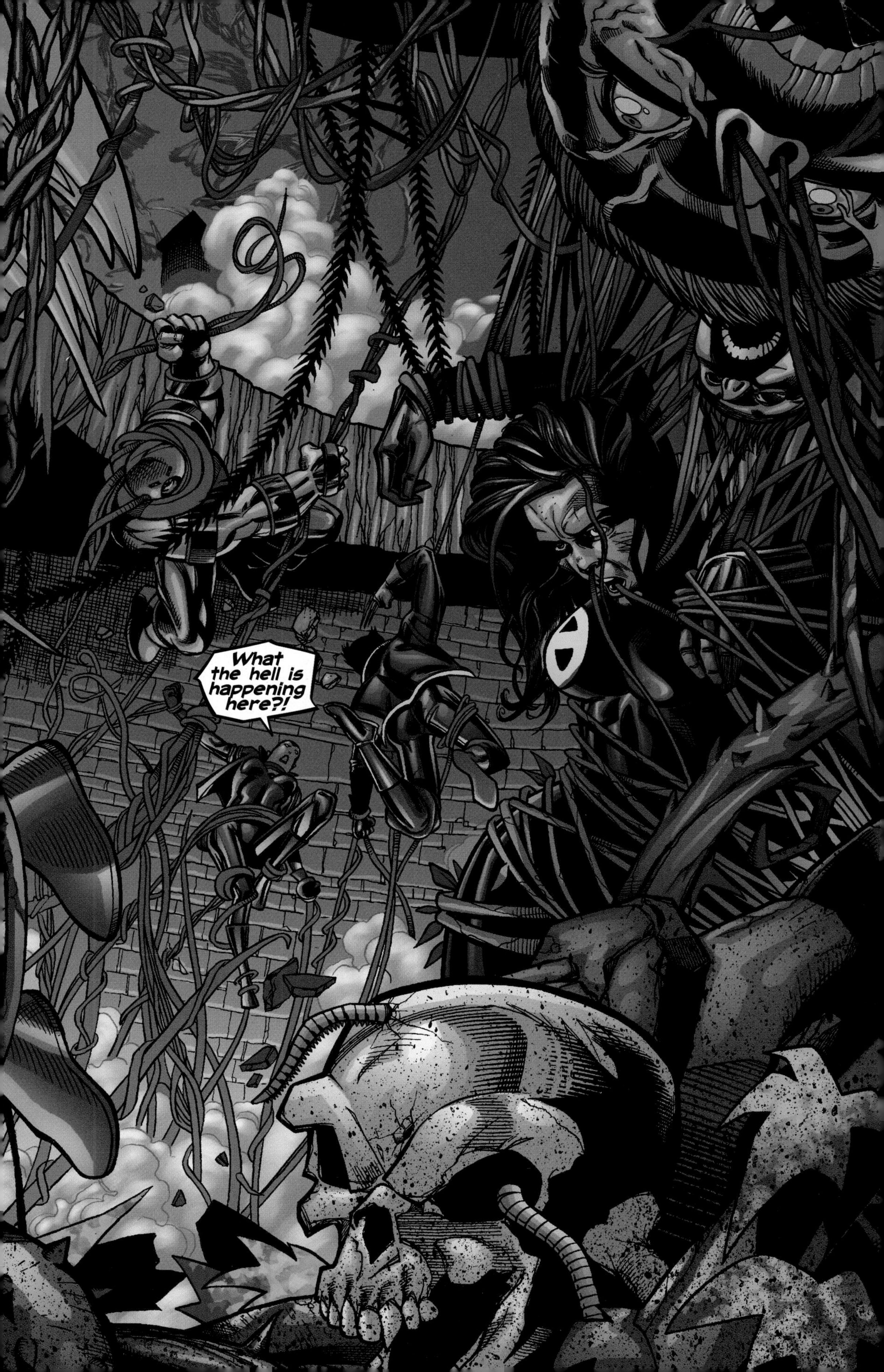
What the hell is happening here?!

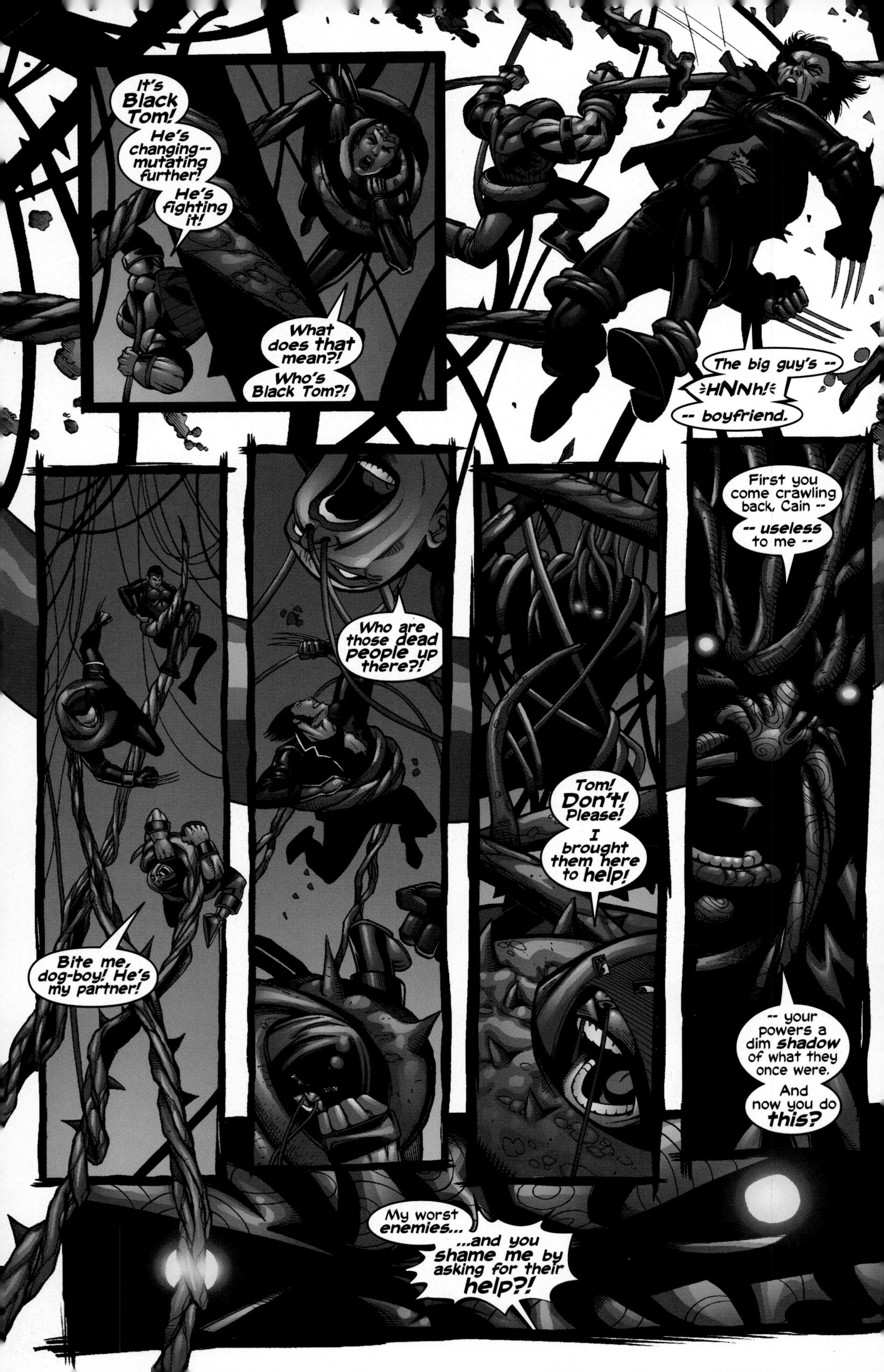

It's Black Tom! He's changing-- mutating further! He's fighting it!
What does that mean?! Who's Black Tom?!
The big guy's -- HNNh! -- boyfriend.
Bite me, dog-boy! He's my partner!
Who are those dead people up there?!
Tom! Don't! Please! I brought them here to help!
First you come crawling back, Cain -- -- useless to me --
-- your powers a dim shadow of what they once were. And now you do this?
My worst enemies... ...and you shame me by asking for their help?!

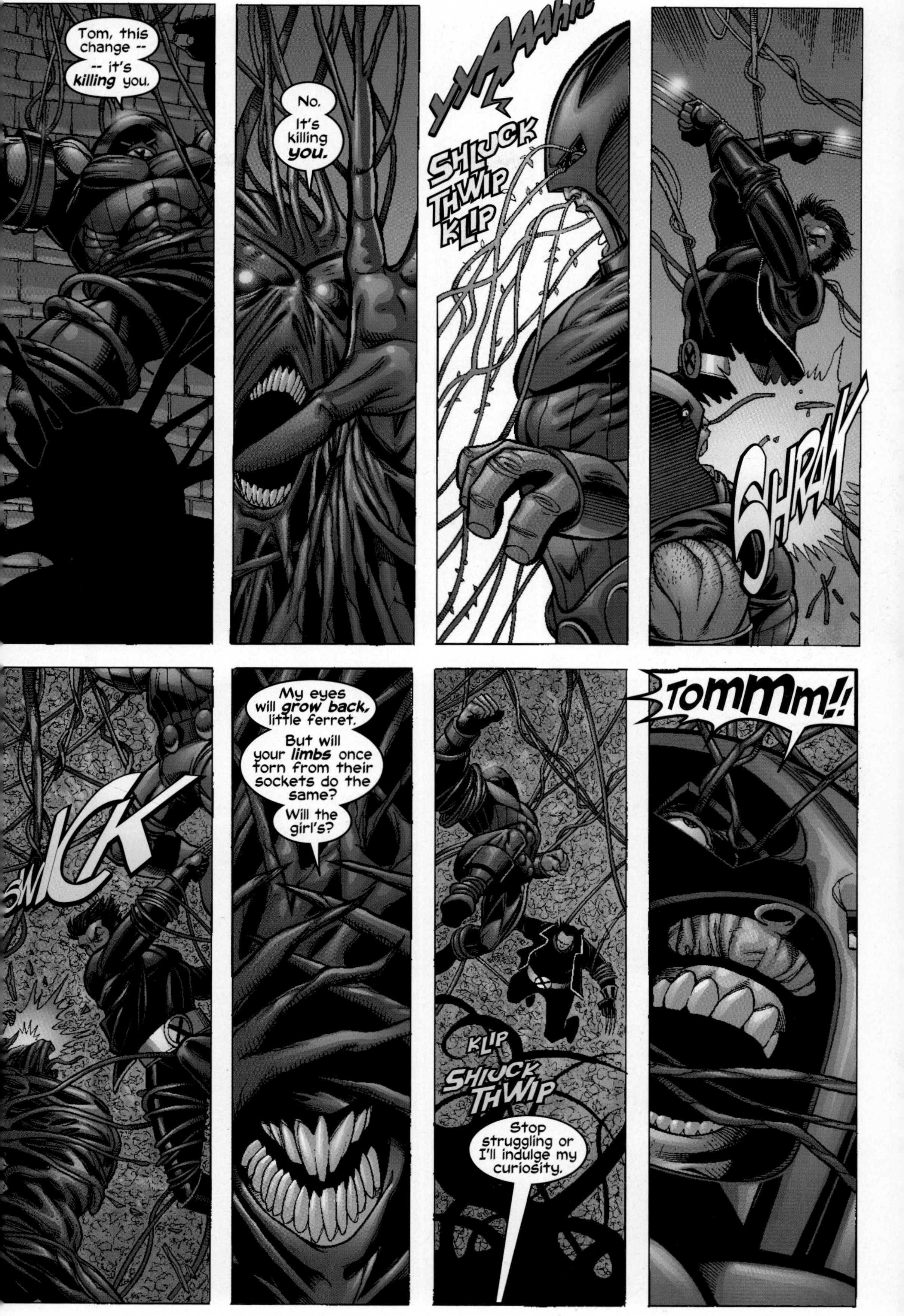

Tom, this change --
-- it's killing you.
No. It's killing you.
YYAAAAhh!
SHLUCK
THWIP
KLIP
SHRAK
SNICK
My eyes will grow back, little ferret.
But will your limbs once torn from their sockets do the same?
Will the girl's?
KLIP
SHLUCK
THWIP
Stop struggling or I'll indulge my curiosity.
TOMMM!!

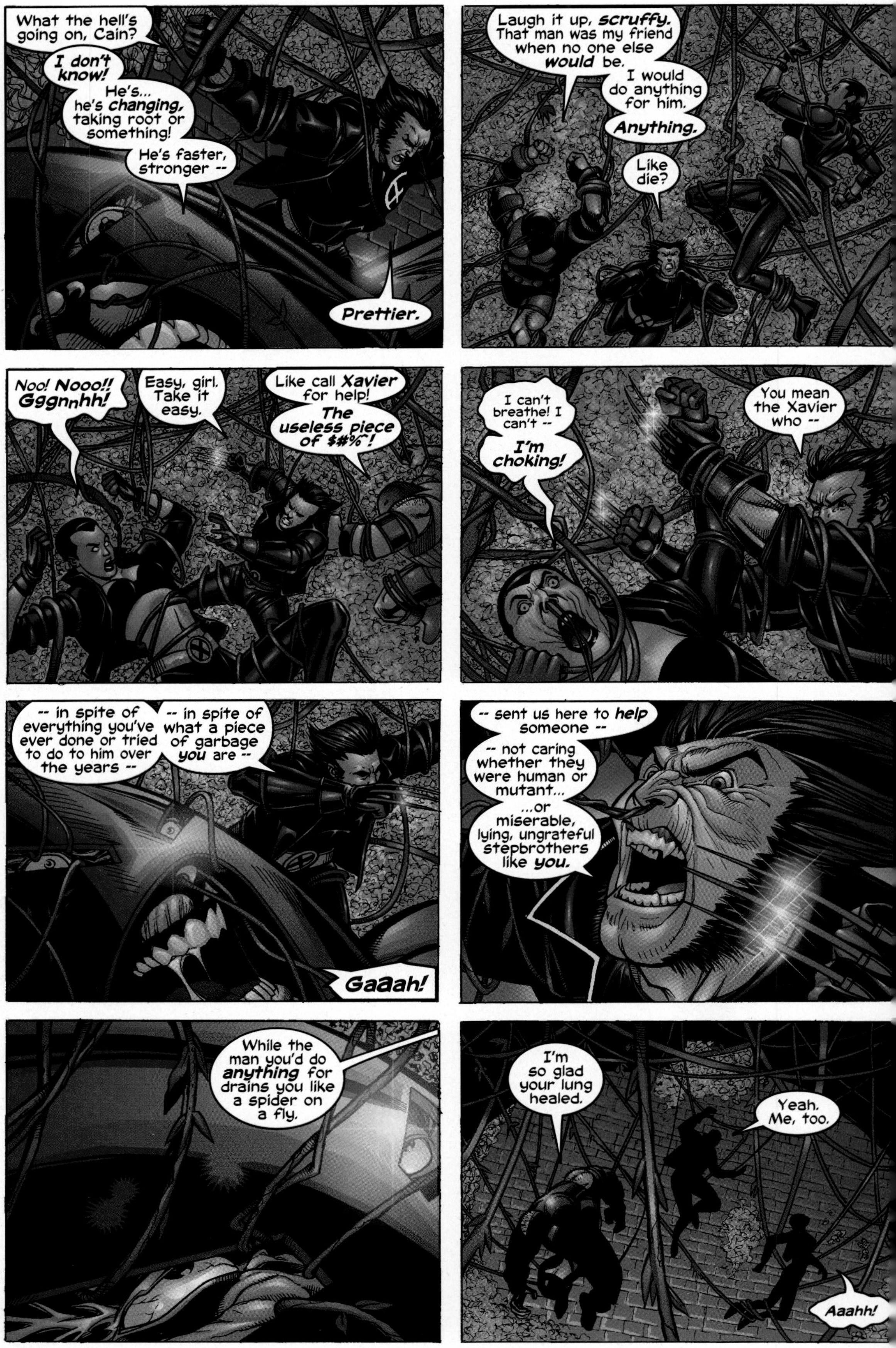
What the hell's going on, Cain?
I don't know!
He's... he's changing, taking root or something!
He's faster, stronger --
Prettier.
Laugh it up, scruffy. That man was my friend when no one else would be.
I would do anything for him.
Anything.
Like die?
Noo! Nooo!! Gggnnhh!
Easy, girl. Take it easy.
Like call Xavier for help! The useless piece of $#%!
I can't breathe! I can't --
I'm choking!
You mean the Xavier who --
-- in spite of everything you've ever done or tried to do to him over the years --
-- in spite of what a piece of garbage you are --
Gaaah!
-- sent us here to help someone --
-- not caring whether they were human or mutant...
...or miserable, lying, ungrateful stepbrothers like you.
While the man you'd do anything for drains you like a spider on a fly.
I'm so glad your lung healed.
Yeah. Me, too.
Aaahh!

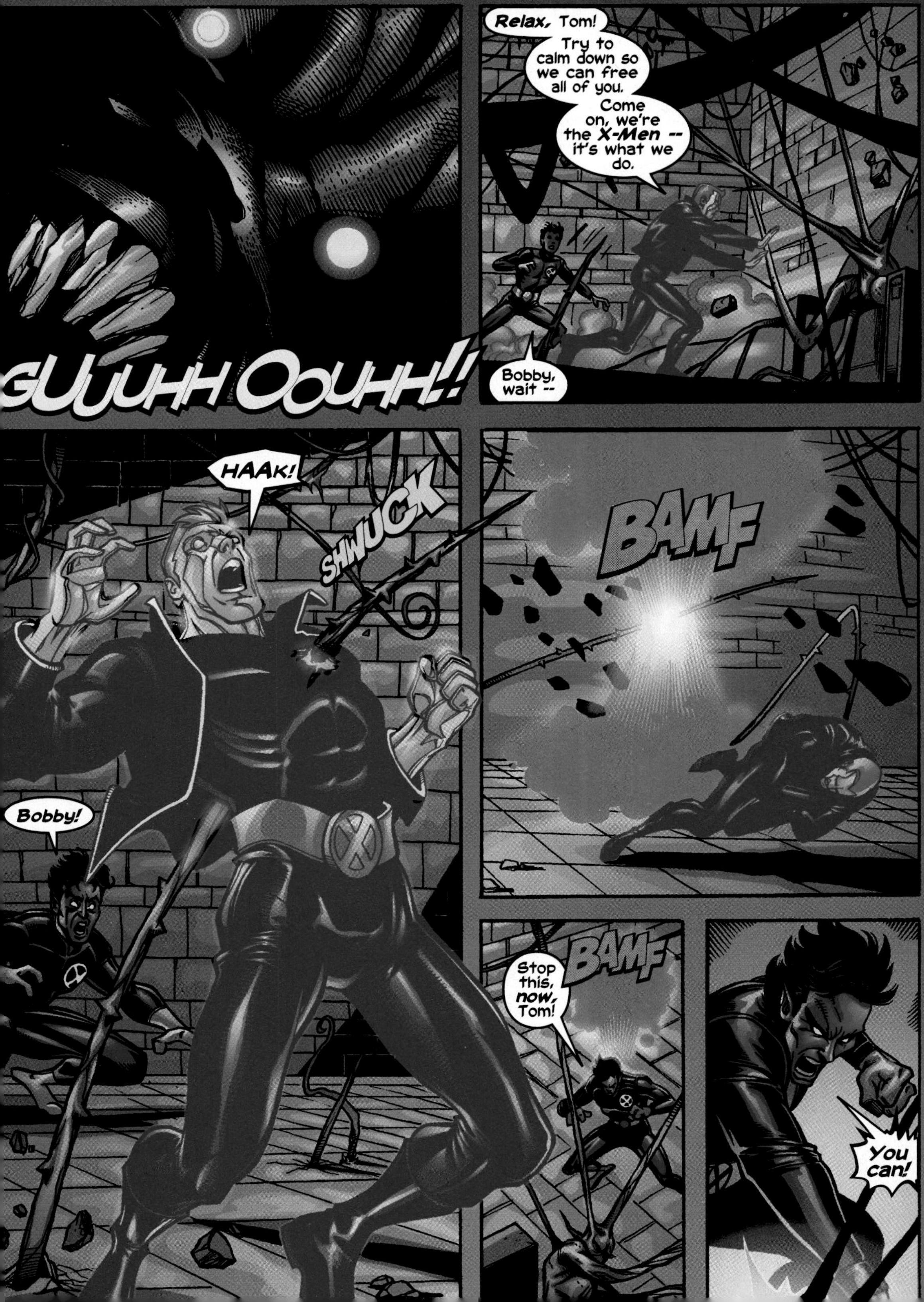
GUUUHH OOUHH!!
Relax, Tom!
Try to calm down so we can free all of you.
Come on, we're the X-Men -- it's what we do.
Bobby, wait --
HAAK!
SHWUCK
Bobby!
BAMF
BAMF
Stop this, now, Tom!
You can!

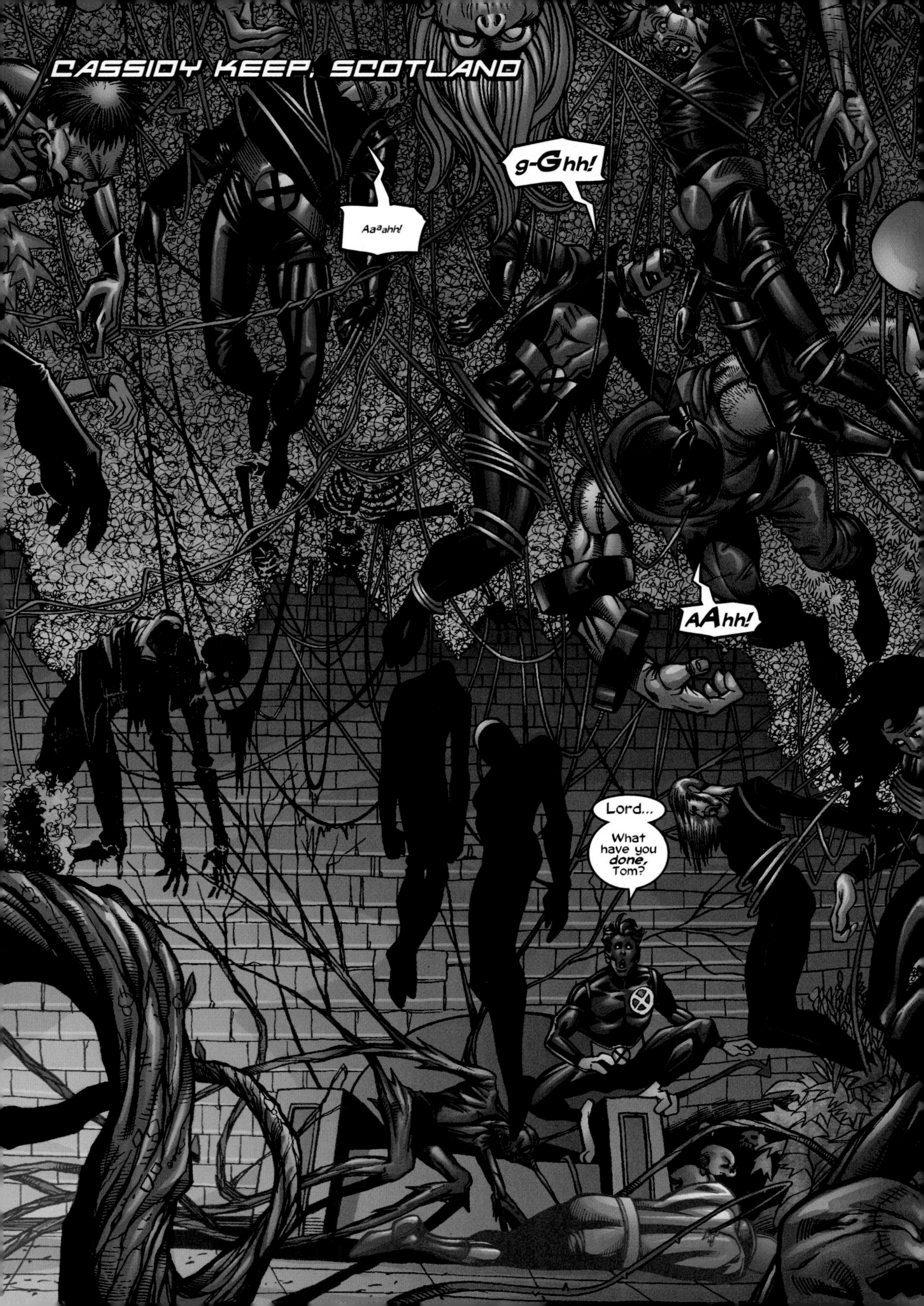
CASSIDY KEEP, SCOTLAND
Aaaahh!
g-Ghh!
AAhh!
Lord...
What have you done, Tom?

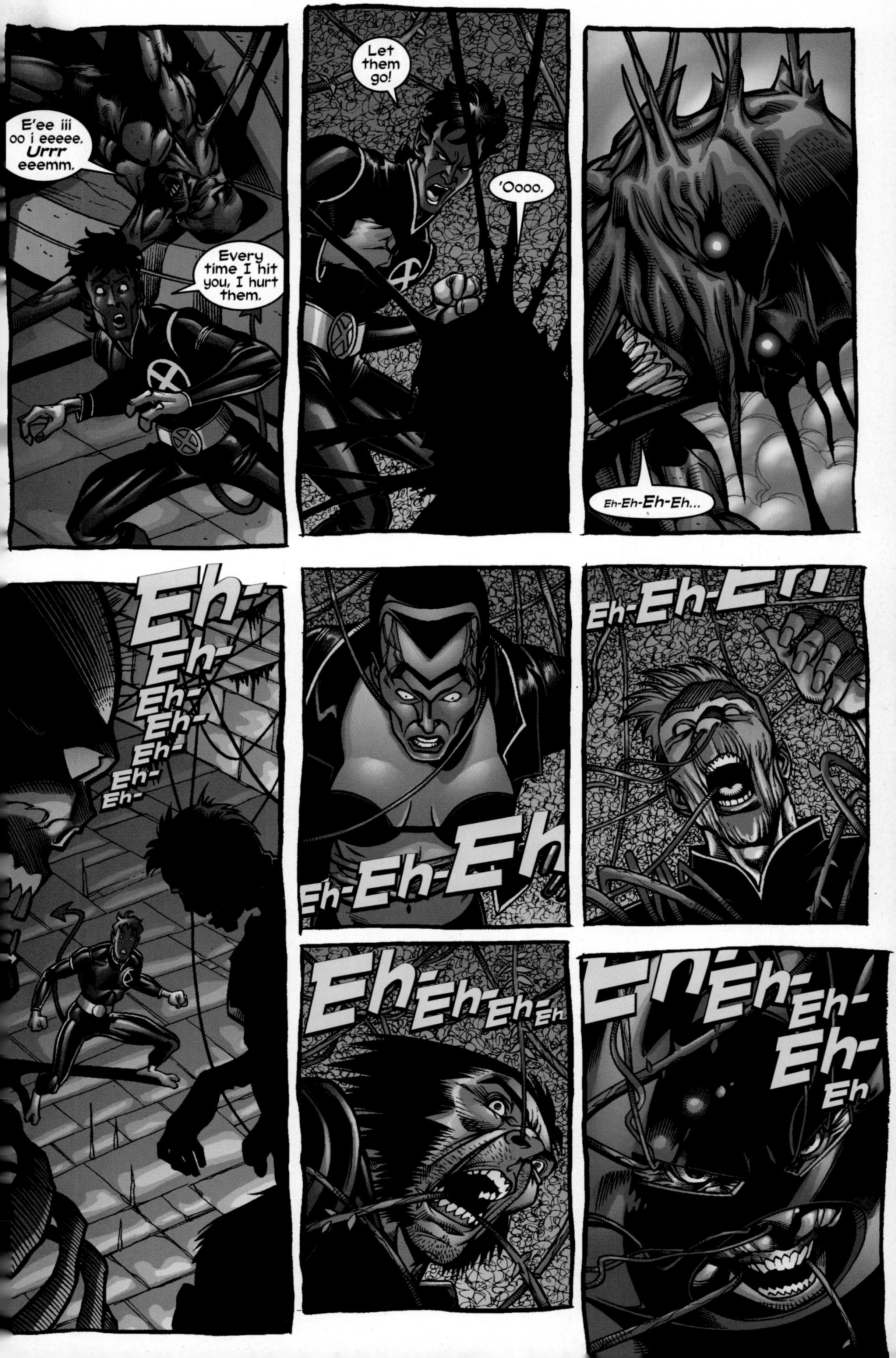
E'ee iii oo i eeeee. Urrr eeemm.
Every time I hit you, I hurt them.
Let them go!
'Oooo.
Eh-Eh-Eh-Eh...
Eh-Eh-Eh-Eh-Eh-Eh-Eh-
Eh-Eh-Eh
Eh-Eh-Eh
Eh-Eh-Eh-Eh
Eh-Eh-Eh-Eh-Eh

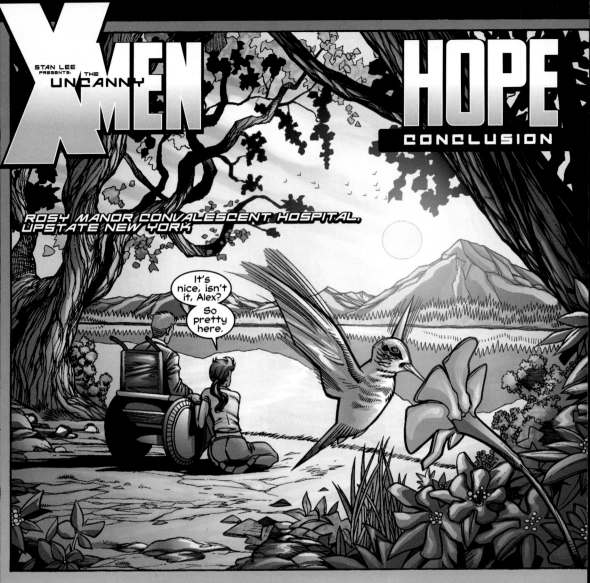

STAN LEE
PRESENTS: THE
**UNCANNY
X-MEN**

HOPE
CONCLUSION

ROSY MANOR CONVALESCENT HOSPITAL,
UPSTATE NEW YORK

It's nice, isn't it, Alex? So pretty here.

A good place to say goodbye... ...not something I ever thought I'd be --

-- I'd be doing.

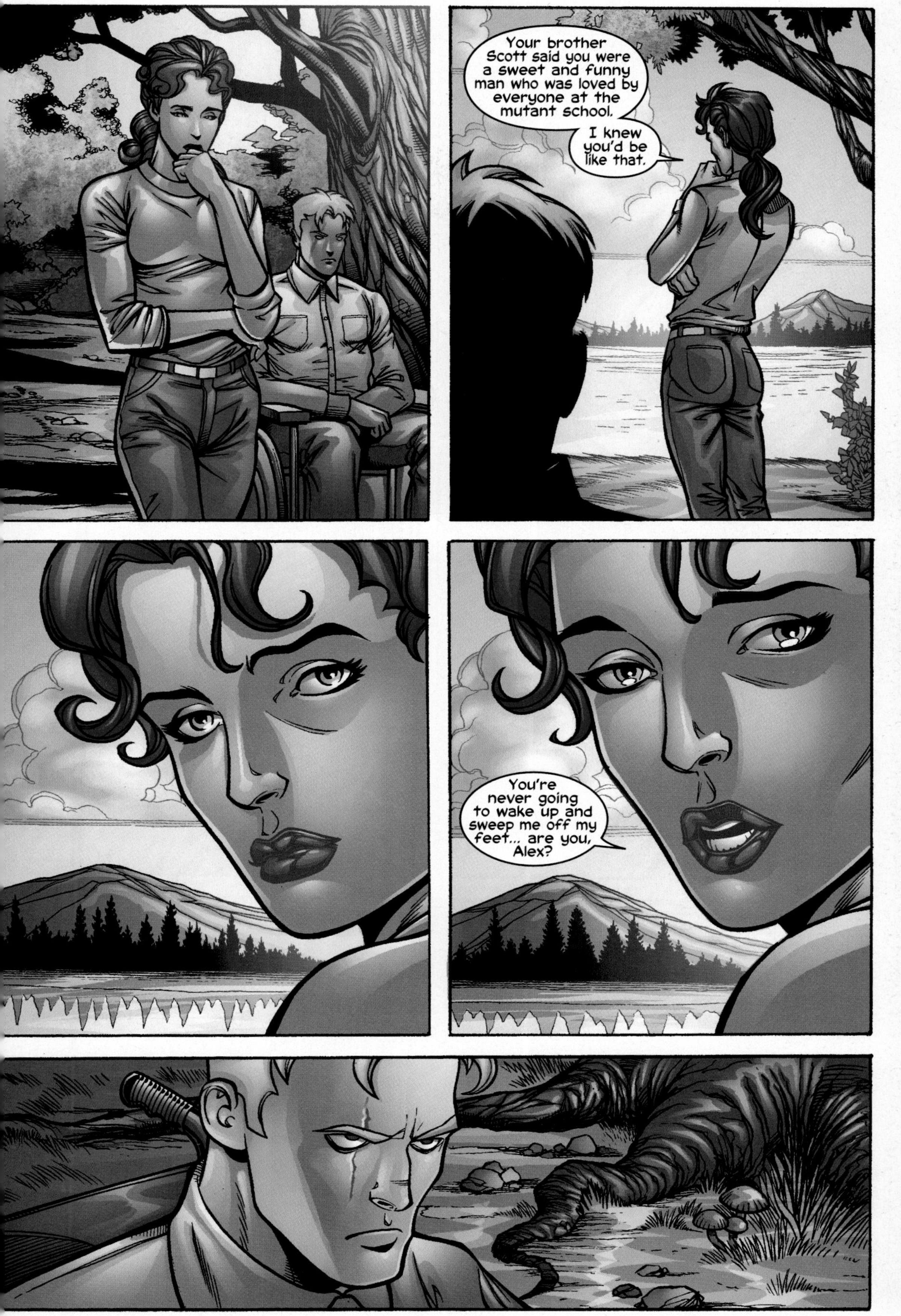
Your brother Scott said you were a sweet and funny man who was loved by everyone at the mutant school.
I knew you'd be like that.
You're never going to wake up and sweep me off my feet... are you, Alex?

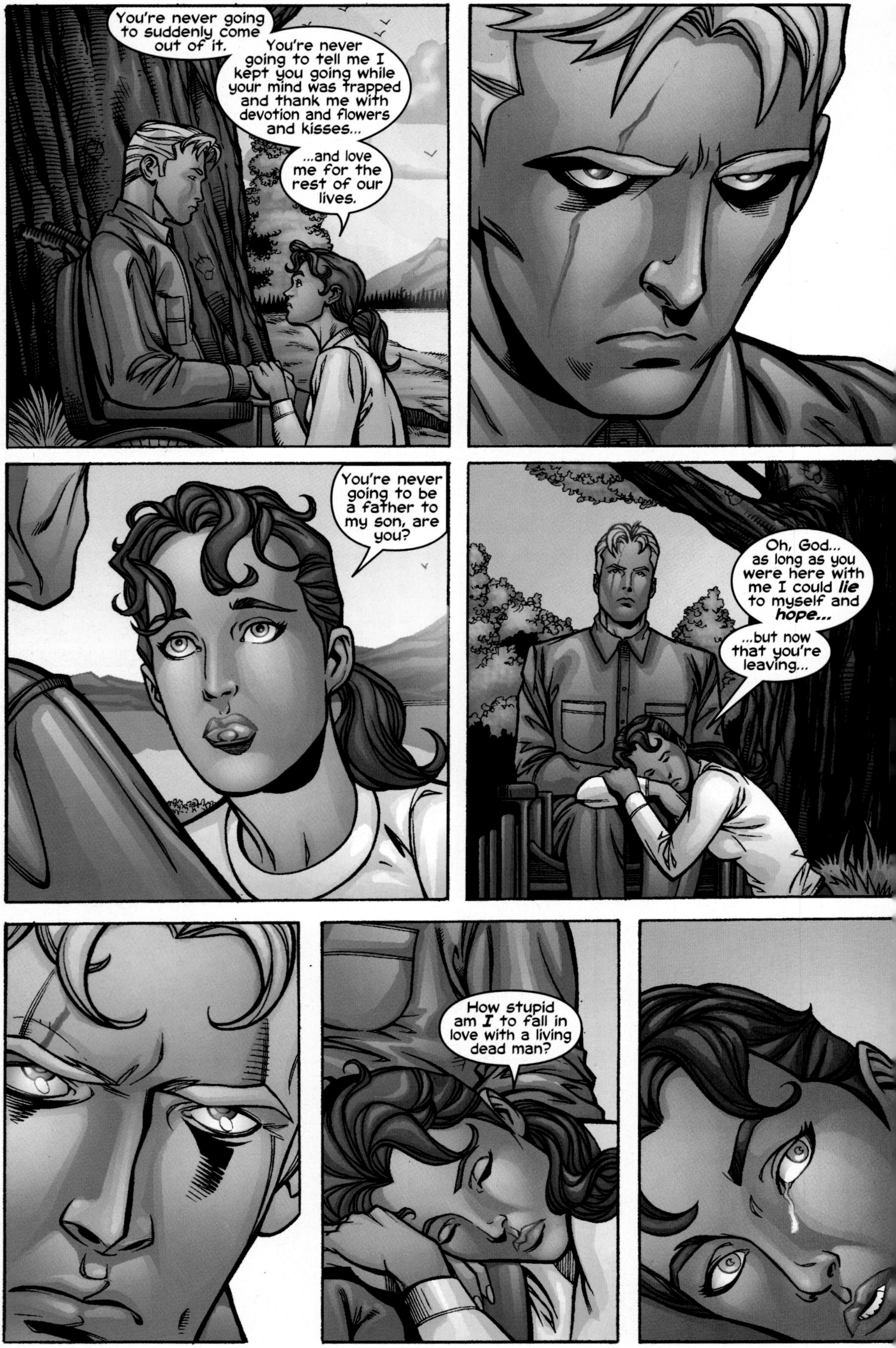
You're never going to suddenly come out of it.
You're never going to tell me I kept you going while your mind was trapped and thank me with devotion and flowers and kisses...
...and love me for the rest of our lives.
You're never going to be a father to my son, are you?
Oh, God... as long as you were here with me I could *lie* to myself and *hope...*
...but now that you're leaving...
How stupid am *I* to fall in love with a living dead man?

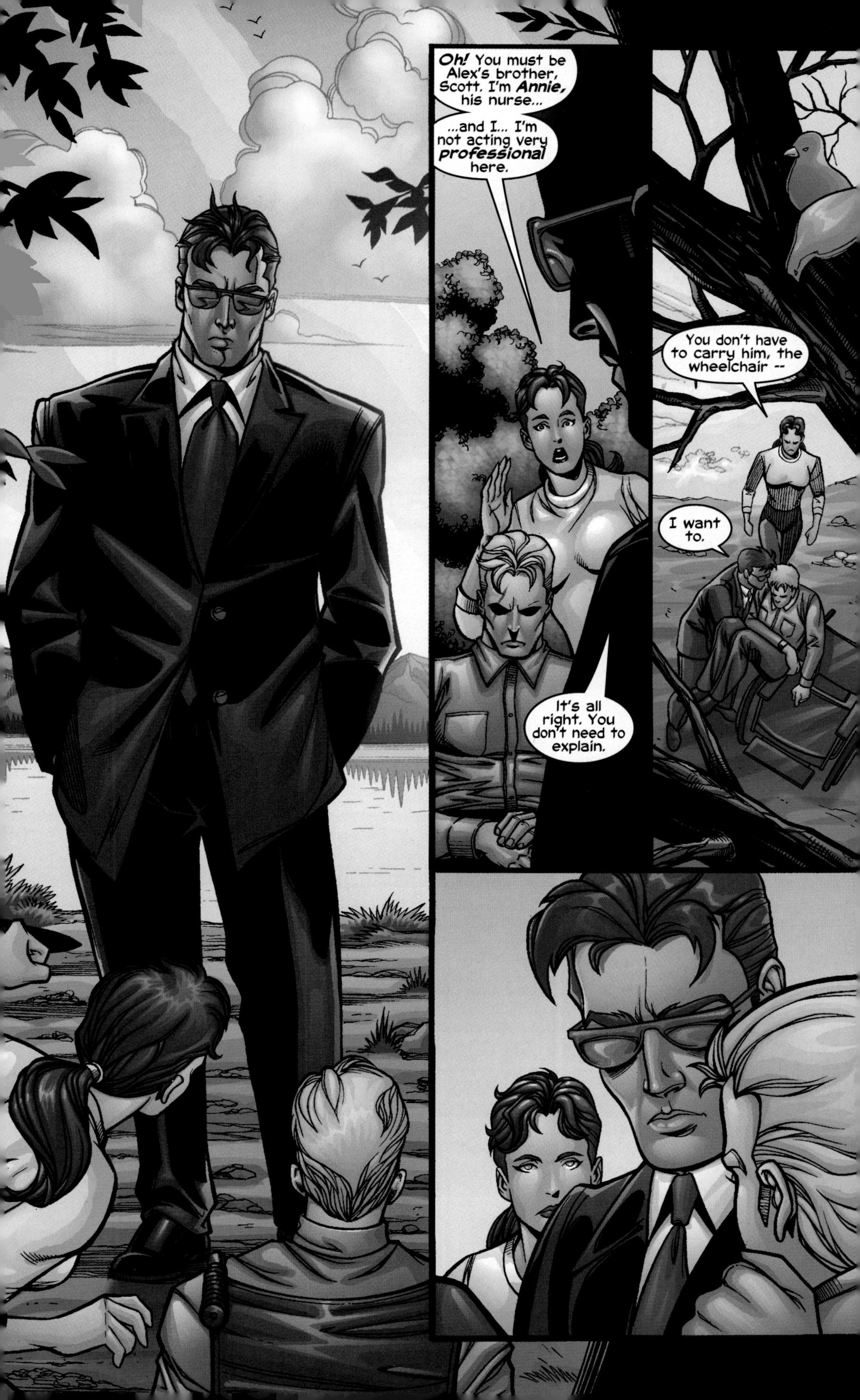

Oh! You must be Alex's brother, Scott. I'm Annie, his nurse...
...and I... I'm not acting very professional here.
It's all right. You don't need to explain.
You don't have to carry him, the wheelchair --
I want to.

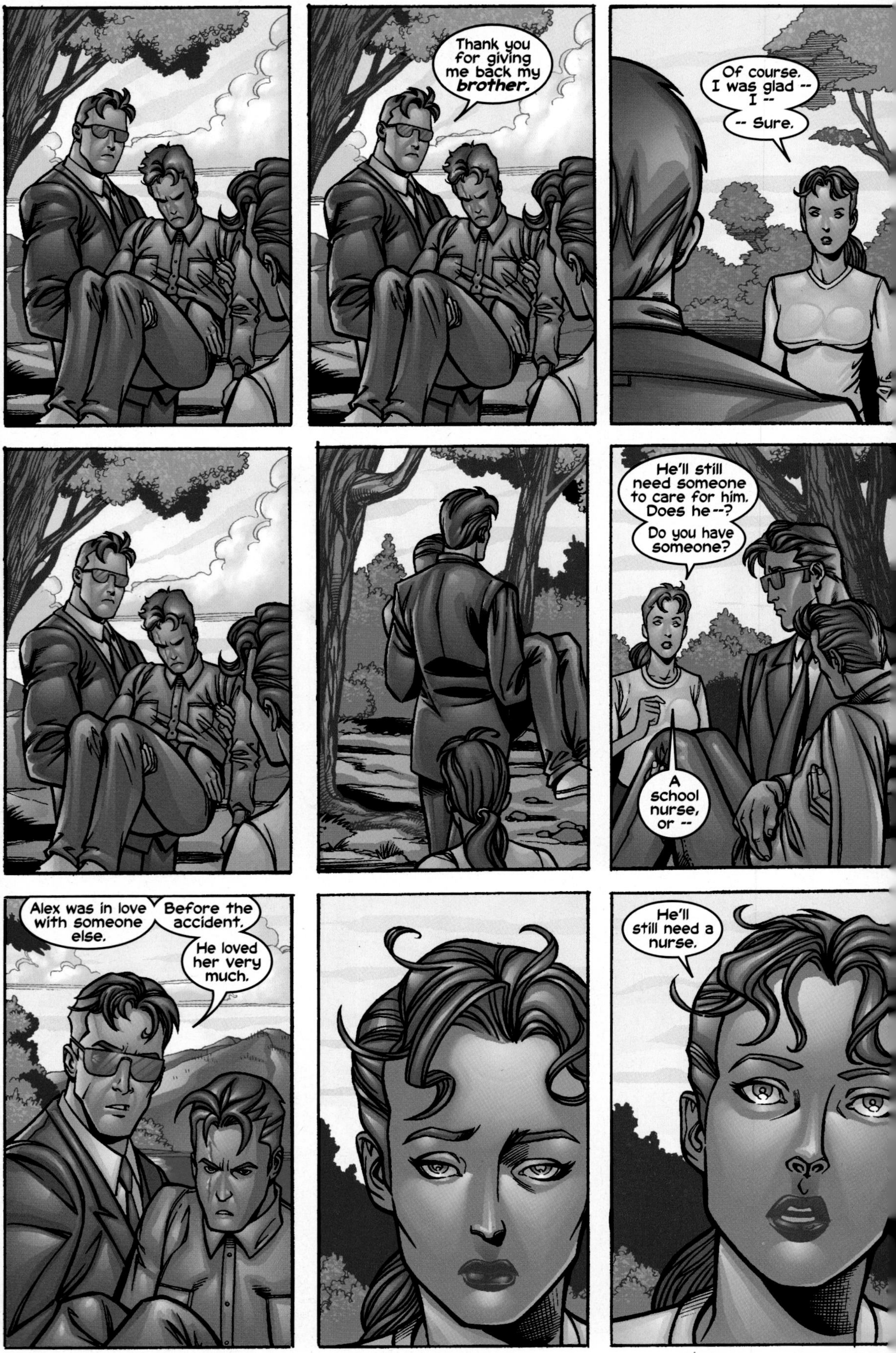
Thank you for giving me back my *brother.*
Of course. I was glad -- I --
-- Sure.
He'll still need someone to care for him. Does he--?
Do you have someone?
A school nurse, or --
Alex was in love with someone else.
Before the accident.
He loved her very much.
He'll still need a nurse.

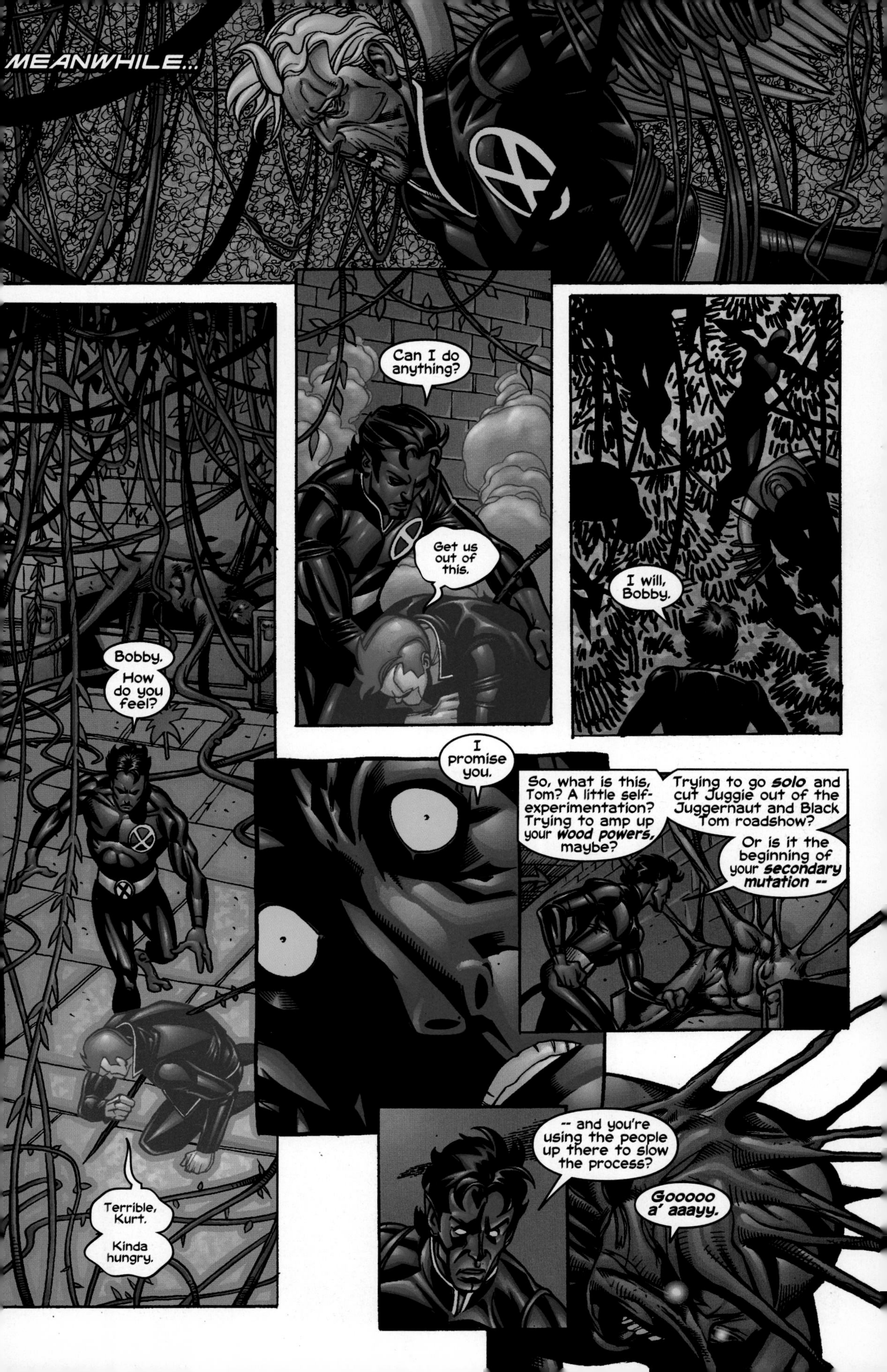
MEANWHILE...
Bobby. How do you feel?
Terrible, Kurt.
Kinda hungry.
Can I do anything?
Get us out of this.
I will, Bobby.
I promise you.
So, what is this, Tom? A little self-experimentation? Trying to amp up your wood powers, maybe?
Trying to go solo and cut Juggie out of the Juggernaut and Black Tom roadshow?
Or is it the beginning of your secondary mutation --
-- and you're using the people up there to slow the process?
Gooooo a' aaayy.

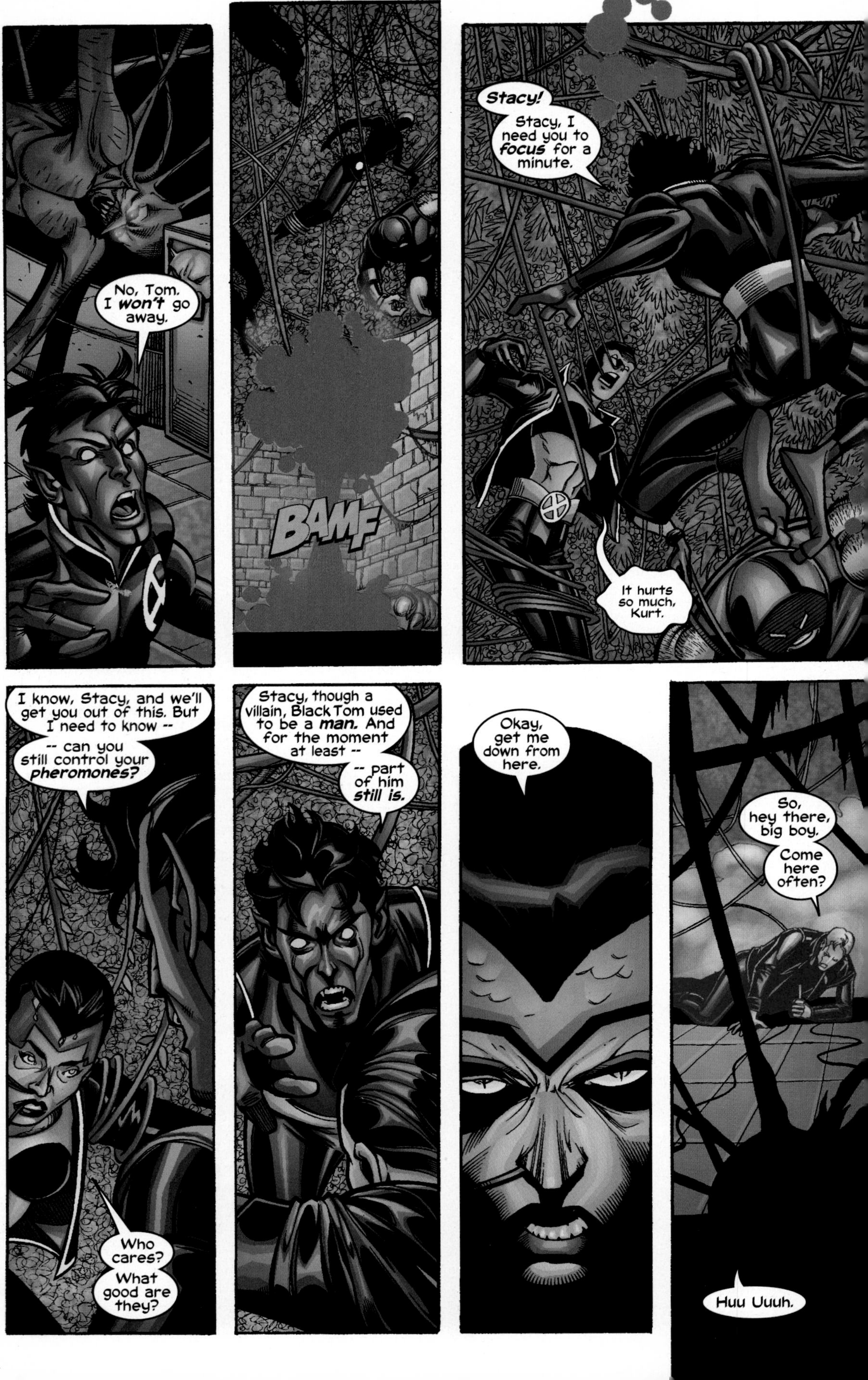

No, Tom. I *won't* go away.
BAMF
Stacy!
Stacy, I need you to *focus* for a minute.
It hurts so much, Kurt.
I know, Stacy, and we'll get you out of this. But I need to know --
-- can you still control your *pheromones?*
Who cares? What good are they?
Stacy, though a villain, Black Tom used to be a *man.* And for the moment at least --
-- part of him *still is.*
Okay, get me down from here.
So, hey there, big boy.
Come here often?
Huu Uuuh.

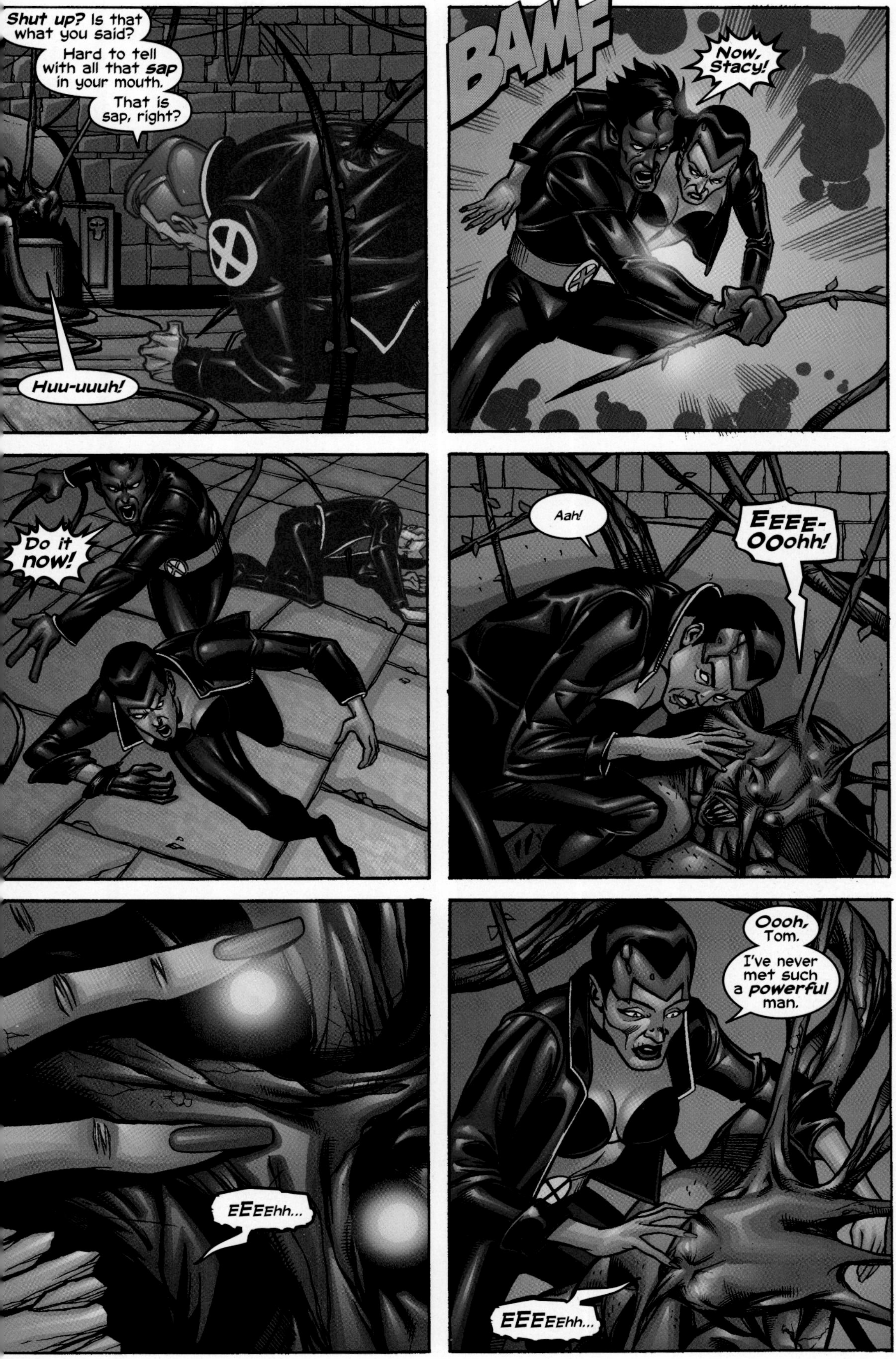

Shut up? Is that what you said?
Hard to tell with all that sap in your mouth.
That is sap, right?
Huu-uuuh!
BAMF
Now, Stacy!
Do it now!
Aah!
EEEE-OOohh!
EEEehh...
Oooh, Tom.
I've never met such a powerful man.
EEEEehh...

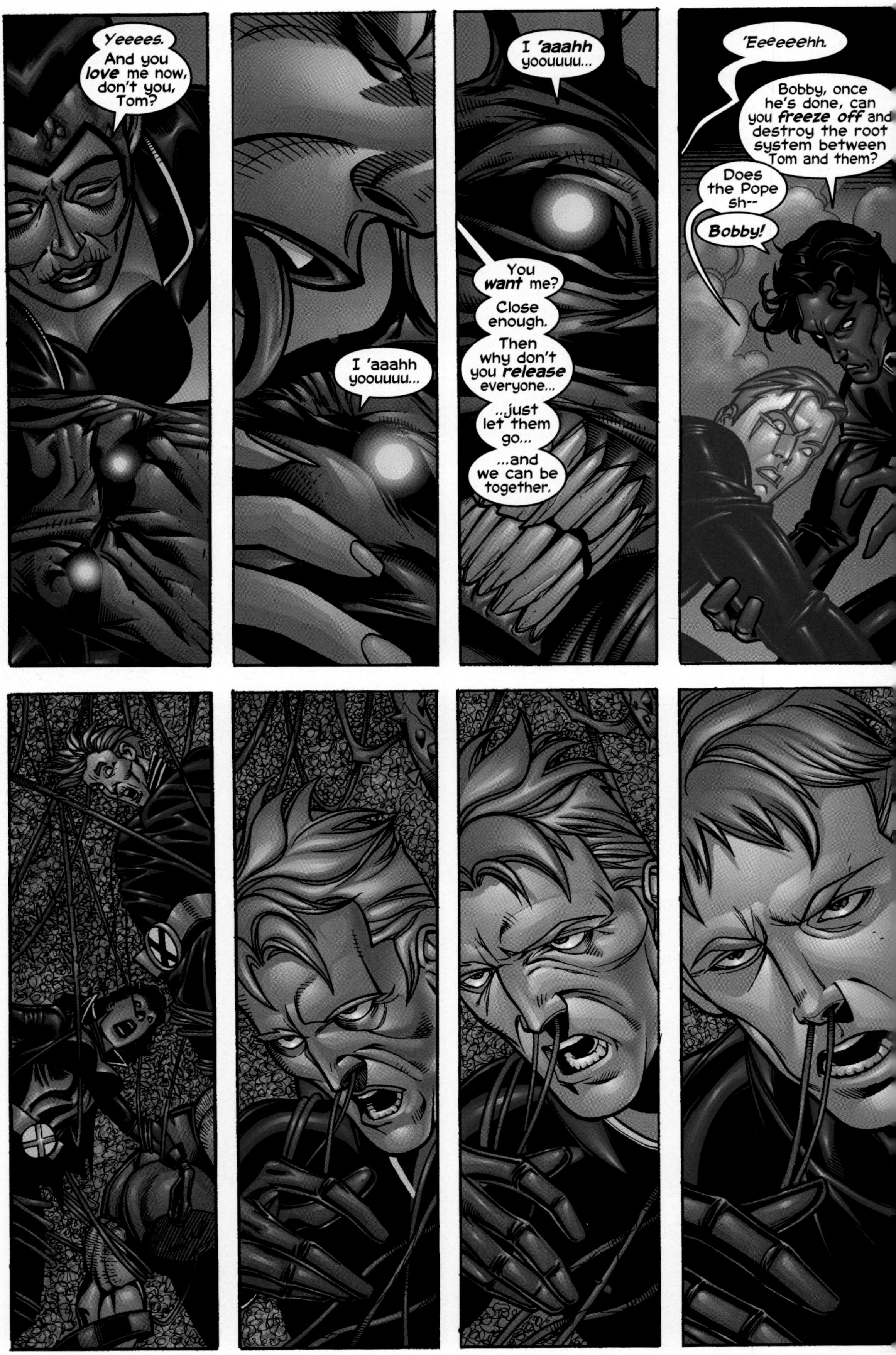
Yeeees. And you love me now, don't you, Tom?
I 'aaahh yoouuuu...
I 'aaahh yoouuuu...
You want me?
Close enough.
Then why don't you release everyone...
..just let them go...
...and we can be together.
'Eeeeeehh.
Bobby, once he's done, can you freeze off and destroy the root system between Tom and them?
Does the Pope sh--
Bobby!

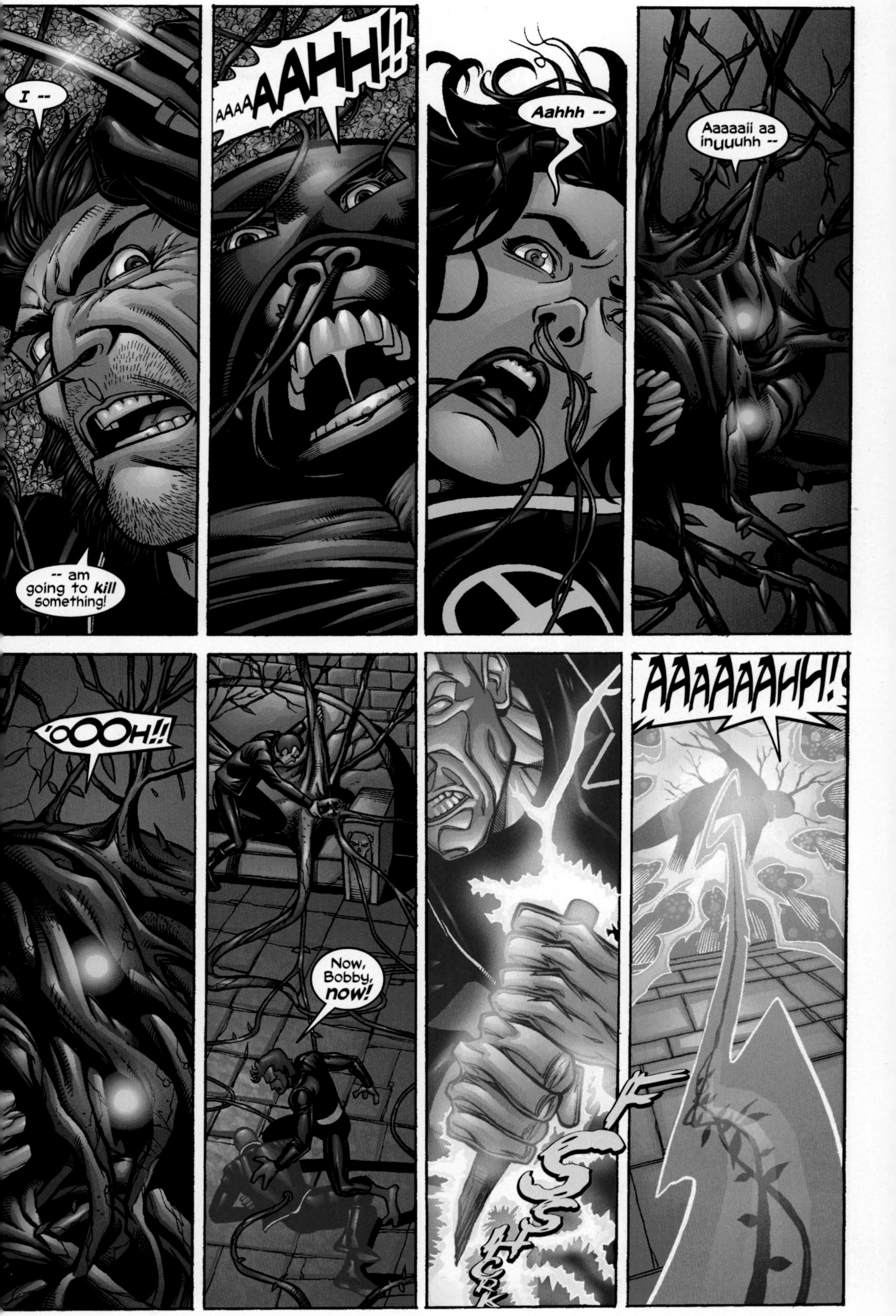

I --
-- am going to *kill* something!
AAAAAAHH!!
Aahhh --
Aaaaaii aa inyuuhh --
'OOOH!!
Now, Bobby, *now!*
FSSHCRK
AAAAAAHH!!

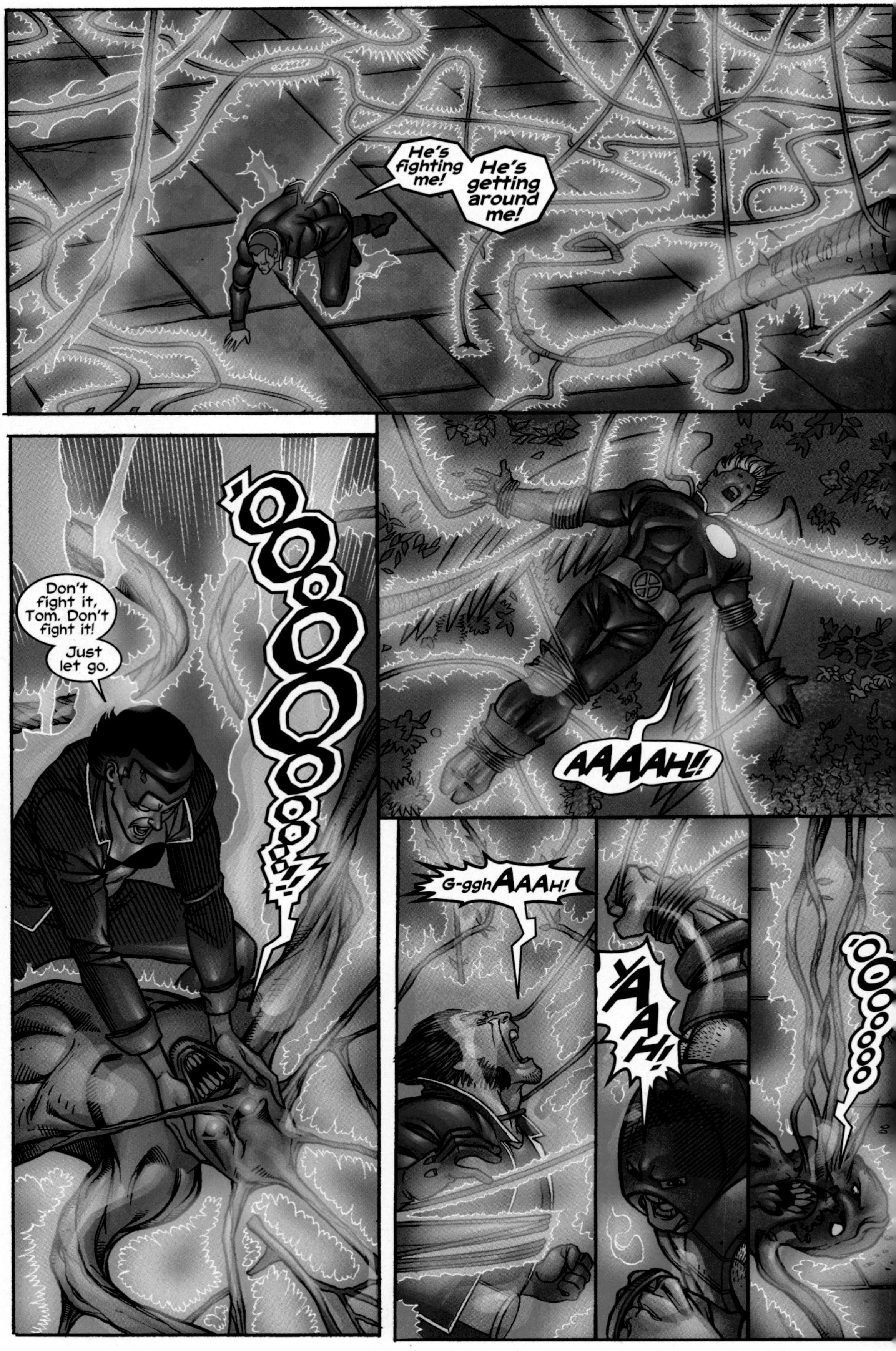
He's fighting me!
He's getting around me!
Don't fight it, Tom. Don't fight it!
Just let go.
OOOOOOOOOO!!
AAAAH!!
G-gghAAAH!
YAAH!
OOOOOOO

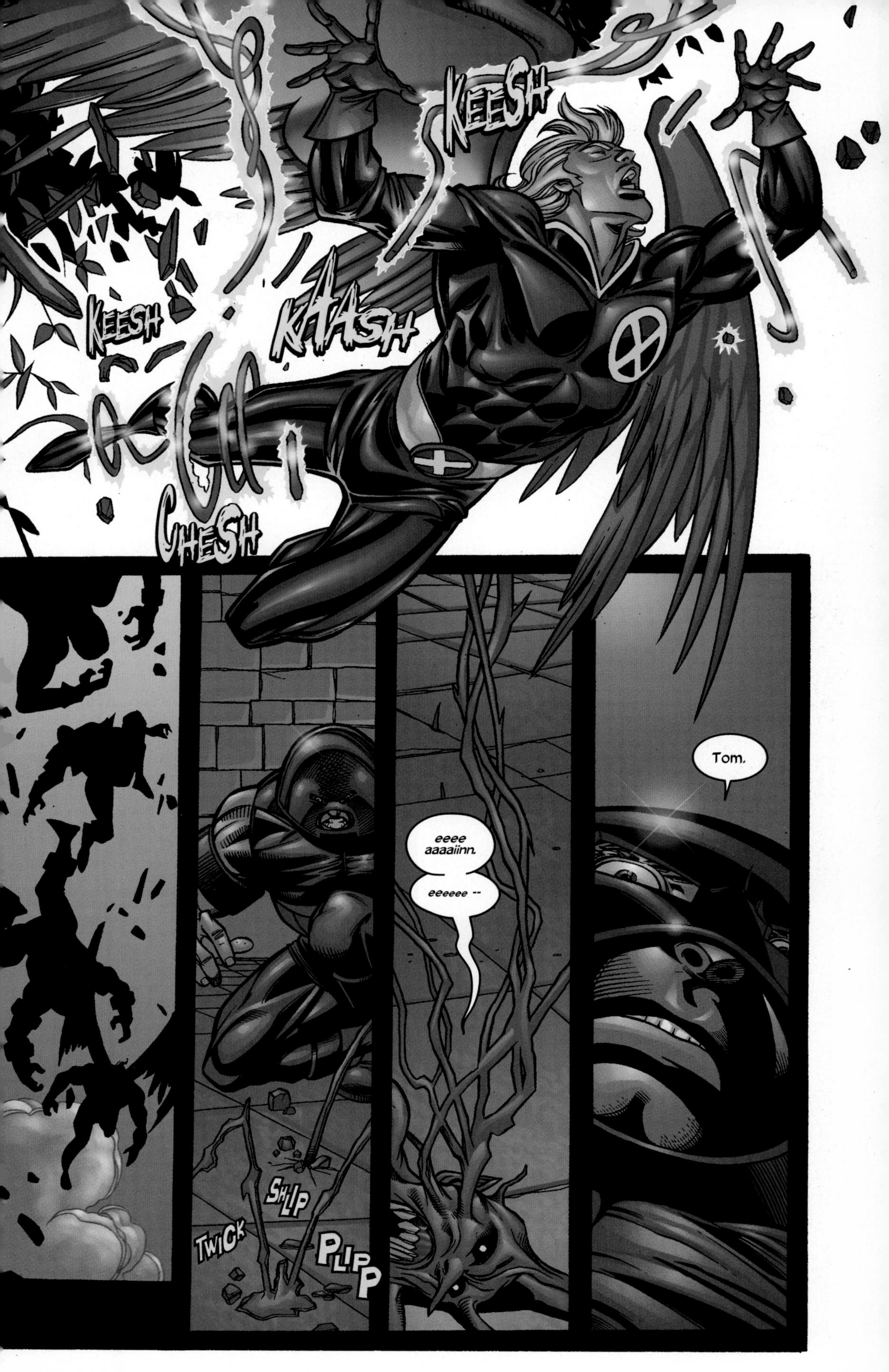
KEESH
KEESH
KAASH
CHESH
eeee aaaaiinn.
eeeee --
SHLIP
TWICK
PLIPP
Tom.

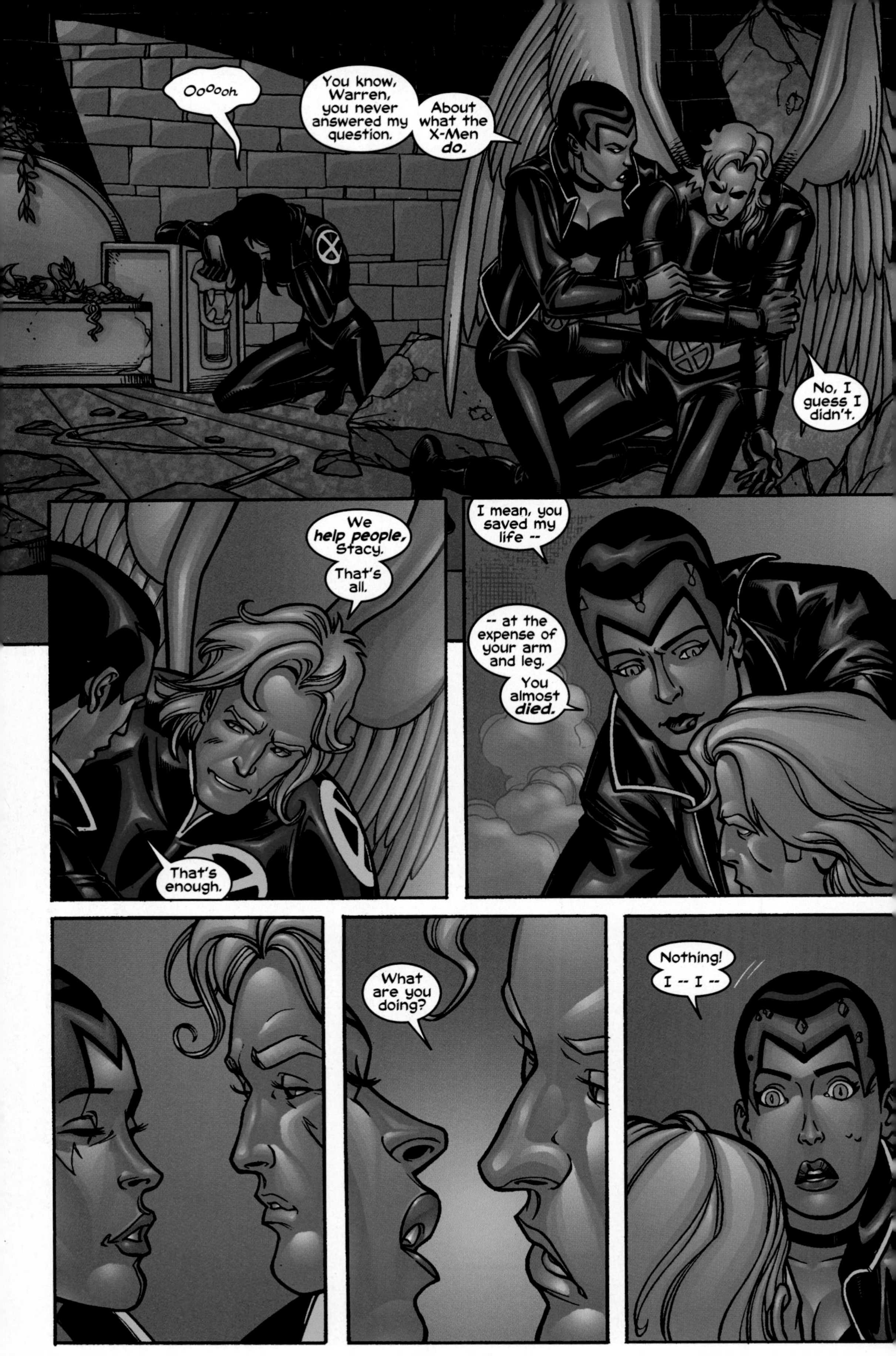
Oooooh.
You know, Warren, you never answered my question.
About what the X-Men *do.*
No, I guess I didn't.
We *help people,* Stacy.
That's all.
That's enough.
I mean, you saved my life --
-- at the expense of your arm and leg.
You almost *died.*
What are you doing?
Nothing!
I -- I --

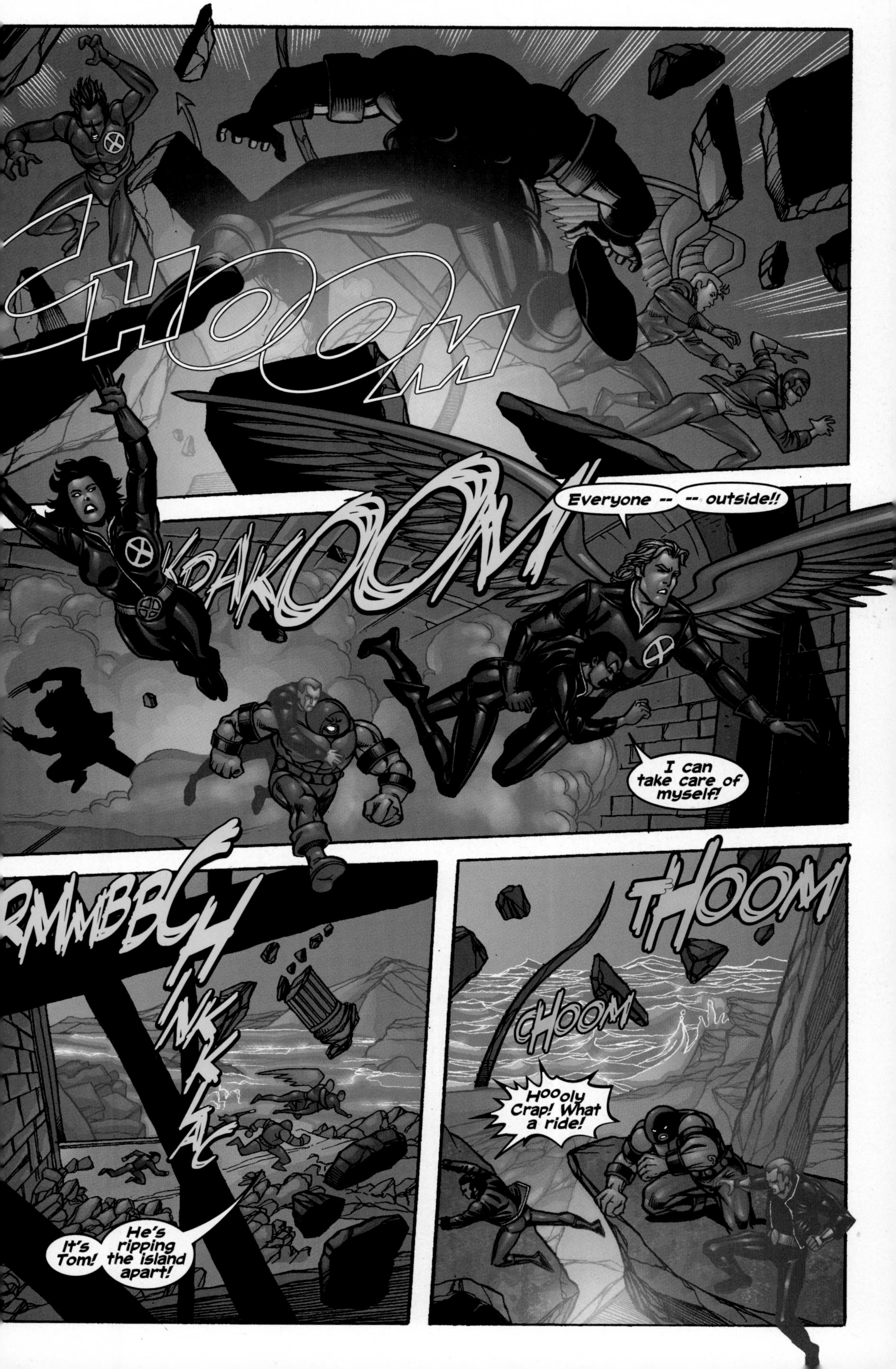
CHOOOM
KRAKOOM
Everyone -- -- outside!!
I can take care of myself!
RMMBBCH
INKLAC
It's Tom!
He's ripping the island apart!
THOOM
CHOOM
HOOoly Crap! What a ride!

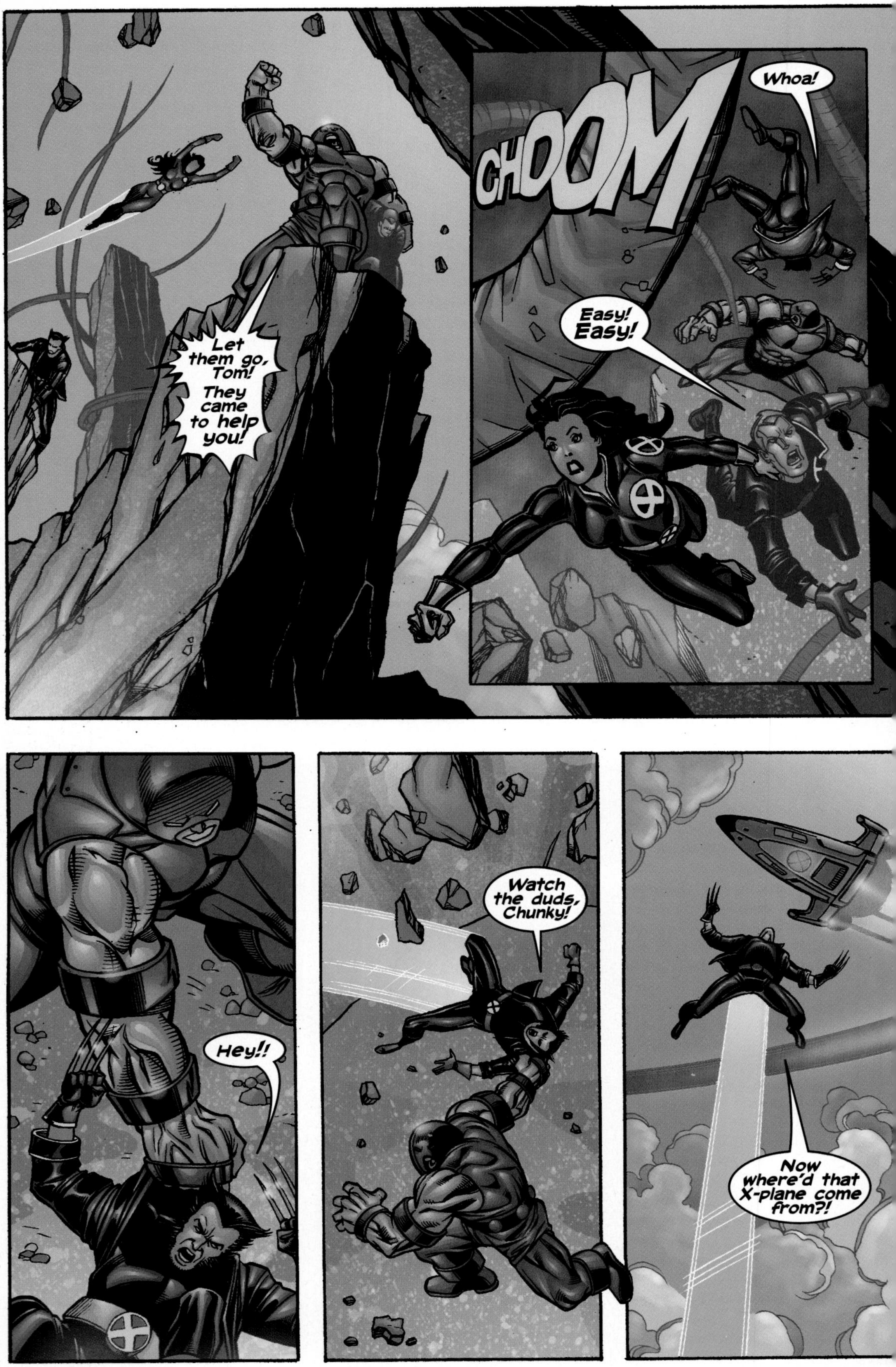
Let them go, Tom! They came to help you!
CHOOM
Whoa!
Easy! Easy!
Hey!!
Watch the duds, Chunky!
Now where'd that X-plane come from?!

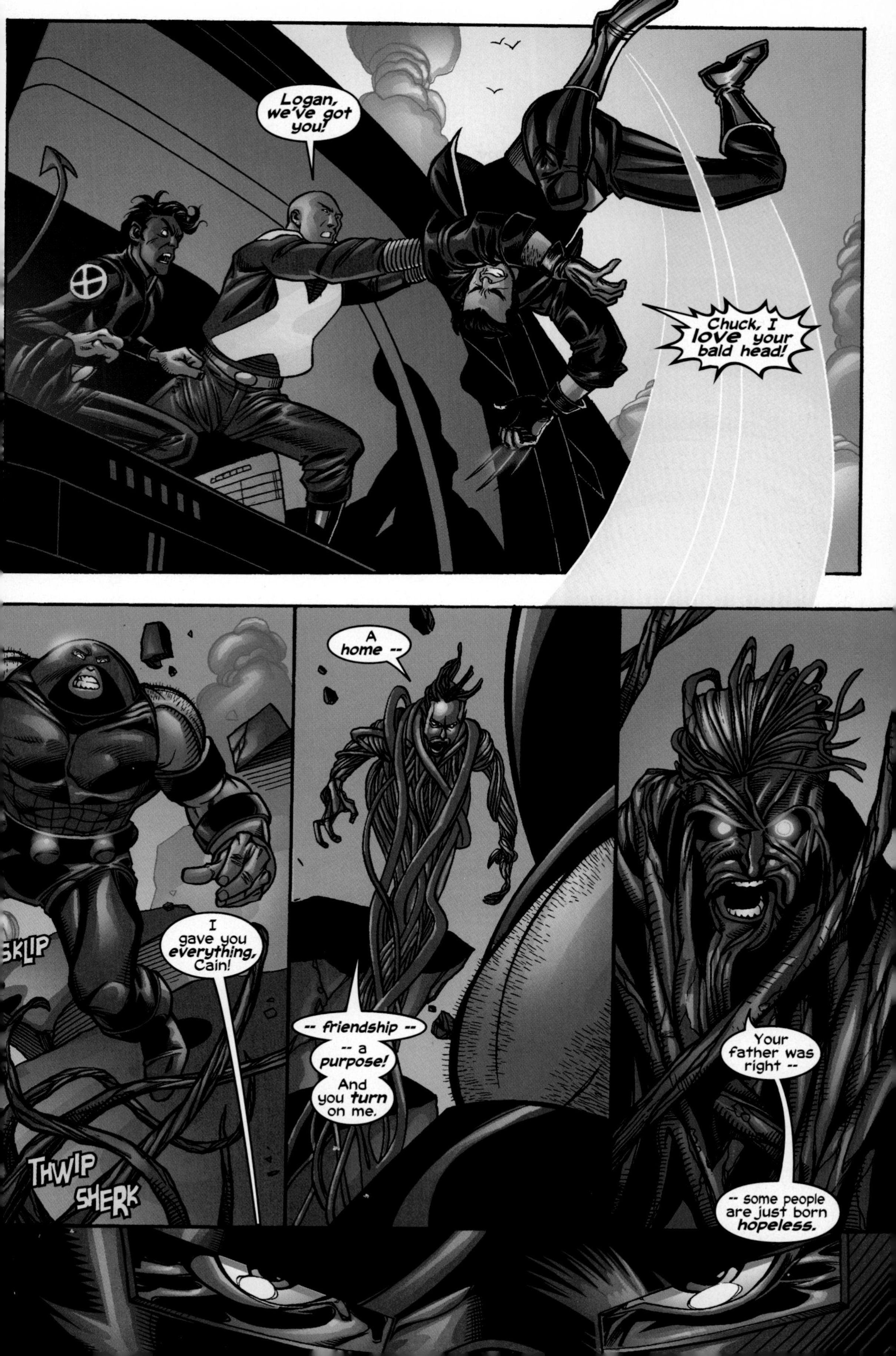
Logan, we've got you!
Chuck, I love your bald head!
SKLIP
I gave you everything, Cain!
THWIP
SHERK
A home --
-- friendship --
-- a purpose!
And you turn on me.
Your father was right --
-- some people are just born hopeless.

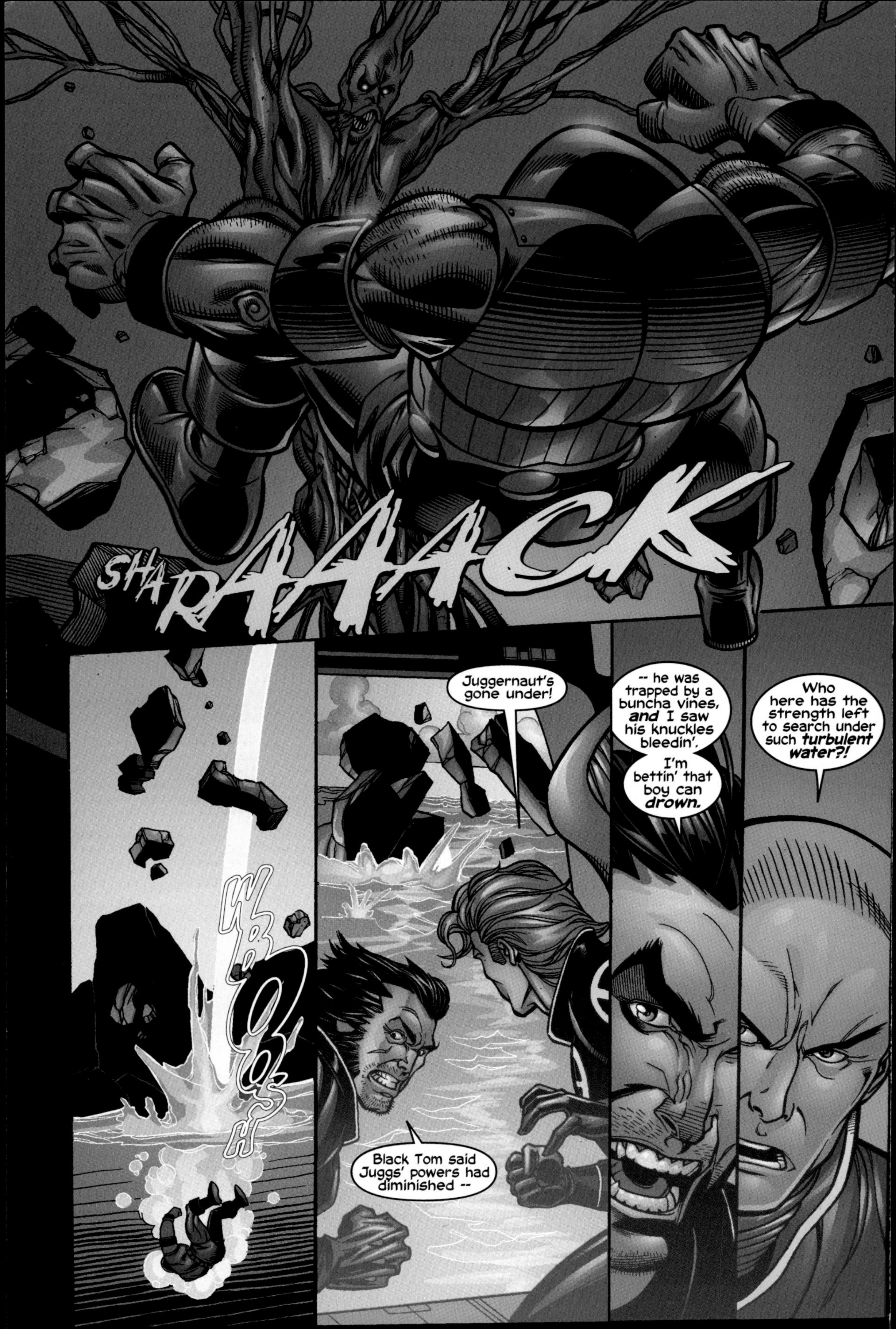
SHARAAACK
WHOOSSH
Juggernaut's gone under!
Black Tom said Juggs' powers had diminished --
-- he was trapped by a buncha vines, and I saw his knuckles bleedin'.
I'm bettin' that boy can drown.
Who here has the strength left to search under such turbulent water?!

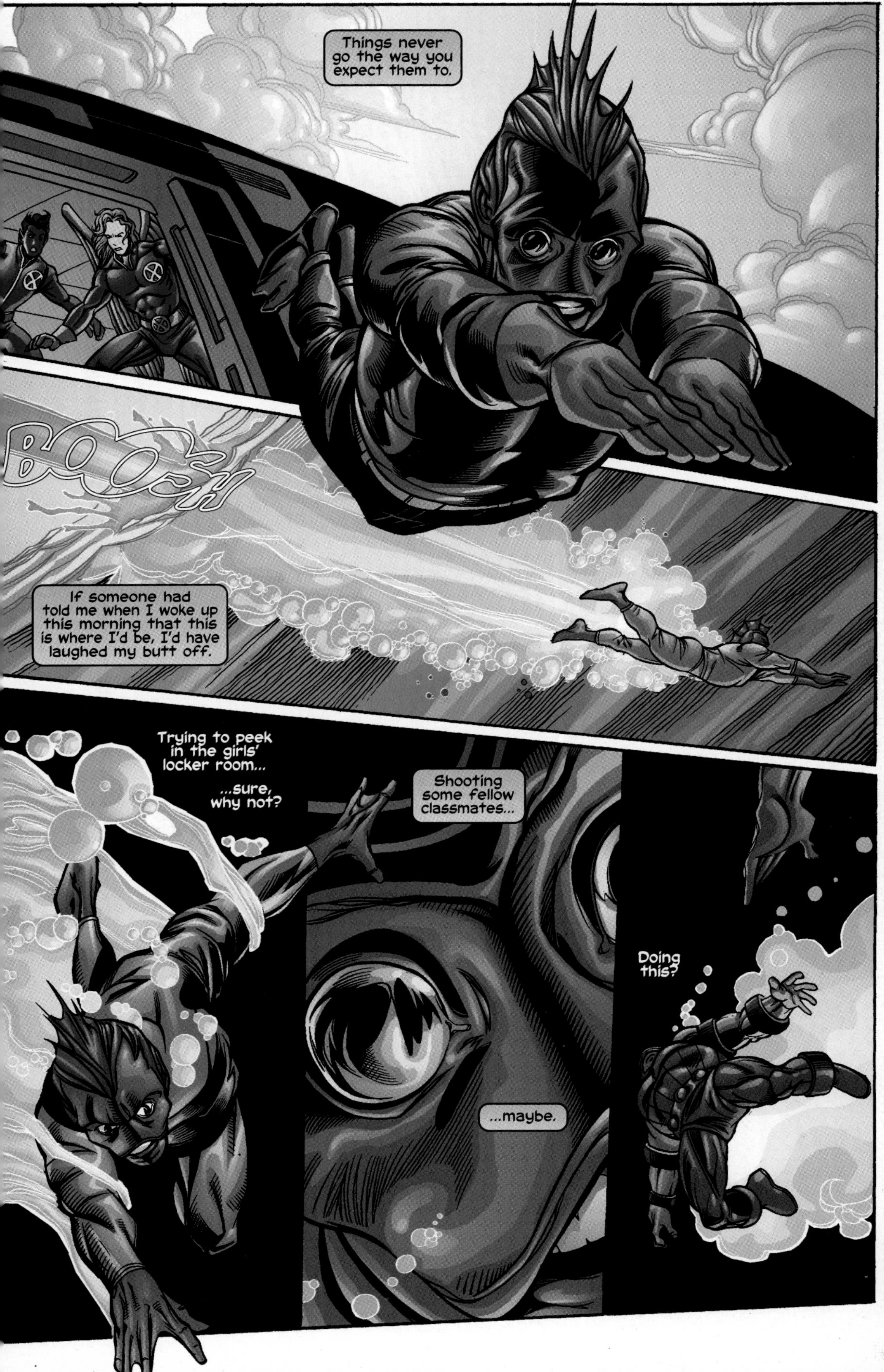
Things never go the way you expect them to.
BOOSH
If someone had told me when I woke up this morning that this is where I'd be, I'd have laughed my butt off.
Trying to peek in the girls' locker room...
...sure, why not?
Shooting some fellow classmates...
...maybe.
Doing this?

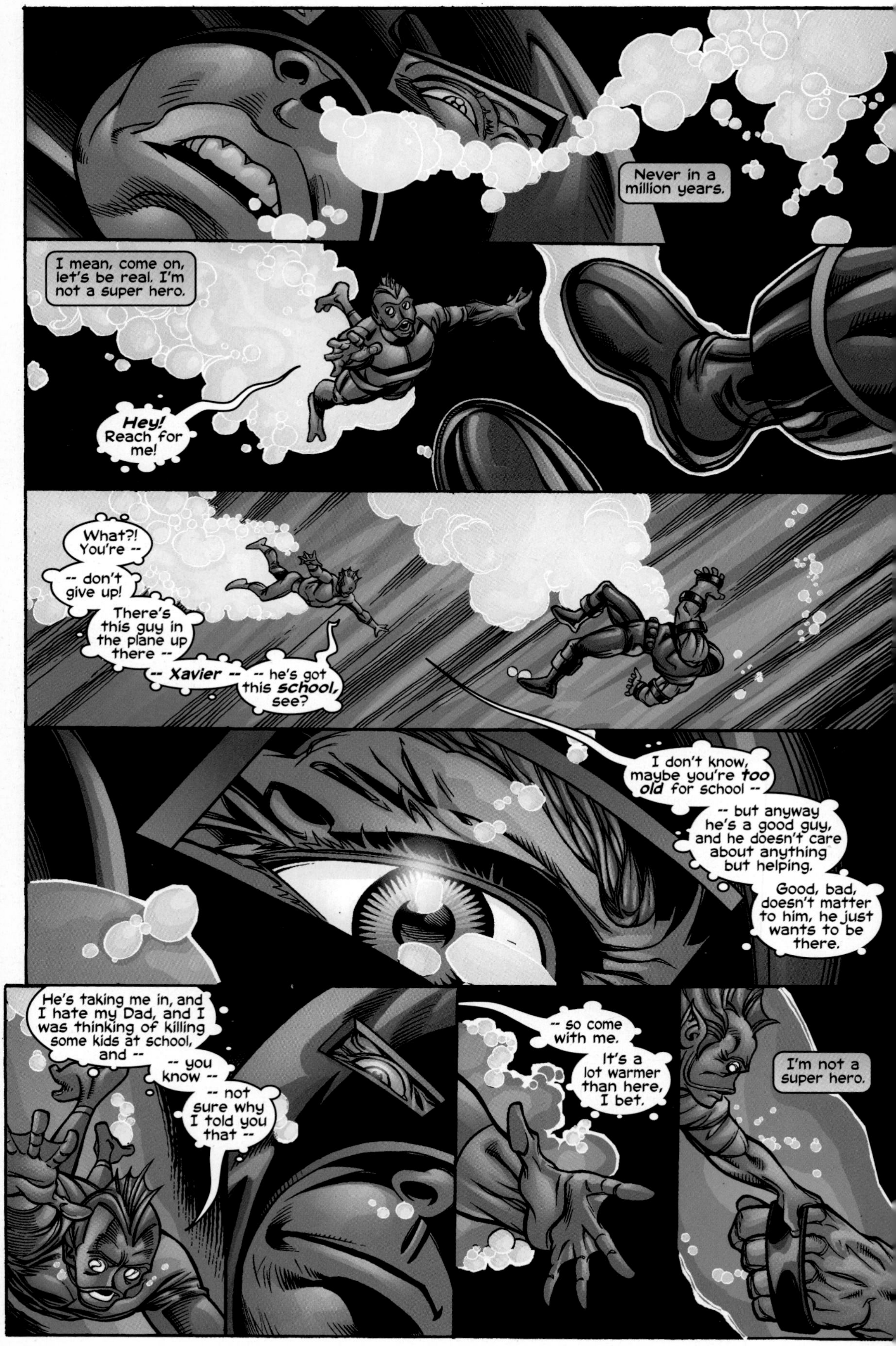
Never in a million years.
I mean, come on, let's be real. I'm not a super hero.
Hey! Reach for me!
What?! You're --
-- don't give up!
There's this guy in the plane up there --
-- Xavier --
-- he's got this school, see?
I don't know, maybe you're too old for school --
-- but anyway he's a good guy, and he doesn't care about anything but helping.
Good, bad, doesn't matter to him, he just wants to be there.
He's taking me in, and I hate my Dad, and I was thinking of killing some kids at school, and --
-- you know --
-- not sure why I told you that --
-- so come with me.
It's a lot warmer than here, I bet.
I'm not a super hero.

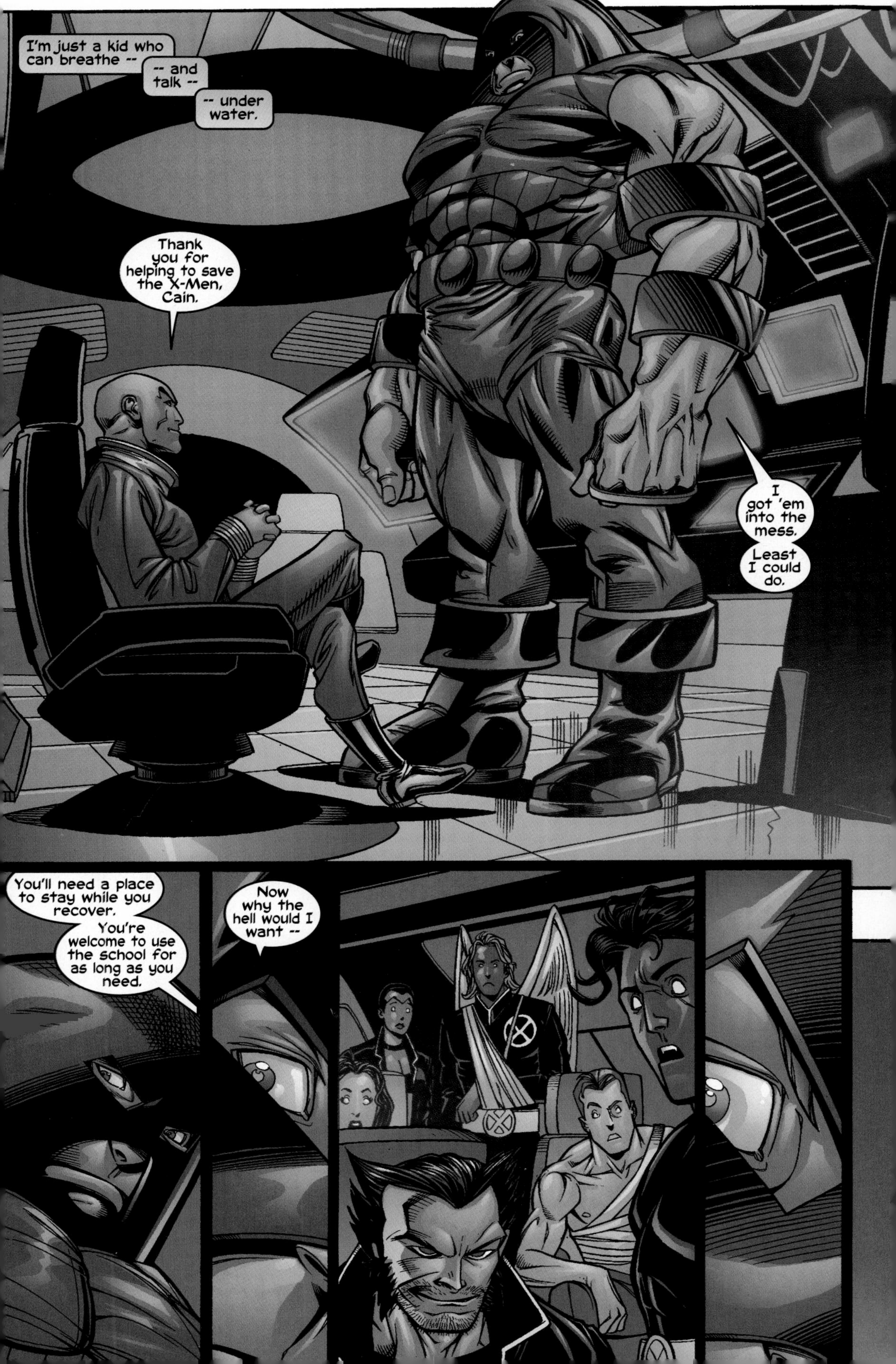
I'm just a kid who can breathe --
-- and talk --
-- under water.
Thank you for helping to save the X-Men, Cain.
I got 'em into the mess.
Least I could do.
You'll need a place to stay while you recover.
You're welcome to use the school for as long as you need.
Now why the hell would I want --

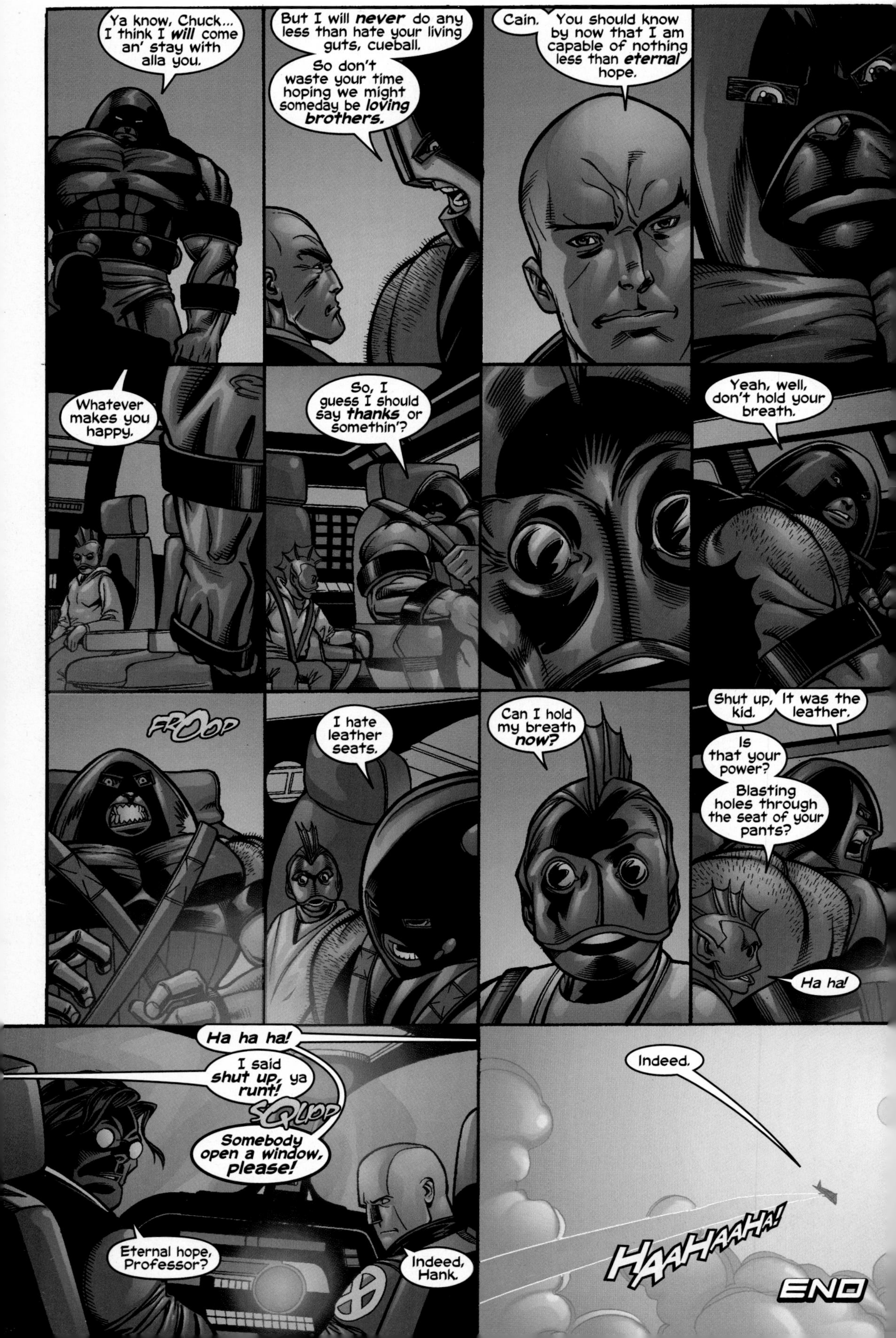
Ya know, Chuck... I think I *will* come an' stay with alla you.
But I will *never* do any less than hate your living guts, cueball.
So don't waste your time hoping we might someday be *loving brothers.*
Cain.
You should know by now that I am capable of nothing less than *eternal* hope.
Whatever makes you happy.
So, I guess I should say *thanks* or somethin'?
Yeah, well, don't hold your breath.
FROOP
I hate leather seats.
Can I hold my breath *now?*
Shut up, kid.
It was the leather.
Is that your power?
Blasting holes through the seat of your pants?
Ha ha!
Ha ha ha!
I said *shut up,* ya *runt!*
SQUOP
Somebody open a window, please!
Eternal hope, Professor?
Indeed, Hank.
Indeed.
HAHAAHA!
END

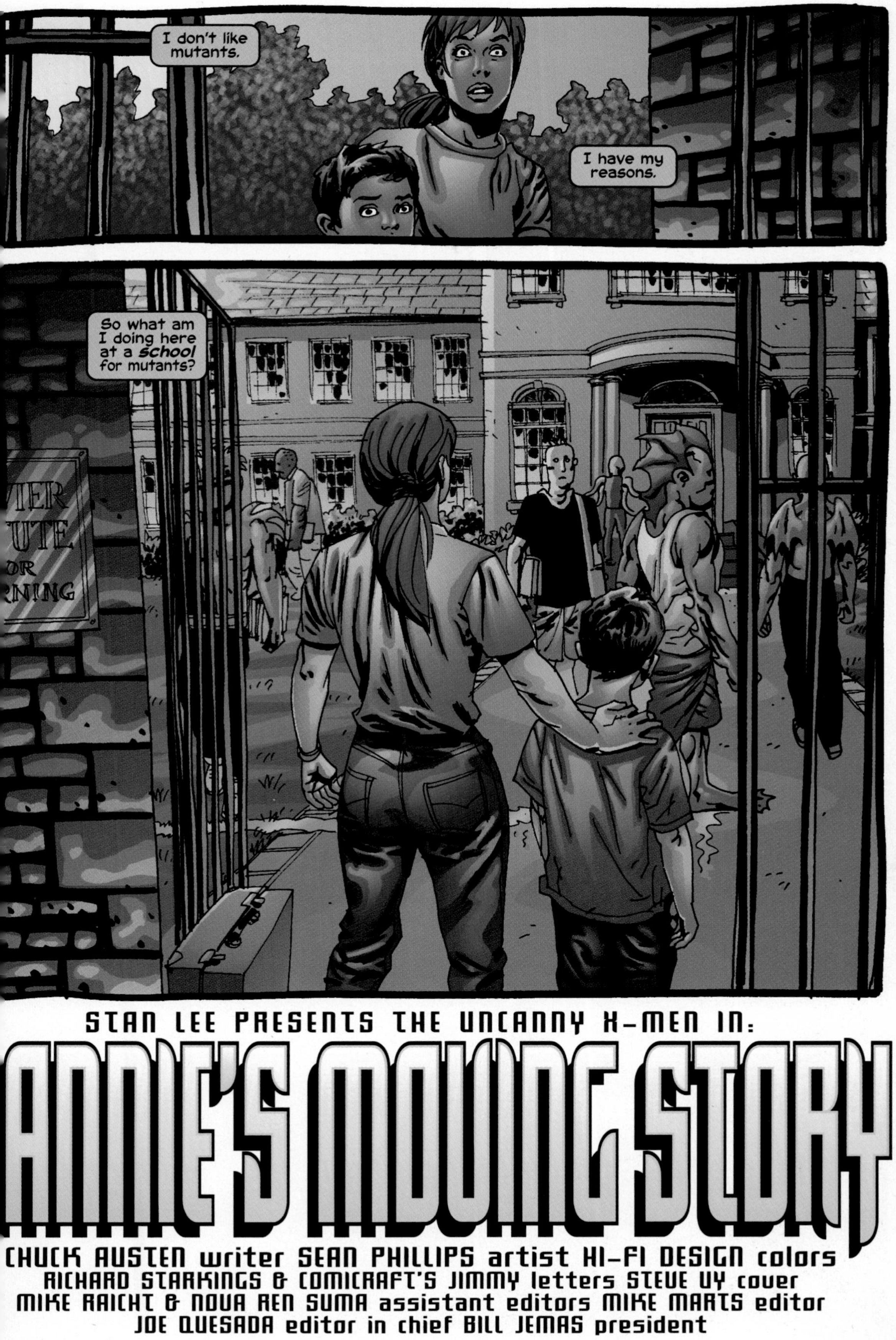
I don't like mutants.
I have my reasons.
So what am I doing here at a *school* for mutants?

STAN LEE PRESENTS THE UNCANNY X-MEN IN:

ANNIE'S MOVING STORY

CHUCK AUSTEN writer SEAN PHILLIPS artist HI-FI DESIGN colors
RICHARD STARKINGS & COMICRAFT'S JIMMY letters STEVE UY cover
MIKE RAICHT & NOVA REN SUMA assistant editors MIKE MARTS editor
JOE QUESADA editor in chief BILL JEMAS president

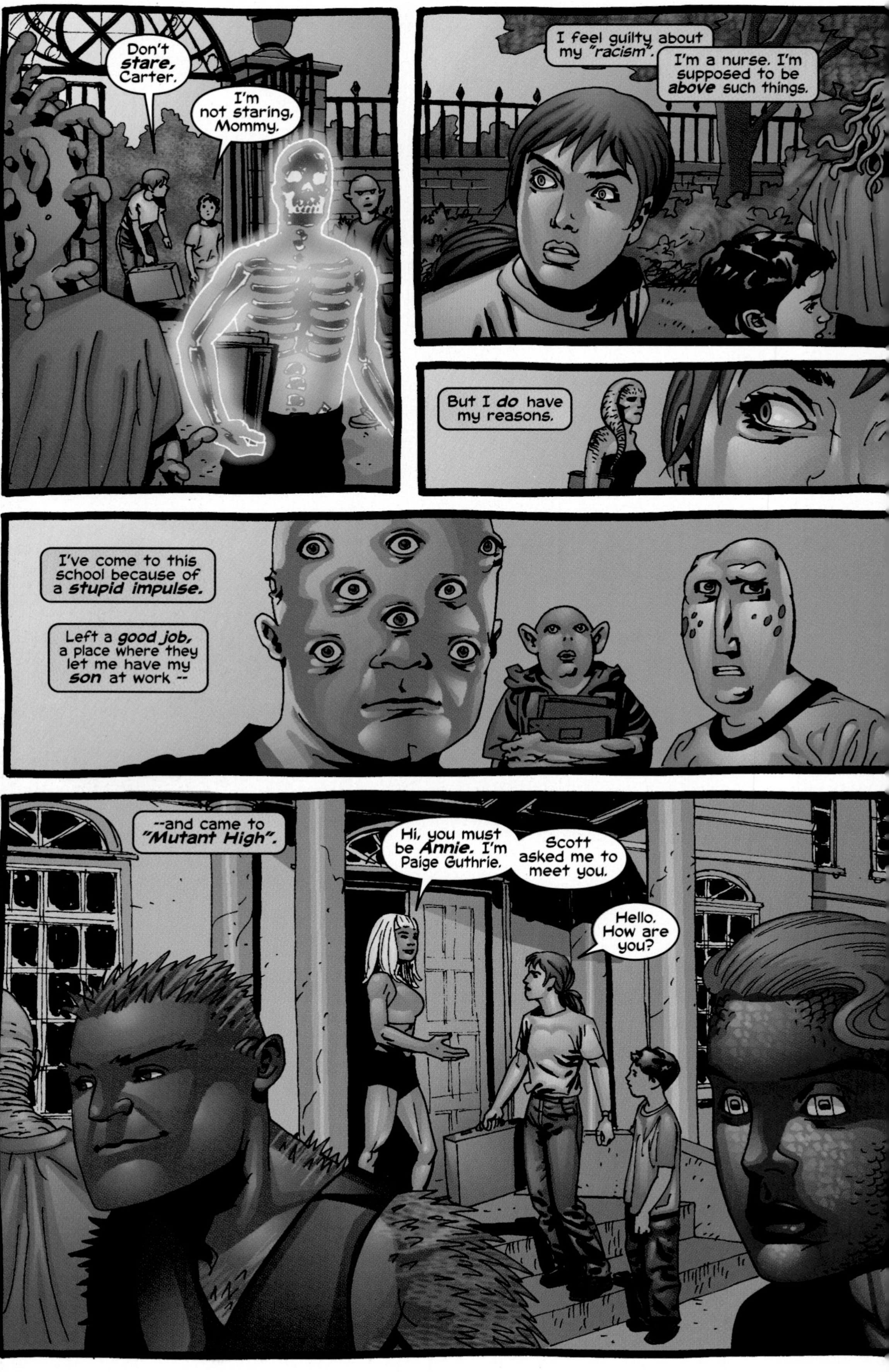

Don't stare, Carter.
I'm not staring, Mommy.
I feel guilty about my "racism".
I'm a nurse. I'm supposed to be above such things.
But I do have my reasons.
I've come to this school because of a stupid impulse.
Left a good job, a place where they let me have my son at work --
--and came to "Mutant High".
Hi, you must be Annie. I'm Paige Guthrie.
Scott asked me to meet you.
Hello. How are you?

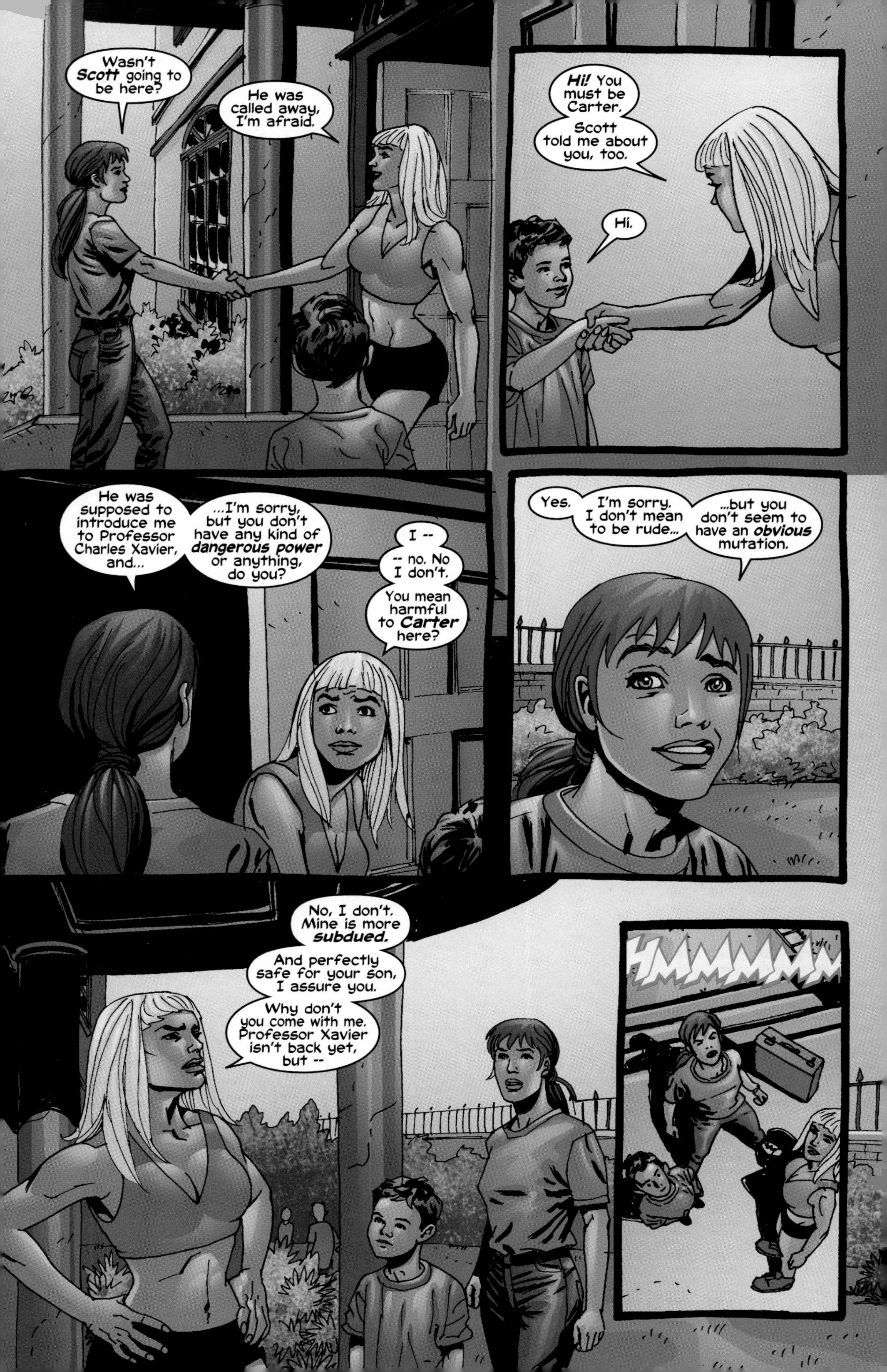
Wasn't Scott going to be here?
He was called away, I'm afraid.
Hi! You must be Carter.
Scott told me about you, too.
Hi.
He was supposed to introduce me to Professor Charles Xavier, and...
...I'm sorry, but you don't have any kind of dangerous power or anything, do you?
I --
-- no. No I don't.
You mean harmful to Carter here?
Yes.
I'm sorry. I don't mean to be rude...
...but you don't seem to have an obvious mutation.
No, I don't. Mine is more subdued.
And perfectly safe for your son, I assure you.
Why don't you come with me. Professor Xavier isn't back yet, but --
HMMMMM

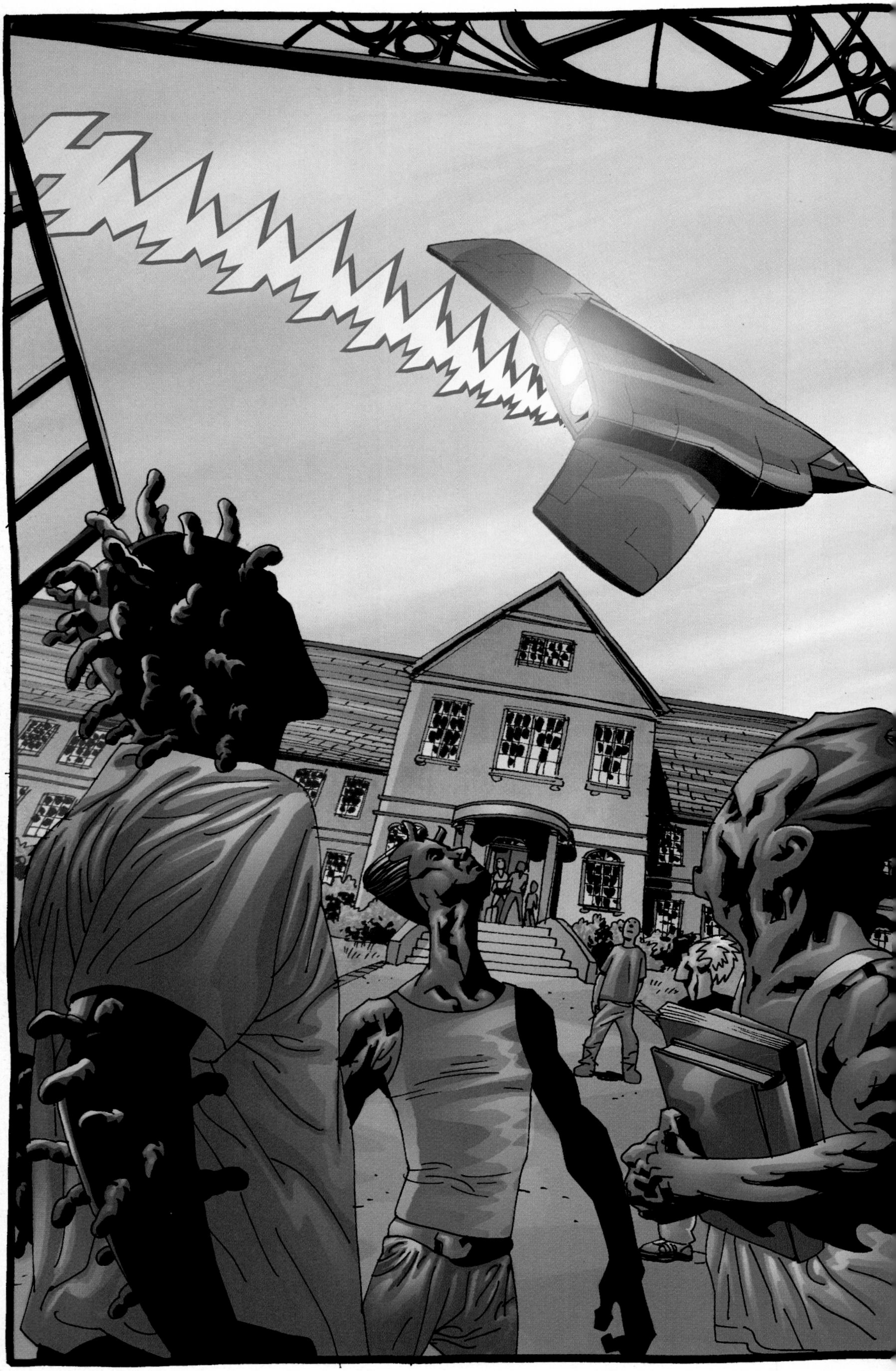

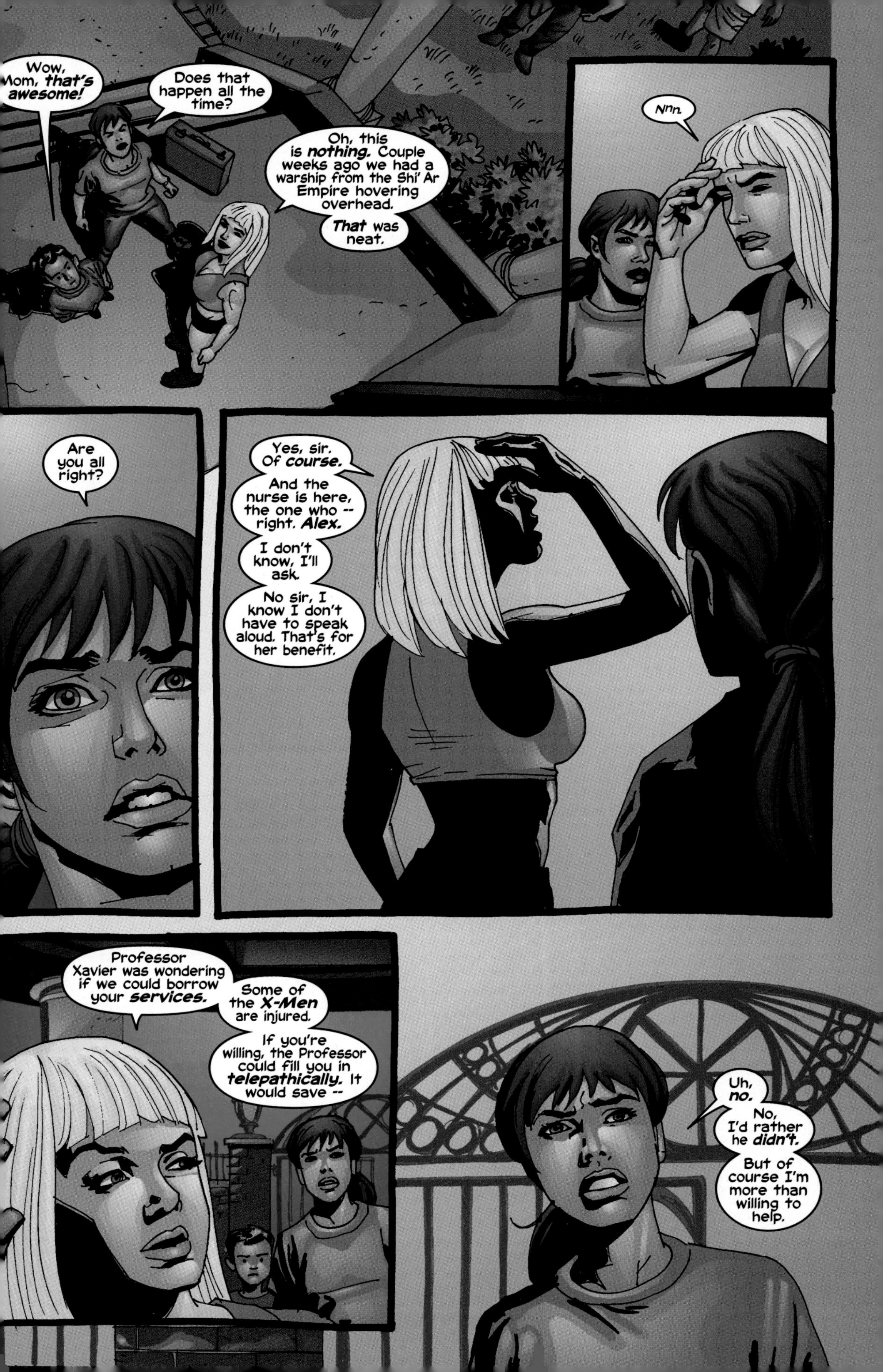
Wow, Mom, that's awesome!
Does that happen all the time?
Oh, this is nothing. Couple weeks ago we had a warship from the Shi' Ar Empire hovering overhead.
That was neat.
Nnn.
Are you all right?
Yes, sir. Of course.
And the nurse is here, the one who -- right. Alex.
I don't know, I'll ask.
No sir, I know I don't have to speak aloud. That's for her benefit.
Professor Xavier was wondering if we could borrow your services.
Some of the X-Men are injured.
If you're willing, the Professor could fill you in telepathically. It would save --
Uh, no.
No, I'd rather he didn't.
But of course I'm more than willing to help.

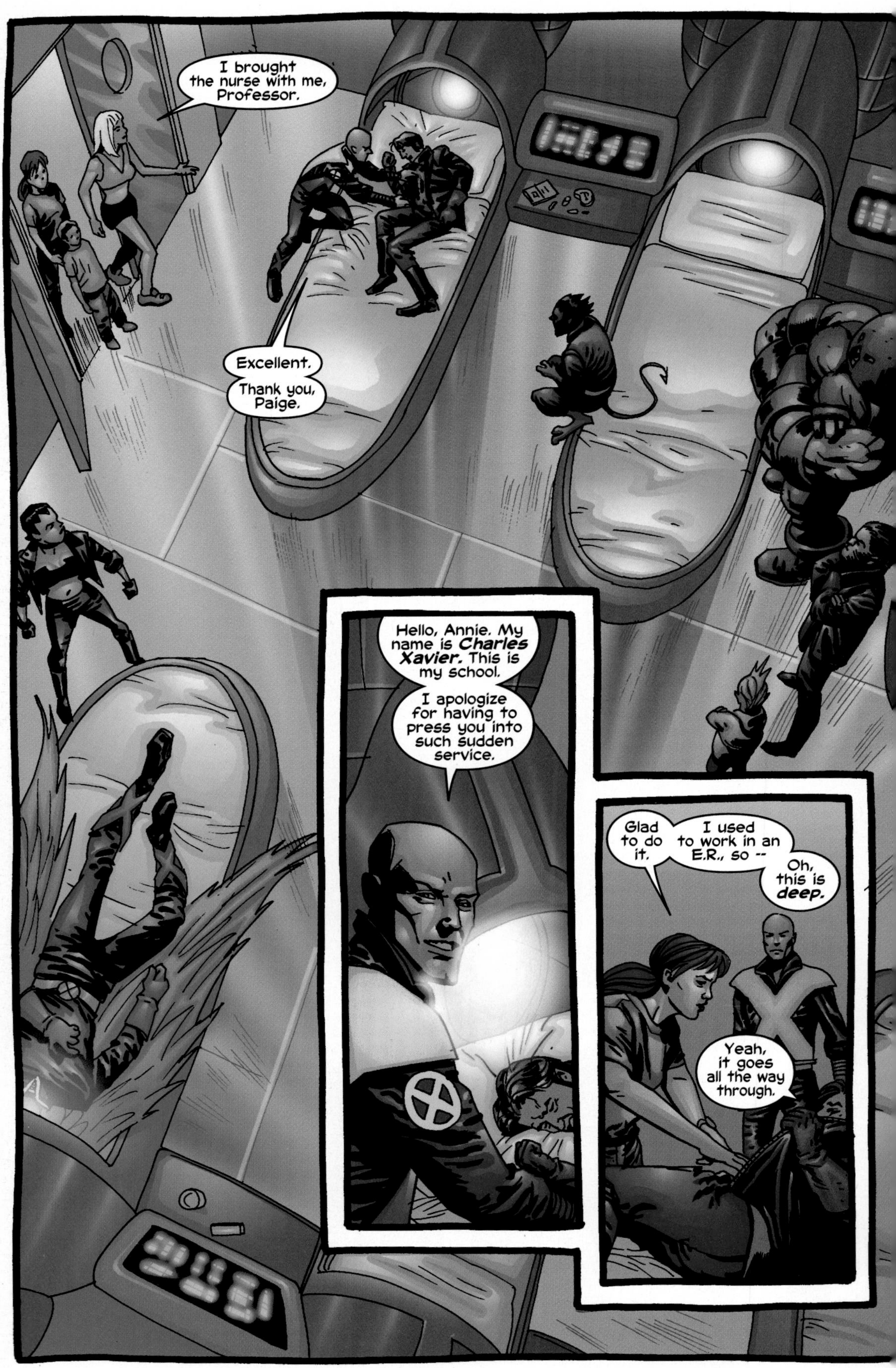
I brought the nurse with me, Professor.
Excellent.
Thank you, Paige.
Hello, Annie. My name is **Charles Xavier.** This is my school.
I apologize for having to press you into such sudden service.
Glad to do it.
I used to work in an E.R., so --
Oh, this is **deep.**
Yeah, it goes all the way through.

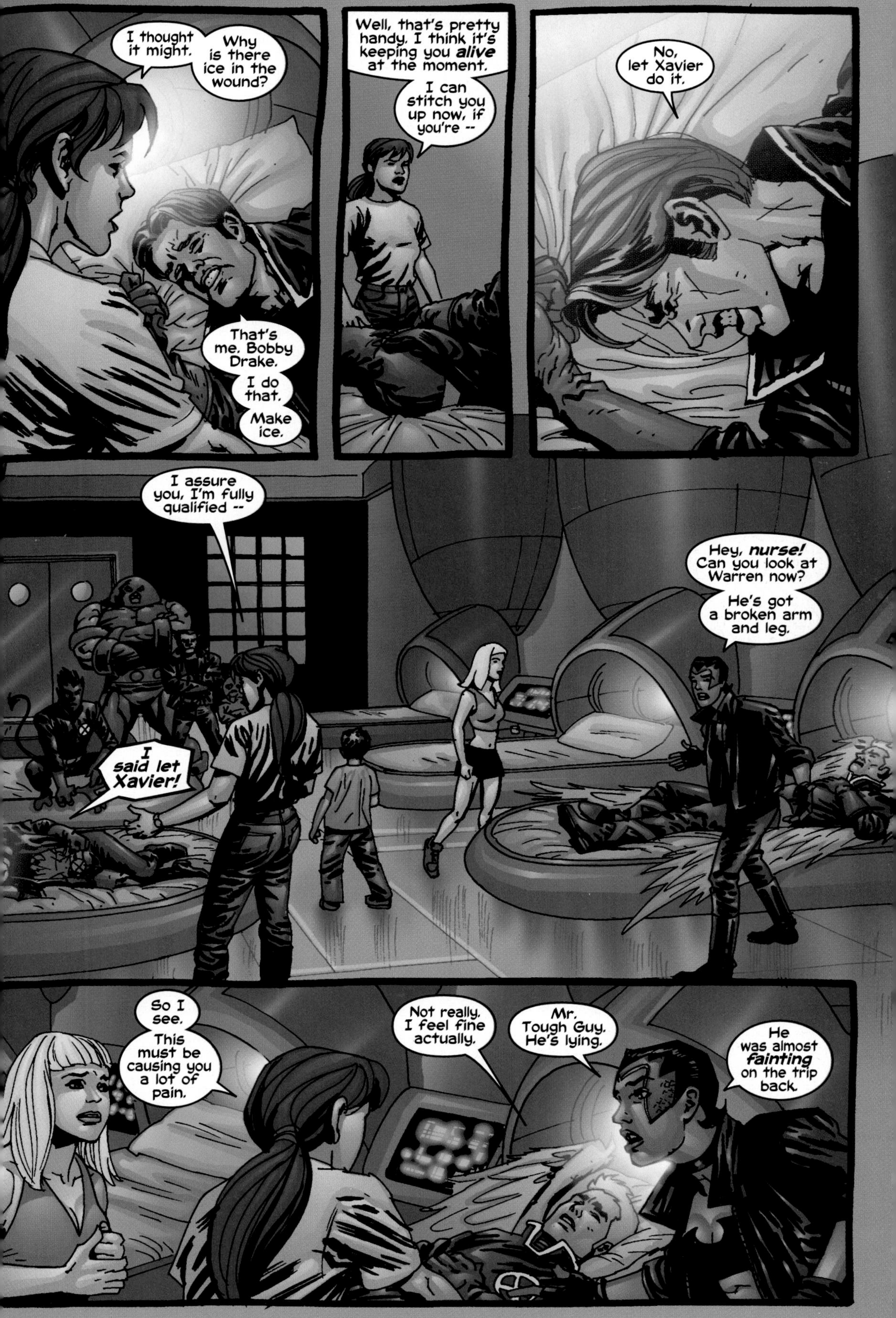

I thought it might.
Why is there ice in the wound?
That's me. Bobby Drake.
I do that.
Make ice.
Well, that's pretty handy, I think it's keeping you alive at the moment.
I can stitch you up now, if you're --
No, let Xavier do it.
I assure you, I'm fully qualified --
I said let Xavier!
Hey, nurse! Can you look at Warren now?
He's got a broken arm and leg.
So I see.
This must be causing you a lot of pain.
Not really. I feel fine actually.
Mr. Tough Guy. He's lying.
He was almost fainting on the trip back.

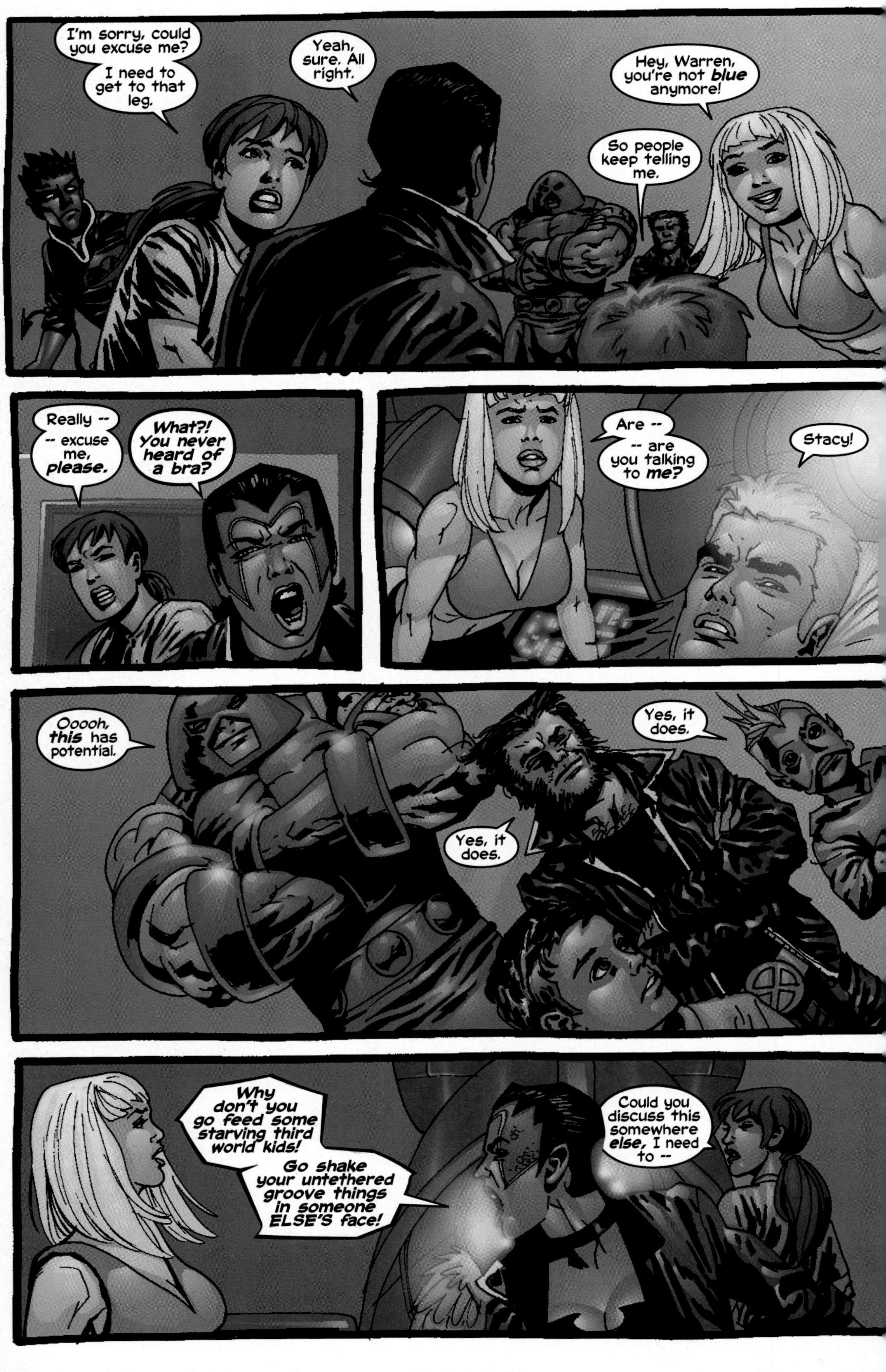
I'm sorry, could you excuse me?
I need to get to that leg.
Yeah, sure. All right.
Hey, Warren, you're not *blue* anymore!
So people keep telling me.
Really --
-- excuse me, *please.*
What?! You never heard of a bra?
Are --
-- are you talking to *me?*
Stacy!
Ooooh, *this* has potential.
Yes, it does.
Yes, it does.
Why don't you go feed some starving third world kids!
Go shake your untethered groove things in someone ELSE'S face!
Could you discuss this somewhere *else*, I need to --

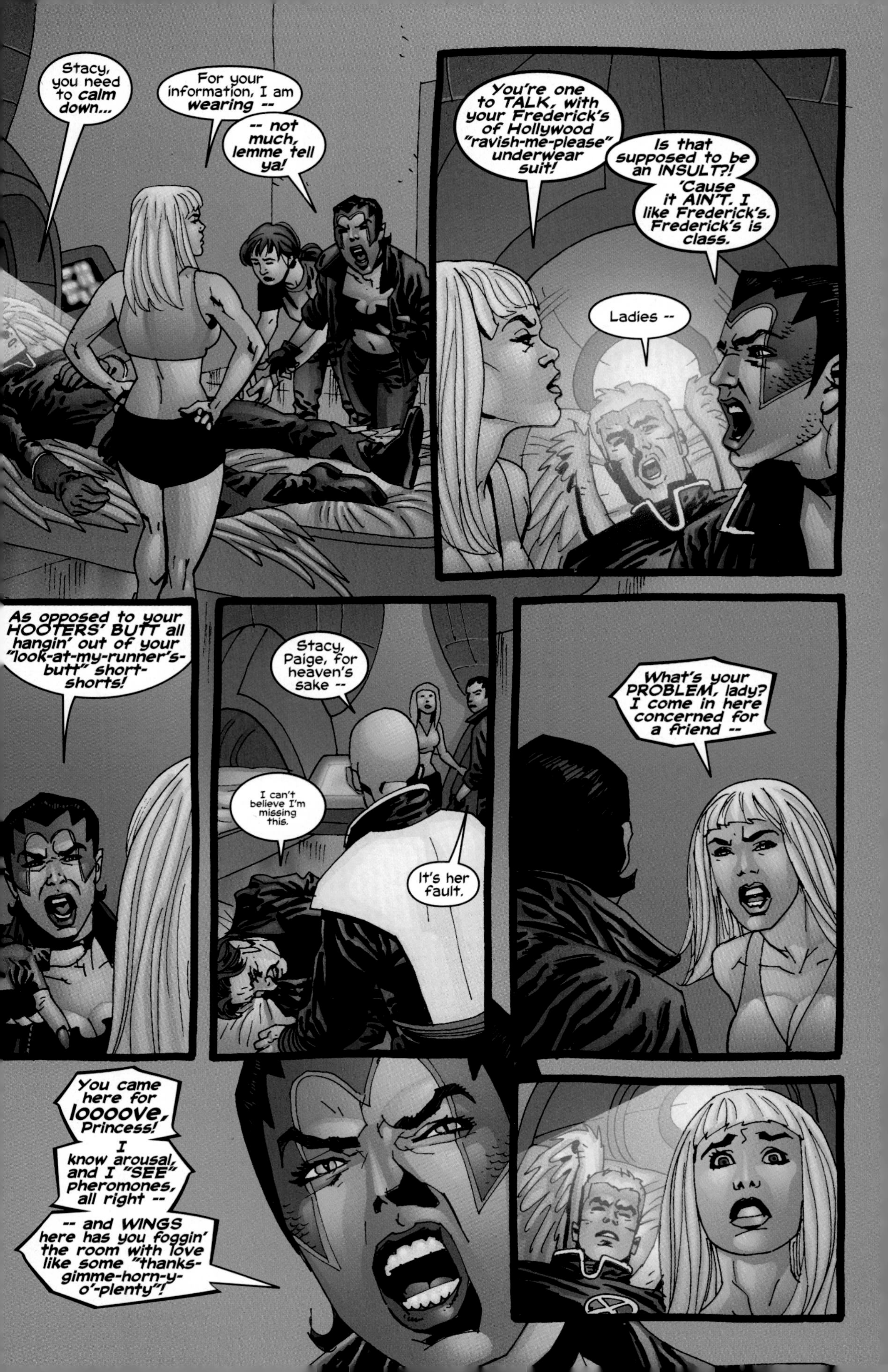

Stacy, you need to calm down...
For your information, I am wearing --
-- not much, lemme tell ya!
You're one to TALK, with your Frederick's of Hollywood "ravish-me-please" underwear suit!
Is that supposed to be an INSULT?!
'Cause it AIN'T. I like Frederick's. Frederick's is class.
Ladies --
As opposed to your HOOTERS' BUTT all hangin' out of your "look-at-my-runner's-butt" short-shorts!
Stacy, Paige, for heaven's sake --
I can't believe I'm missing this.
It's her fault.
What's your PROBLEM, lady? I come in here concerned for a friend --
You came here for loooove, Princess!
I know arousal, and I "SEE" pheromones, all right --
-- and WINGS here has you foggin' the room with love like some "thanks-gimme-horn-y-o'-plenty"!

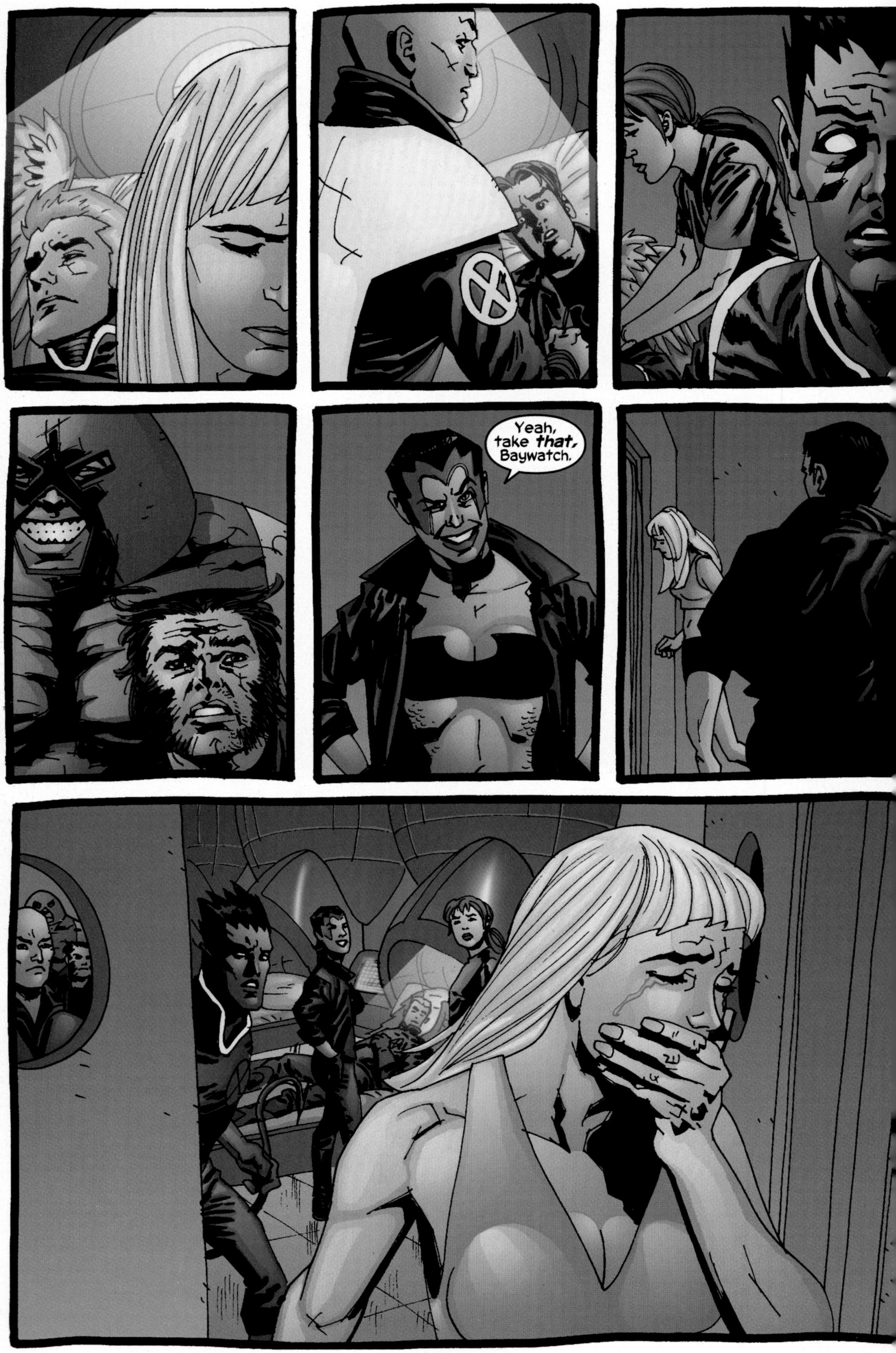
Yeah, take *that,* Baywatch.

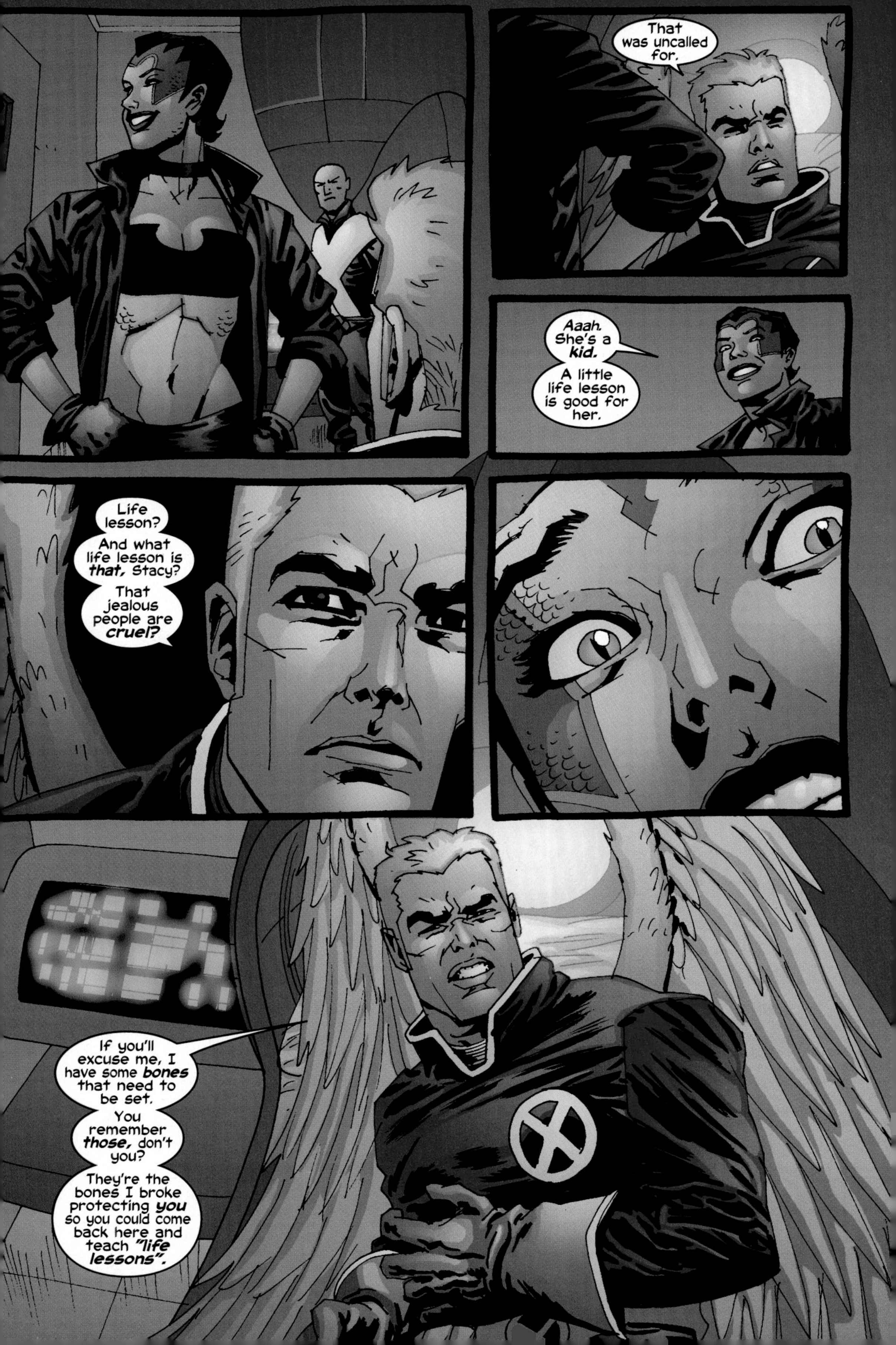
That was uncalled for.
Aaah. She's a kid.
A little life lesson is good for her.
Life lesson?
And what life lesson is that, Stacy?
That jealous people are cruel?
If you'll excuse me, I have some bones that need to be set.
You remember those, don't you?
They're the bones I broke protecting you so you could come back here and teach "life lessons".

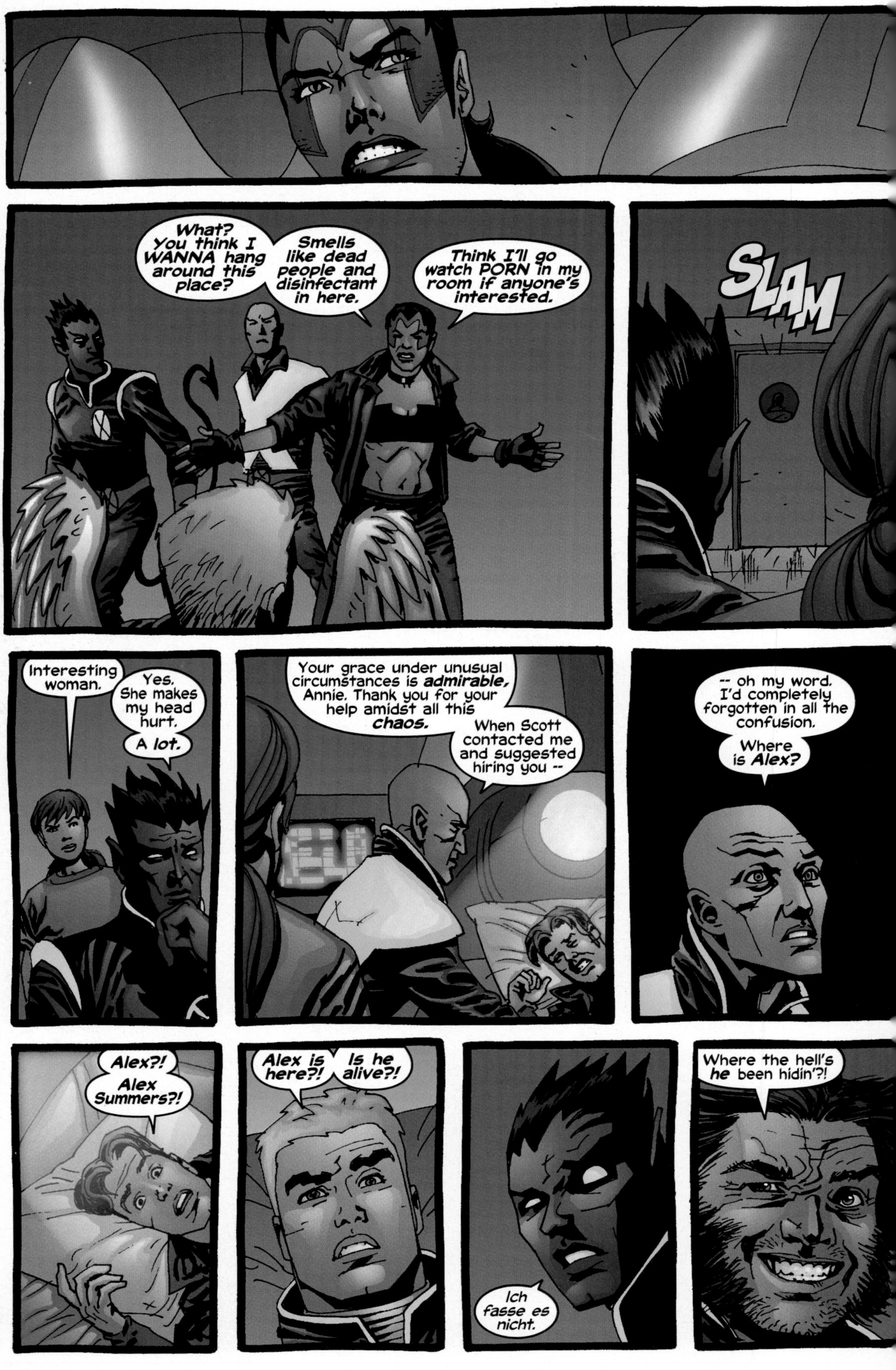
What? You think I WANNA hang around this place?
Smells like dead people and disinfectant in here.
Think I'll go watch PORN in my room if anyone's interested.
SLAM
Interesting woman.
Yes. She makes my head hurt.
A lot.
Your grace under unusual circumstances is admirable, Annie. Thank you for your help amidst all this chaos.
When Scott contacted me and suggested hiring you --
-- oh my word. I'd completely forgotten in all the confusion.
Where is Alex?
Alex?! Alex Summers?!
Alex is here?!
Is he alive?!
Ich fasse es nicht.
Where the hell's he been hidin'?!

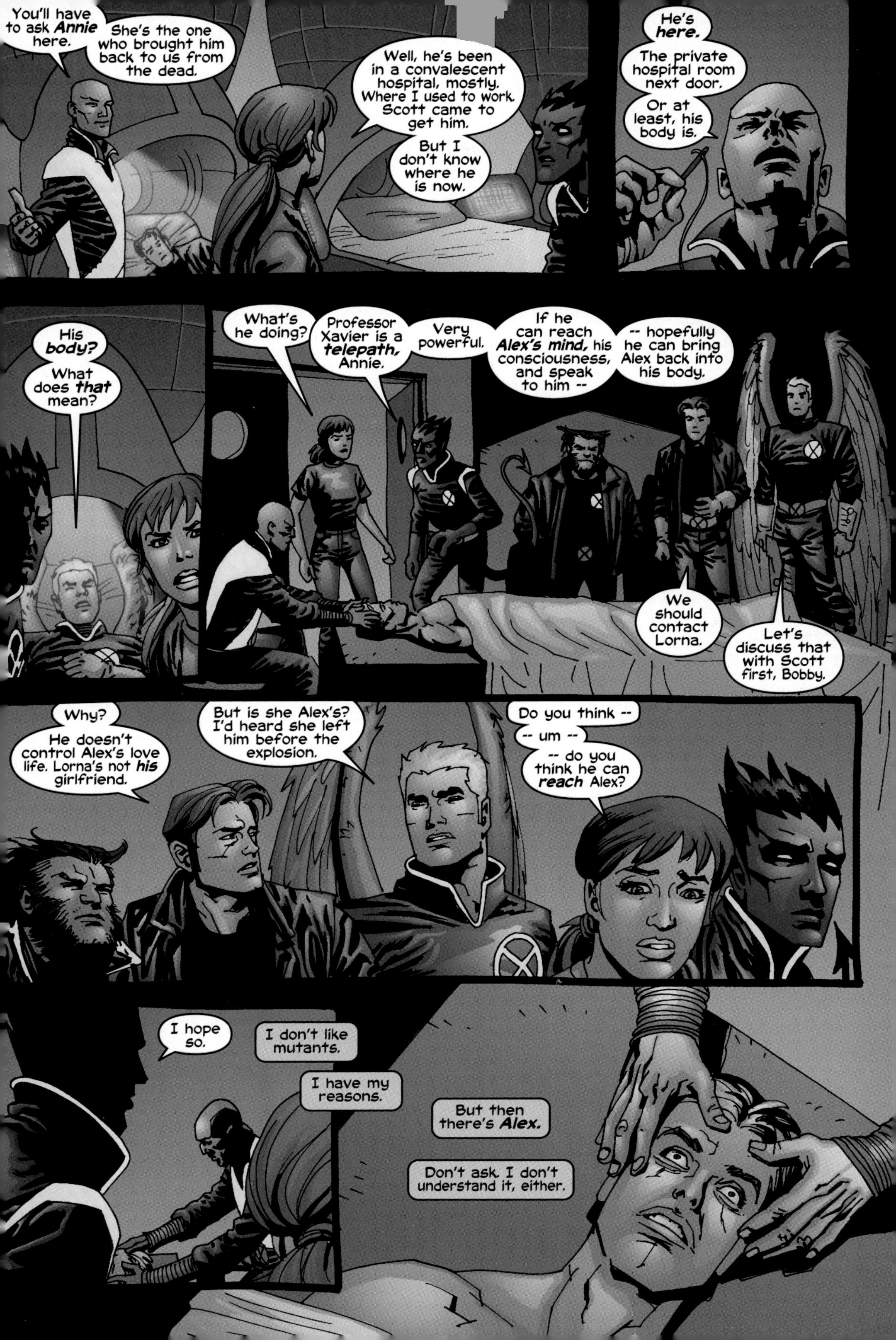

You'll have to ask Annie here.
She's the one who brought him back to us from the dead.
Well, he's been in a convalescent hospital, mostly. Where I used to work. Scott came to get him.
But I don't know where he is now.
He's here.
The private hospital room next door.
Or at least, his body is.
His body?
What does that mean?
What's he doing?
Professor Xavier is a telepath, Annie.
Very powerful.
If he can reach Alex's mind, his consciousness, and speak to him --
-- hopefully he can bring Alex back into his body.
We should contact Lorna.
Let's discuss that with Scott first, Bobby.
Why?
He doesn't control Alex's love life. Lorna's not his girlfriend.
But is she Alex's? I'd heard she left him before the explosion.
Do you think --
-- um --
-- do you think he can reach Alex?
I hope so.
I don't like mutants.
I have my reasons.
But then there's Alex.
Don't ask. I don't understand it, either.

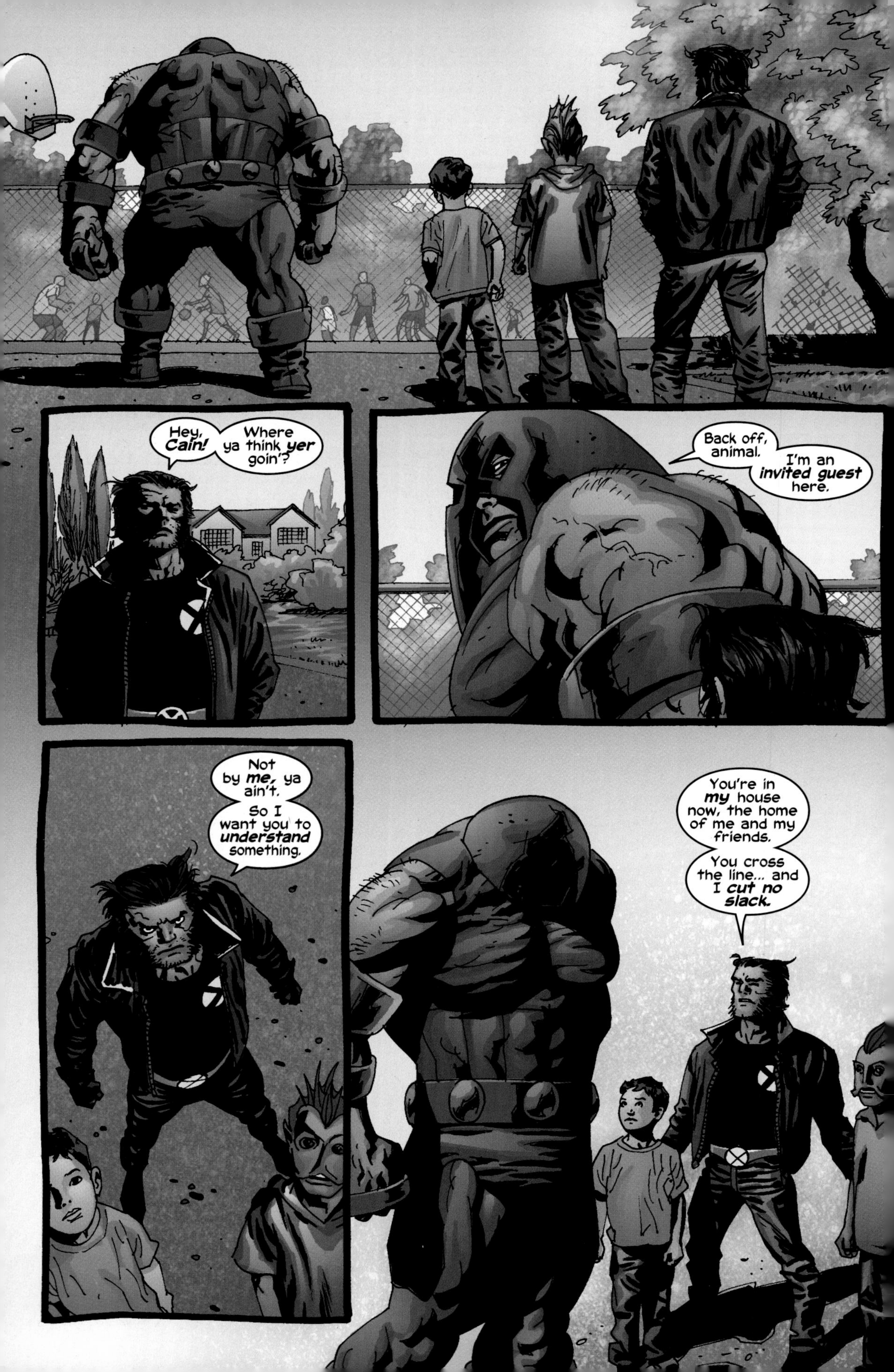
Hey, Cain!
Where ya think yer goin'?
Back off, animal.
I'm an invited guest here.
Not by me, ya ain't.
So I want you to understand something.
You're in my house now, the home of me and my friends.
You cross the line... and I cut no slack.

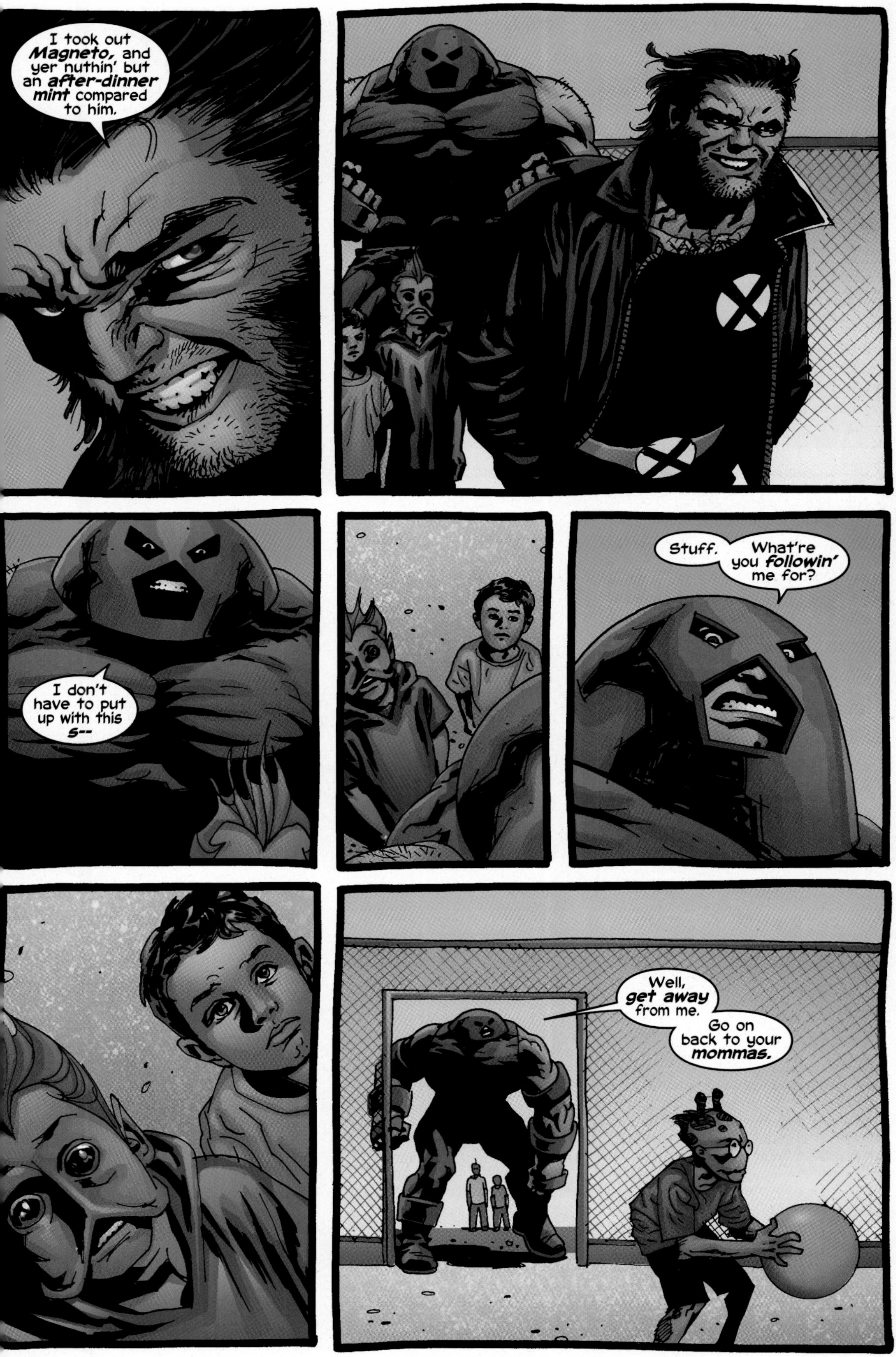
I took out Magneto, and yer nuthin' but an after-dinner mint compared to him.
I don't have to put up with this s--
Stuff.
What're you followin' me for?
Well, get away from me.
Go on back to your mommas.

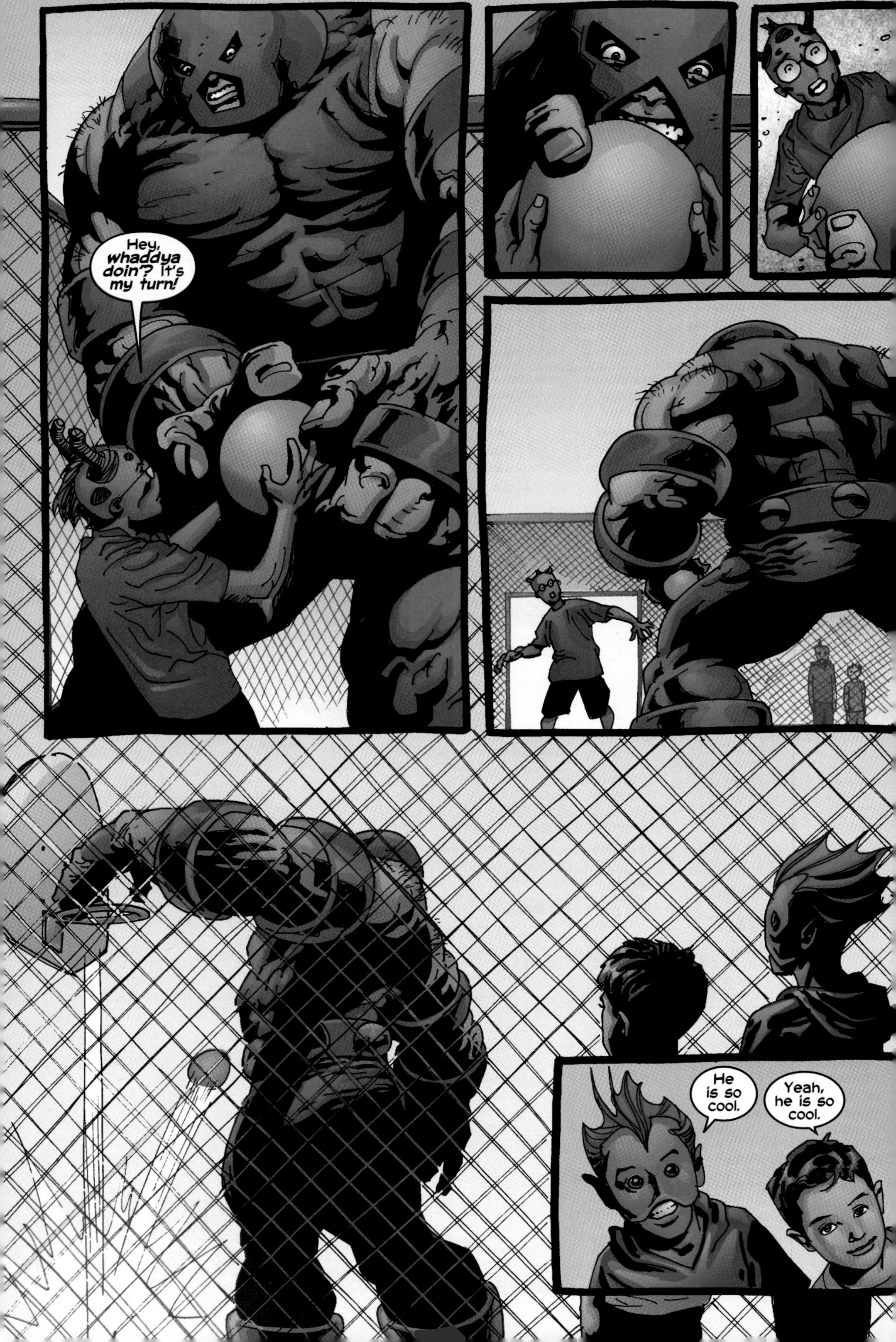
Hey, whaddya doin'? It's my turn!
He is so cool.
Yeah, he is so cool.

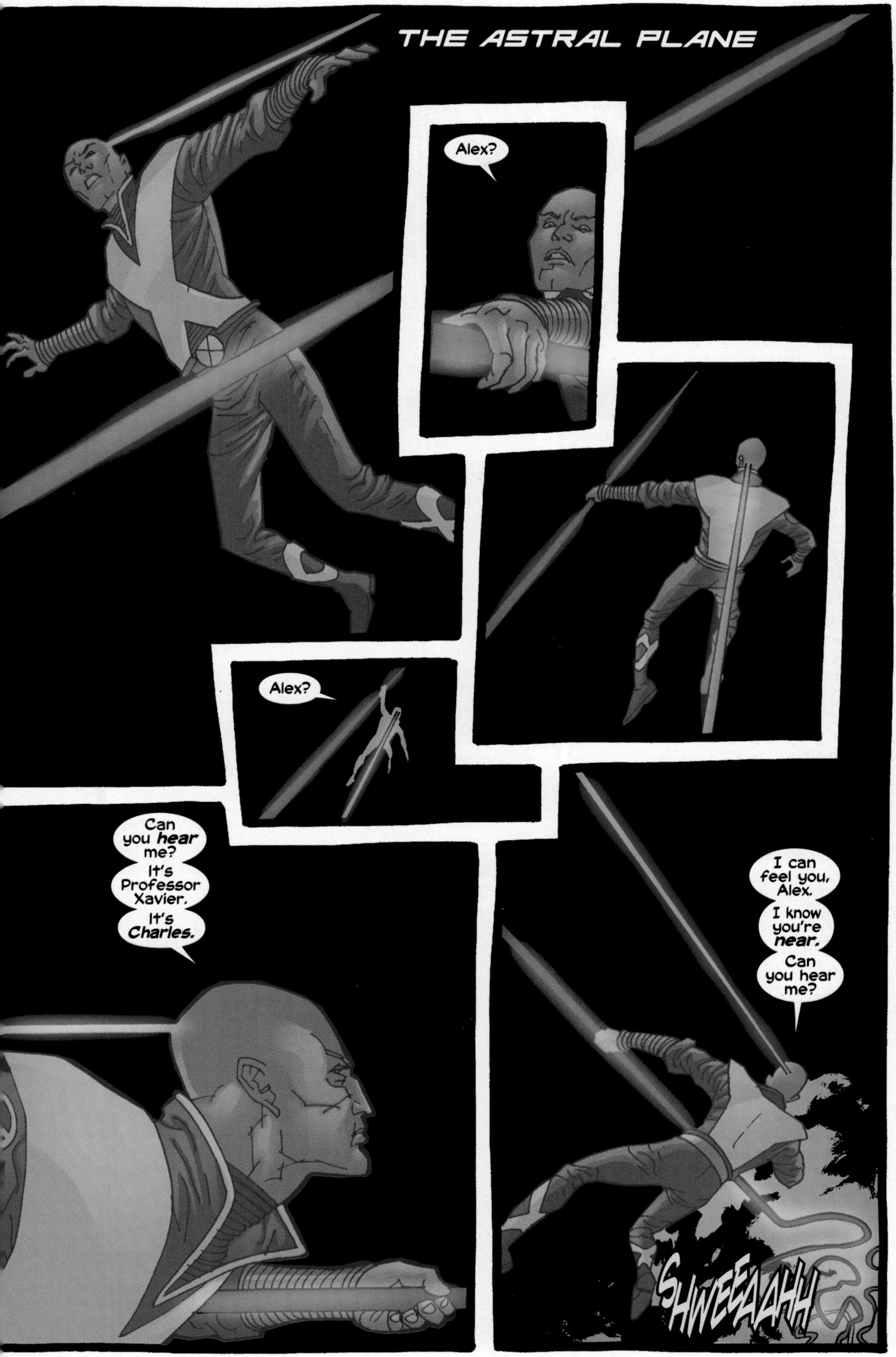
THE ASTRAL PLANE
Alex?
Alex?
Can you hear me? It's Professor Xavier. It's Charles.
I can feel you, Alex. I know you're near. Can you hear me?
SHWEEAAHH

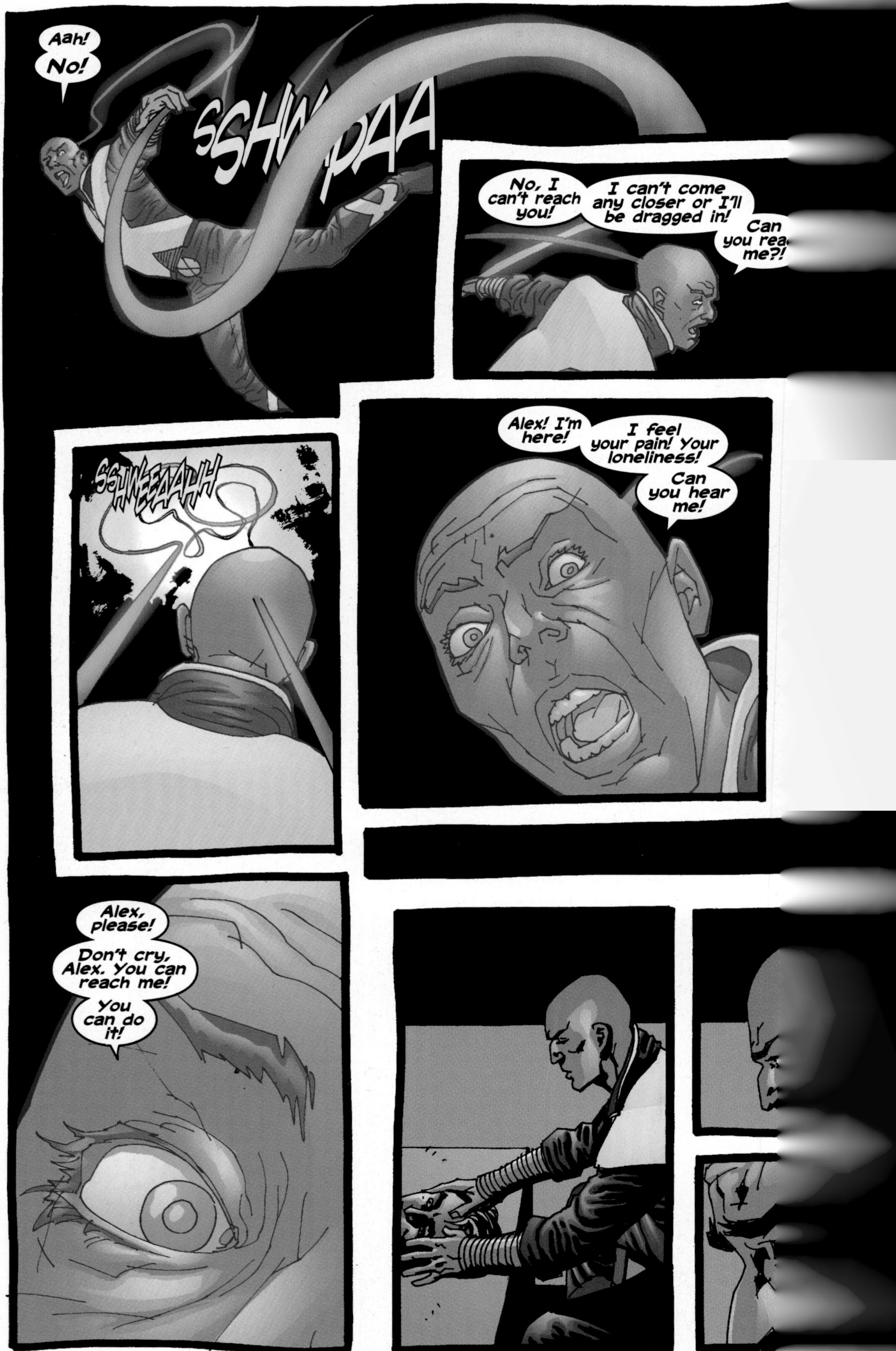
Aah! No!
SSHWPAA
No, I can't reach you!
I can't come any closer or I'll be dragged in!
Can you rea me?!
SSHWEEAAHH
Alex! I'm here!
I feel your pain! Your loneliness!
Can you hear me!
Alex, please!
Don't cry, Alex. You can reach me!
You can do it!

Aaah. The others left?

Yes. They felt it best. It's going on *three hours* now that you've been struggling.

I was *so close.* He is in such anguish. But I can't reach him.

Will you -- -- will you keep trying?

Oh, of course. I'll just... ...I should rest a while, first, I suppose.

Are you all right?

No. No, I'm afraid not.

It's -- --difficult -- --when I can't help one of my -- --one of my *students.*

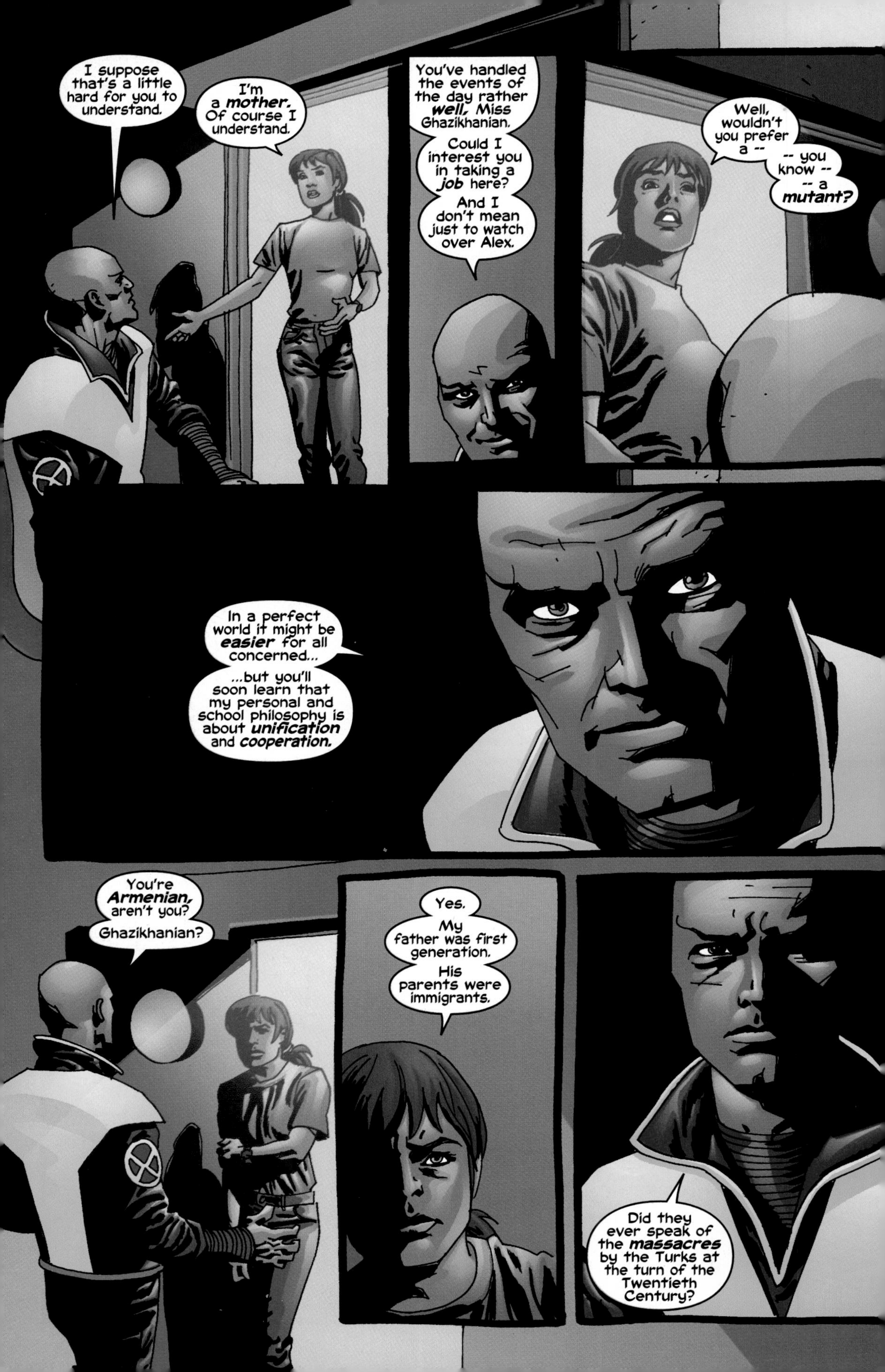
I suppose that's a little hard for you to understand.
I'm a *mother.* Of course I understand.
You've handled the events of the day rather *well,* Miss Ghazikhanian.
Could I interest you in taking a *job* here?
And I don't mean just to watch over Alex.
Well, wouldn't you prefer a --
-- you know --
-- a *mutant?*
In a perfect world it might be *easier* for all concerned...
...but you'll soon learn that my personal and school philosophy is about *unification* and *cooperation.*
You're *Armenian,* aren't you?
Ghazikhanian?
Yes.
My father was first generation.
His parents were immigrants.
Did they ever speak of the *massacres* by the Turks at the turn of the Twentieth Century?

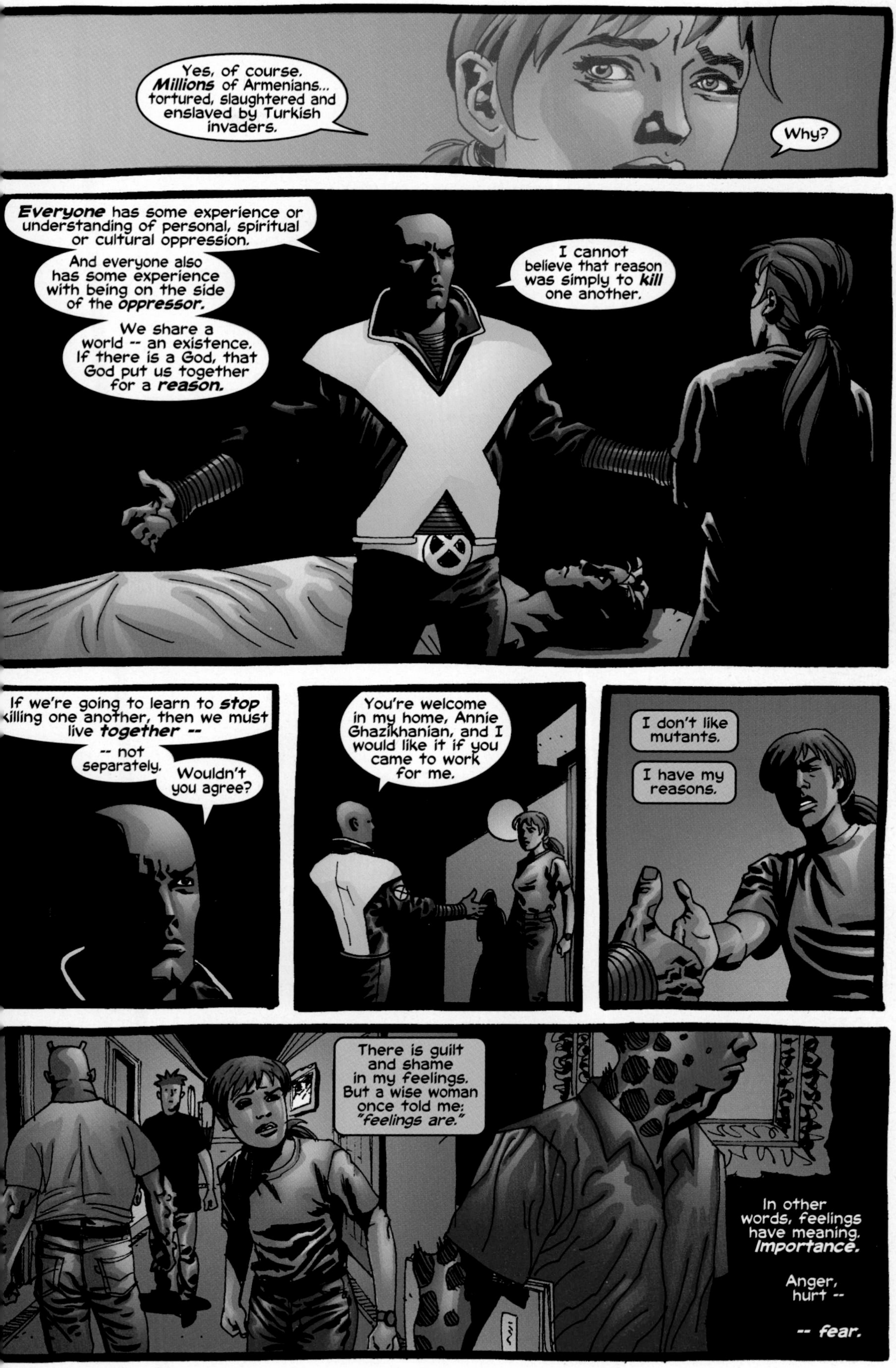
Yes, of course. Millions of Armenians... tortured, slaughtered and enslaved by Turkish invaders.
Why?
Everyone has some experience or understanding of personal, spiritual or cultural oppression.
And everyone also has some experience with being on the side of the oppressor.
We share a world -- an existence. If there is a God, that God put us together for a reason.
I cannot believe that reason was simply to kill one another.
If we're going to learn to stop killing one another, then we must live together --
-- not separately.
Wouldn't you agree?
You're welcome in my home, Annie Ghazikhanian, and I would like it if you came to work for me.
I don't like mutants.
I have my reasons.
There is guilt and shame in my feelings. But a wise woman once told me; "feelings are."
In other words, feelings have meaning. Importance.
Anger, hurt --
-- fear.

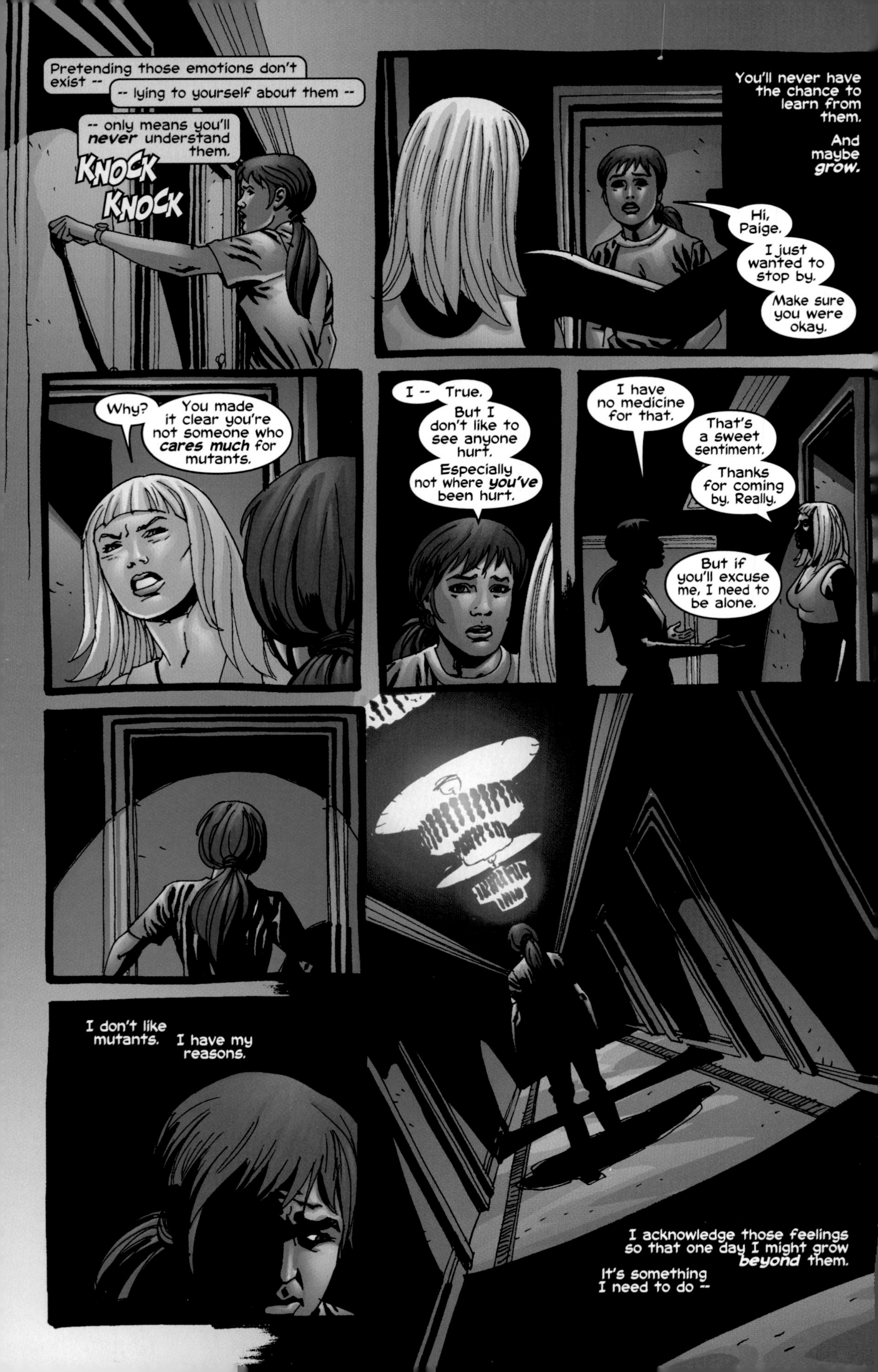
Pretending those emotions don't exist --
-- lying to yourself about them --
-- only means you'll *never* understand them.
KNOCK KNOCK
You'll never have the chance to learn from them.
And maybe *grow.*
Hi, Paige.
I just wanted to stop by.
Make sure you were okay.
Why?
You made it clear you're not someone who *cares much* for mutants.
I -- True.
But I don't like to see anyone hurt.
Especially not where *you've* been hurt.
I have no medicine for that.
That's a sweet sentiment.
Thanks for coming by. Really.
But if you'll excuse me, I need to be alone.
I don't like mutants.
I have my reasons.
I acknowledge those feelings so that one day I might grow *beyond* them.
It's something I need to do --

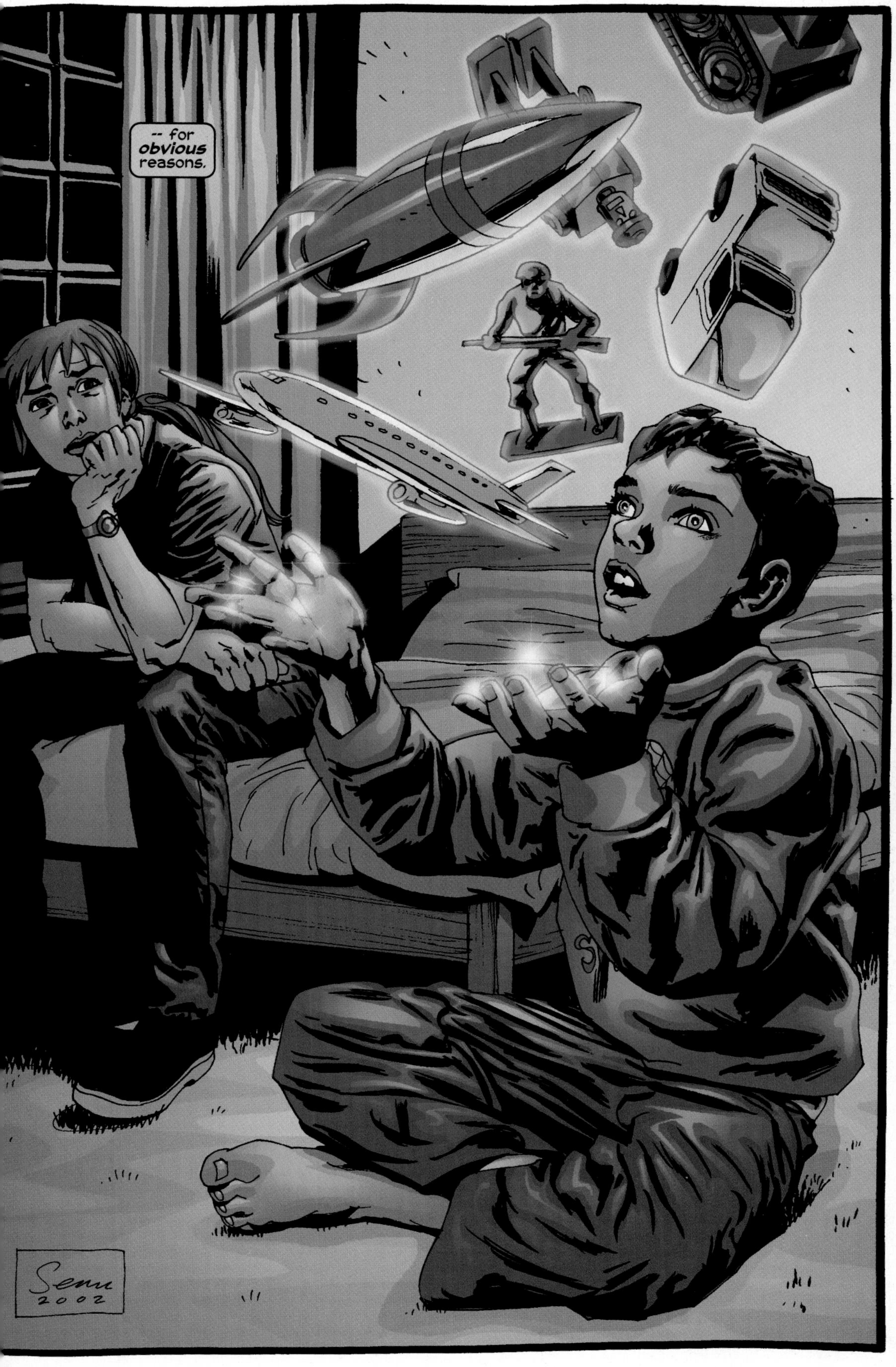
-- for *obvious* reasons.
Seth 2002

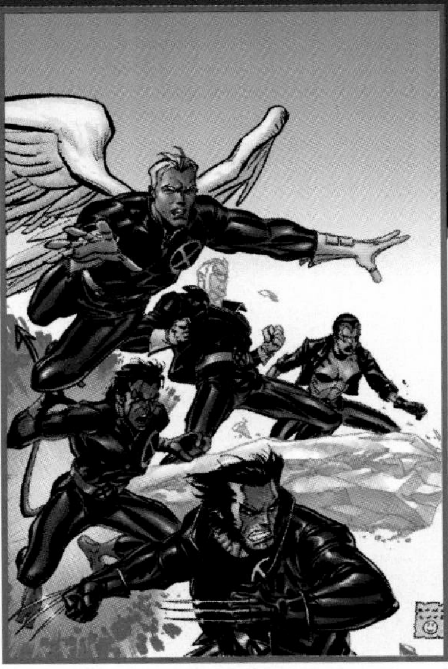

#410

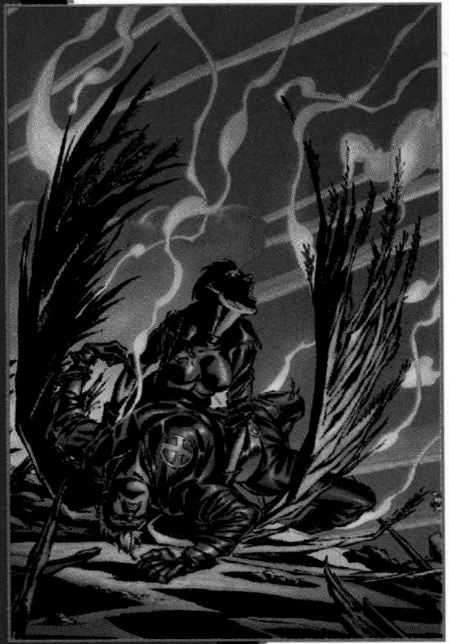

#411

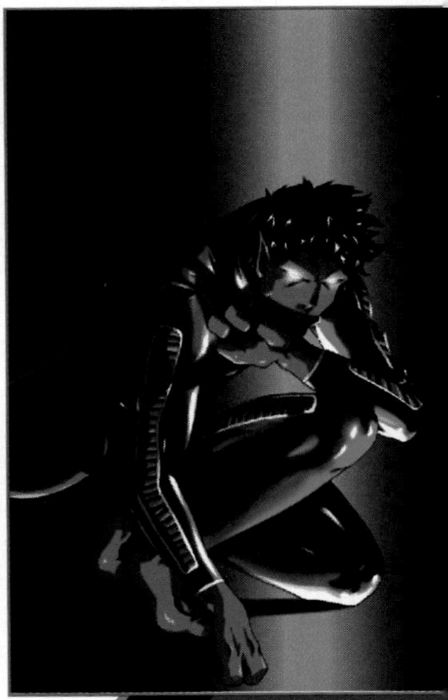

#412

COVER GALLERY

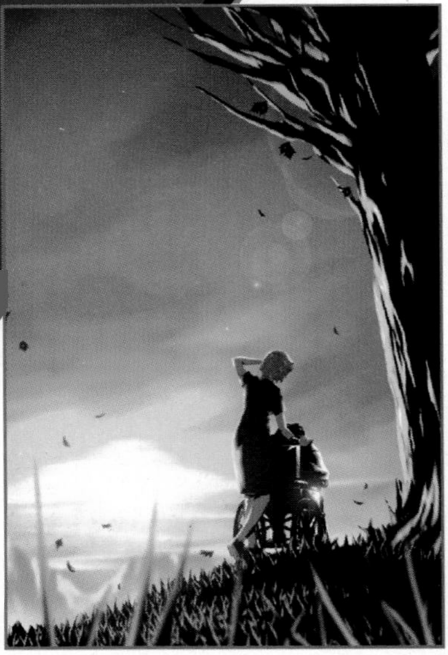

#413

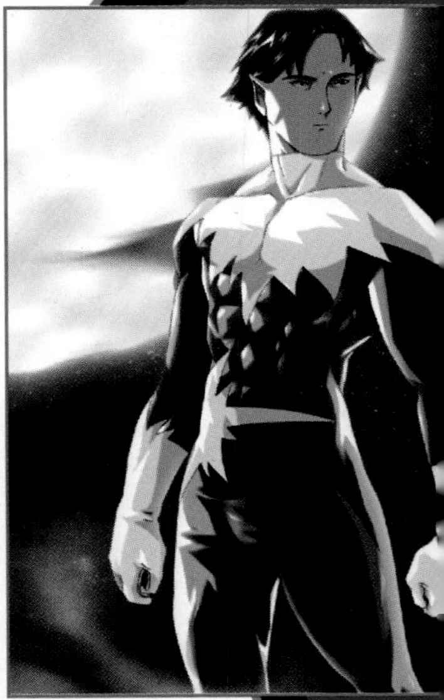

#414

#415

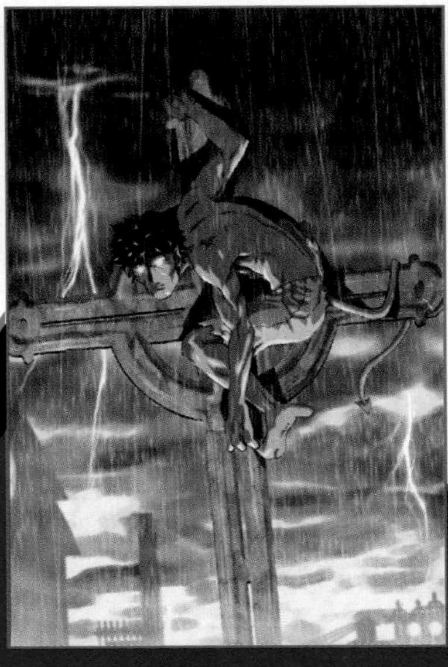

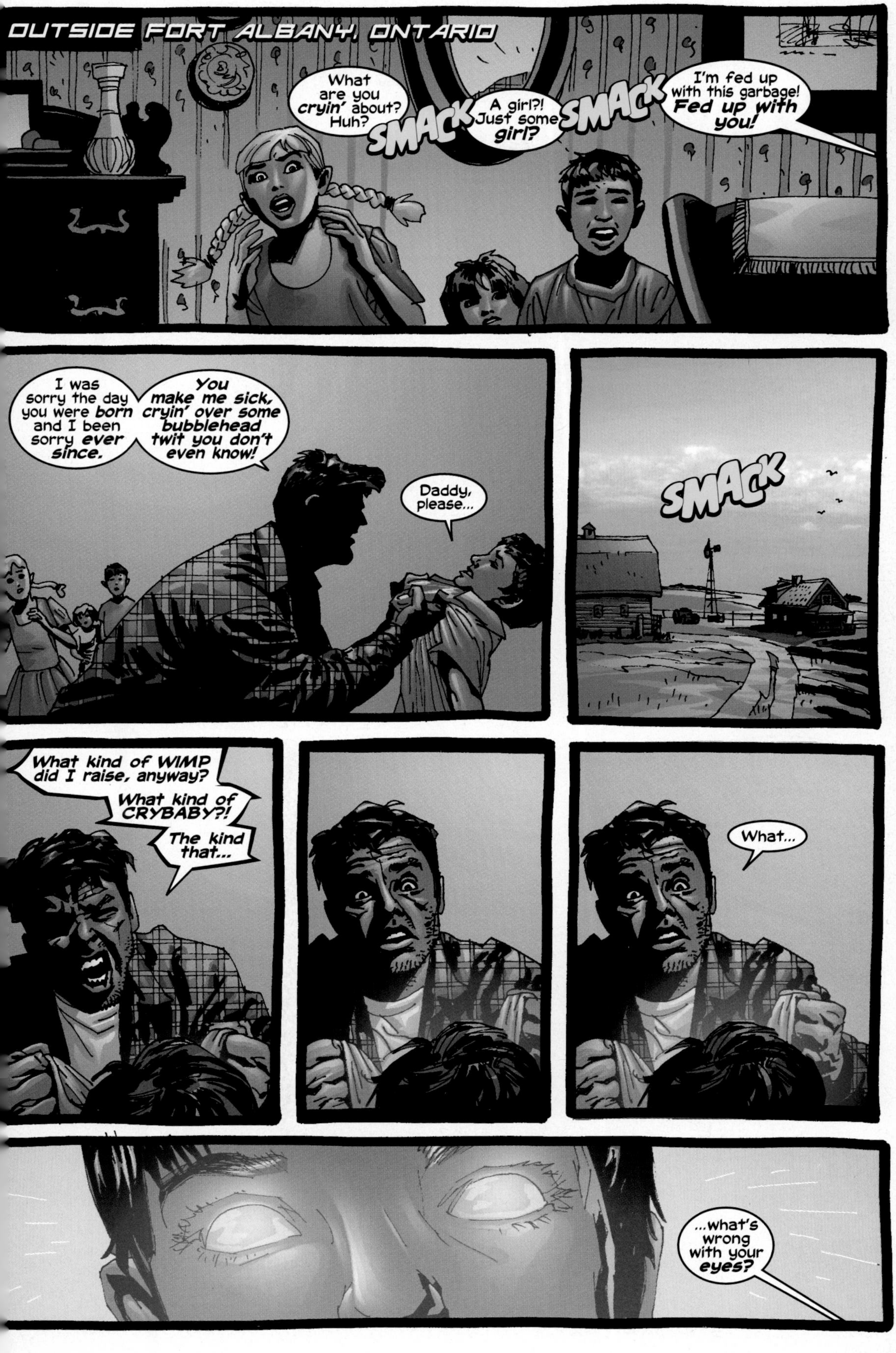
OUTSIDE FORT ALBANY, ONTARIO
What are you cryin' about? Huh?
SMACK
A girl?! Just some girl?
SMACK
I'm fed up with this garbage! Fed up with you!
I was sorry the day you were born and I been sorry ever since.
You make me sick, cryin' over some bubblehead twit you don't even know!
Daddy, please...
SMACK
What kind of WIMP did I raise, anyway?
What kind of CRYBABY?!
The kind that...
What...
...what's wrong with your eyes?

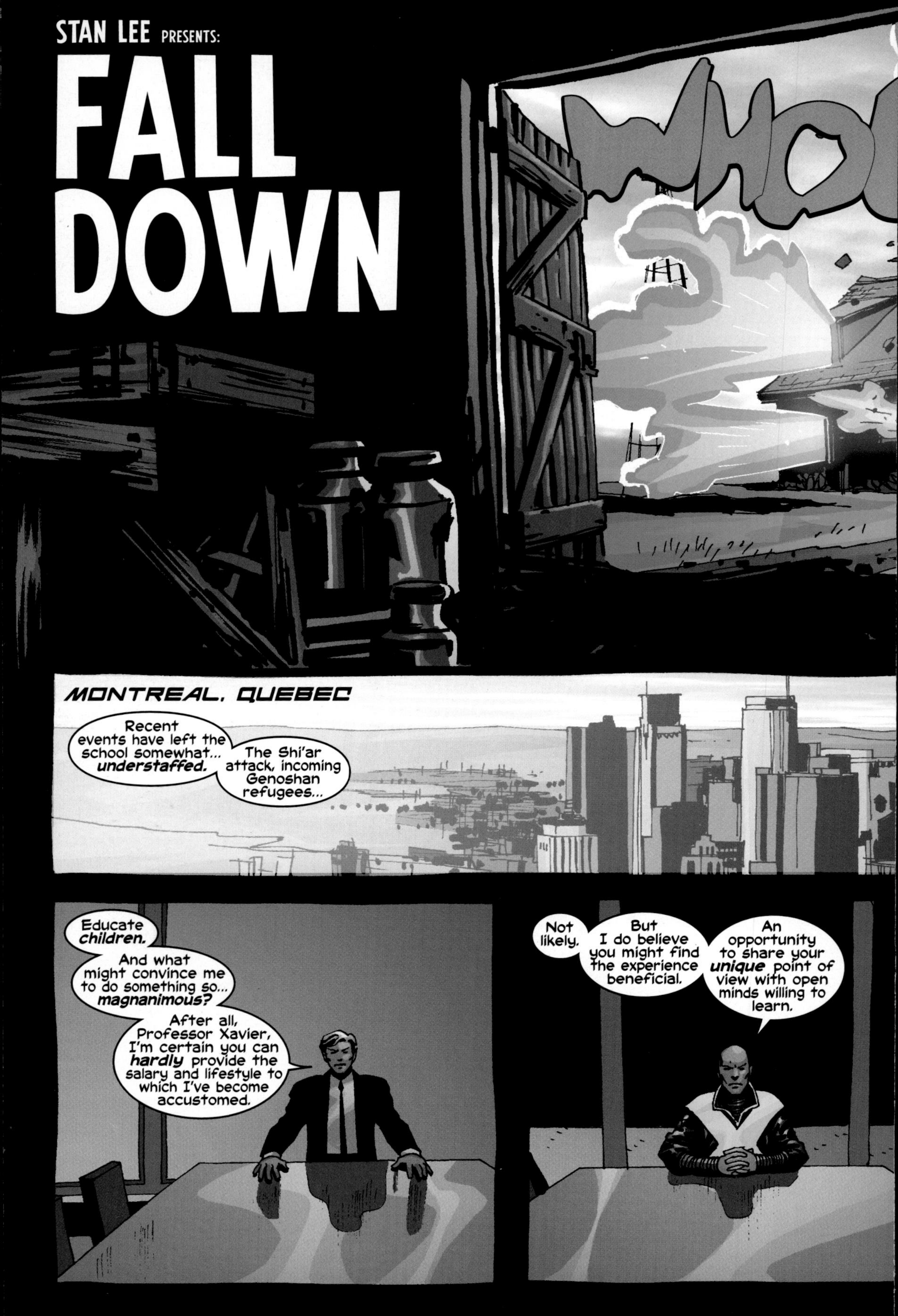
STAN LEE PRESENTS:
FALL DOWN
MONTREAL, QUEBEC
Recent events have left the school somewhat... understaffed.
The Shi'ar attack, incoming Genoshan refugees...
Educate children.
And what might convince me to do something so... magnanimous?
After all, Professor Xavier, I'm certain you can hardly provide the salary and lifestyle to which I've become accustomed.
Not likely.
But I do believe you might find the experience beneficial.
An opportunity to share your unique point of view with open minds willing to learn.

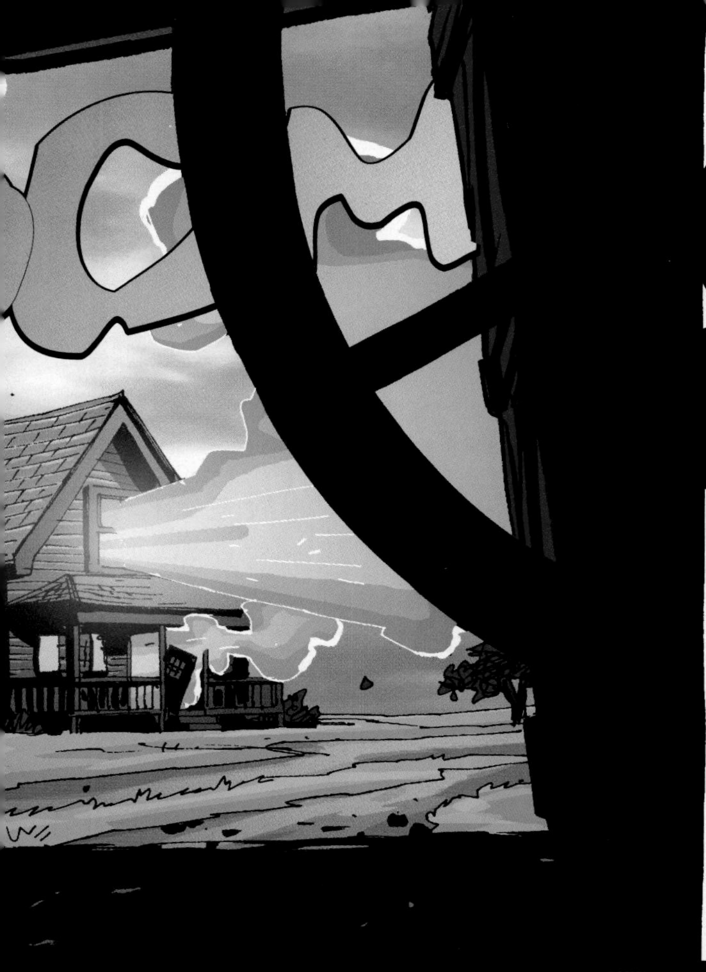

GO BOOM

CHUCK AUSTEN WRITER
SEAN PHILLIPS ARTIST
RICHARD STARKINGS & COMICRAFT'S SAIDA! LETTERS
HI-FI DESIGN COLORS
STEVE UY COVER
MIKE RAICHT & NOVA REN SUMA ASSISTANT EDITORS
MIKE MARTS EDITOR
JOE QUESADA CHIEF
BILL JEMAS PRESIDENT

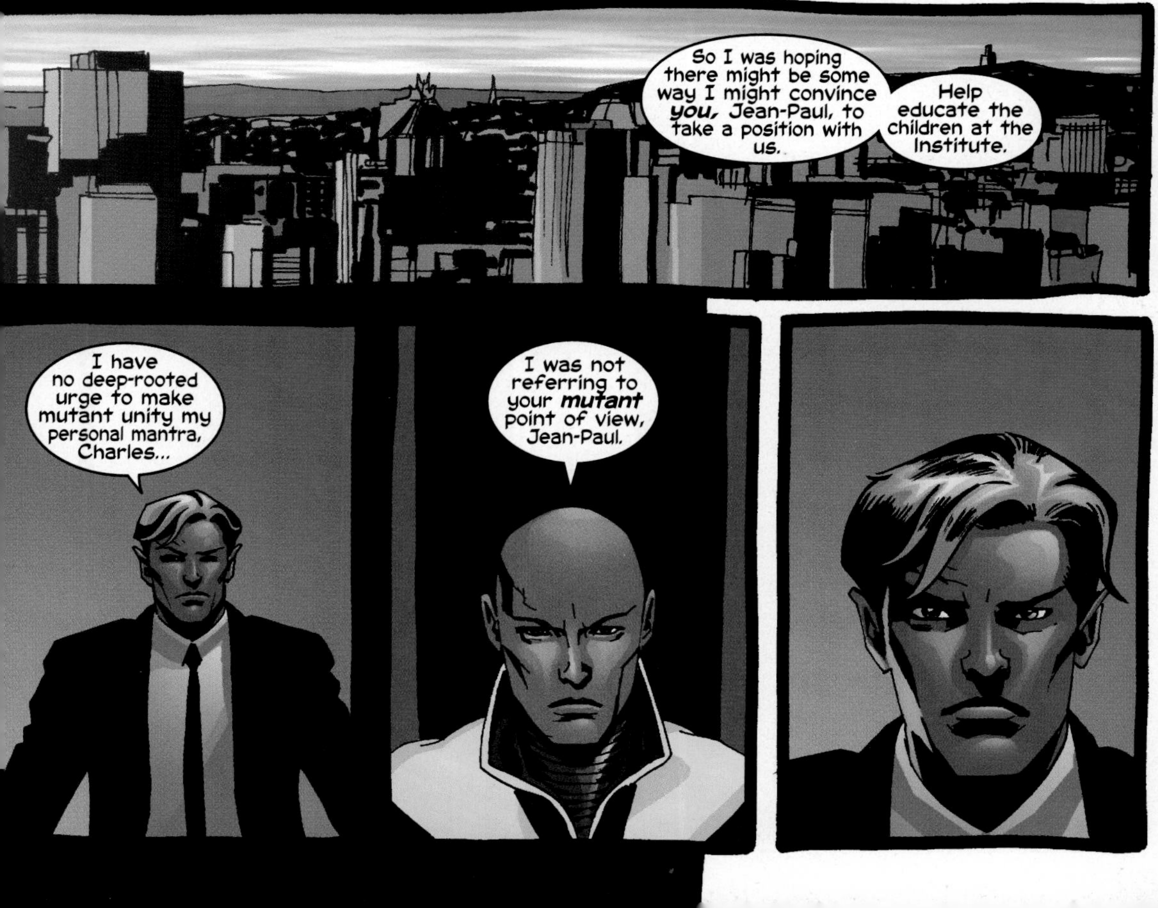
So I was hoping there might be some way I might convince *you,* Jean-Paul, to take a position with us.
Help educate the children at the Institute.
I have no deep-rooted urge to make mutant unity my personal mantra, Charles...
I was not referring to your *mutant* point of view, Jean-Paul.

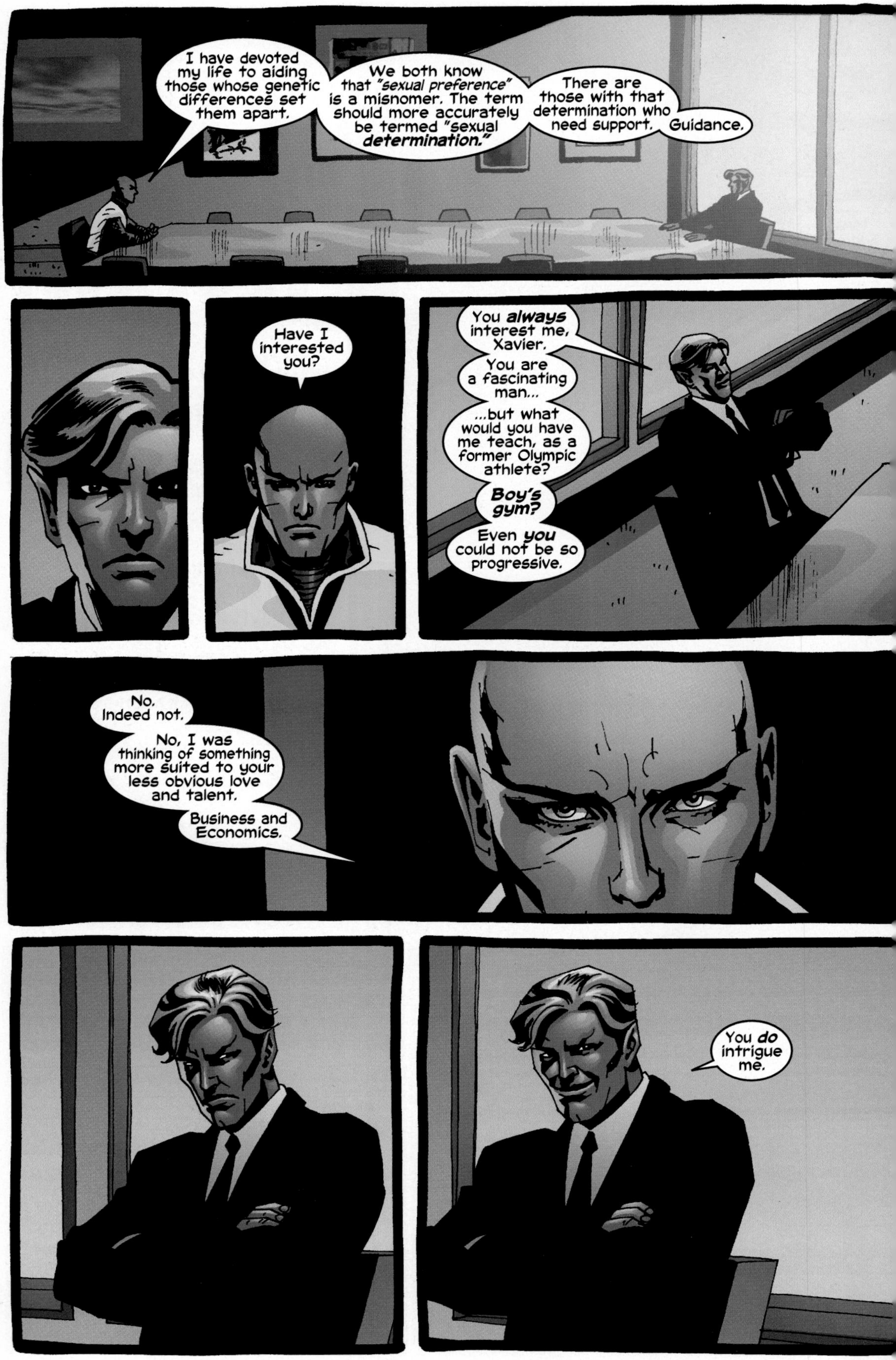
I have devoted my life to aiding those whose genetic differences set them apart.
We both know that "sexual preference" is a misnomer. The term should more accurately be termed "sexual determination."
There are those with that determination who need support.
Guidance.
Have I interested you?
You always interest me, Xavier.
You are a fascinating man...
...but what would you have me teach, as a former Olympic athlete?
Boy's gym?
Even you could not be so progressive.
No. Indeed not.
No, I was thinking of something more suited to your less obvious love and talent.
Business and Economics.
You do intrigue me.

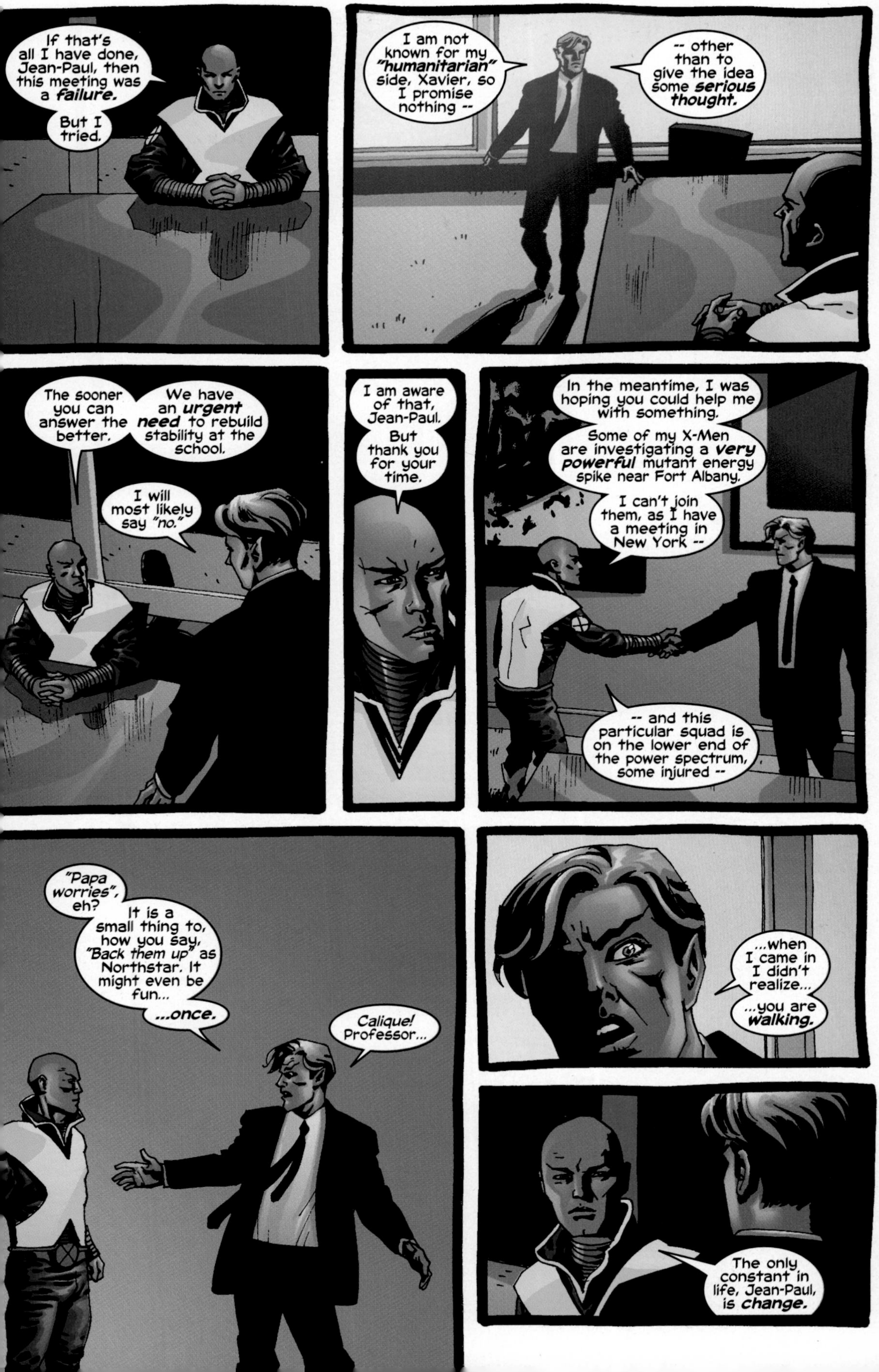
If that's all I have done, Jean-Paul, then this meeting was a ***failure.***
But I tried.
I am not known for my ***"humanitarian"*** side, Xavier, so I promise nothing --
-- other than to give the idea some ***serious thought.***
The sooner you can answer the better.
We have an ***urgent need*** to rebuild stability at the school.
I will most likely say *"no."*
I am aware of that, Jean-Paul.
But thank you for your time.
In the meantime, I was hoping you could help me with something.
Some of my X-Men are investigating a ***very powerful*** mutant energy spike near Fort Albany.
I can't join them, as I have a meeting in New York --
-- and this particular squad is on the lower end of the power spectrum, some injured --
"Papa worries", eh?
It is a small thing to, how you say, *"Back them up"* as Northstar. It might even be fun...
...once.
Calique! Professor...
...when I came in I didn't realize...
...you are ***walking.***
The only constant in life, Jean-Paul, is ***change.***

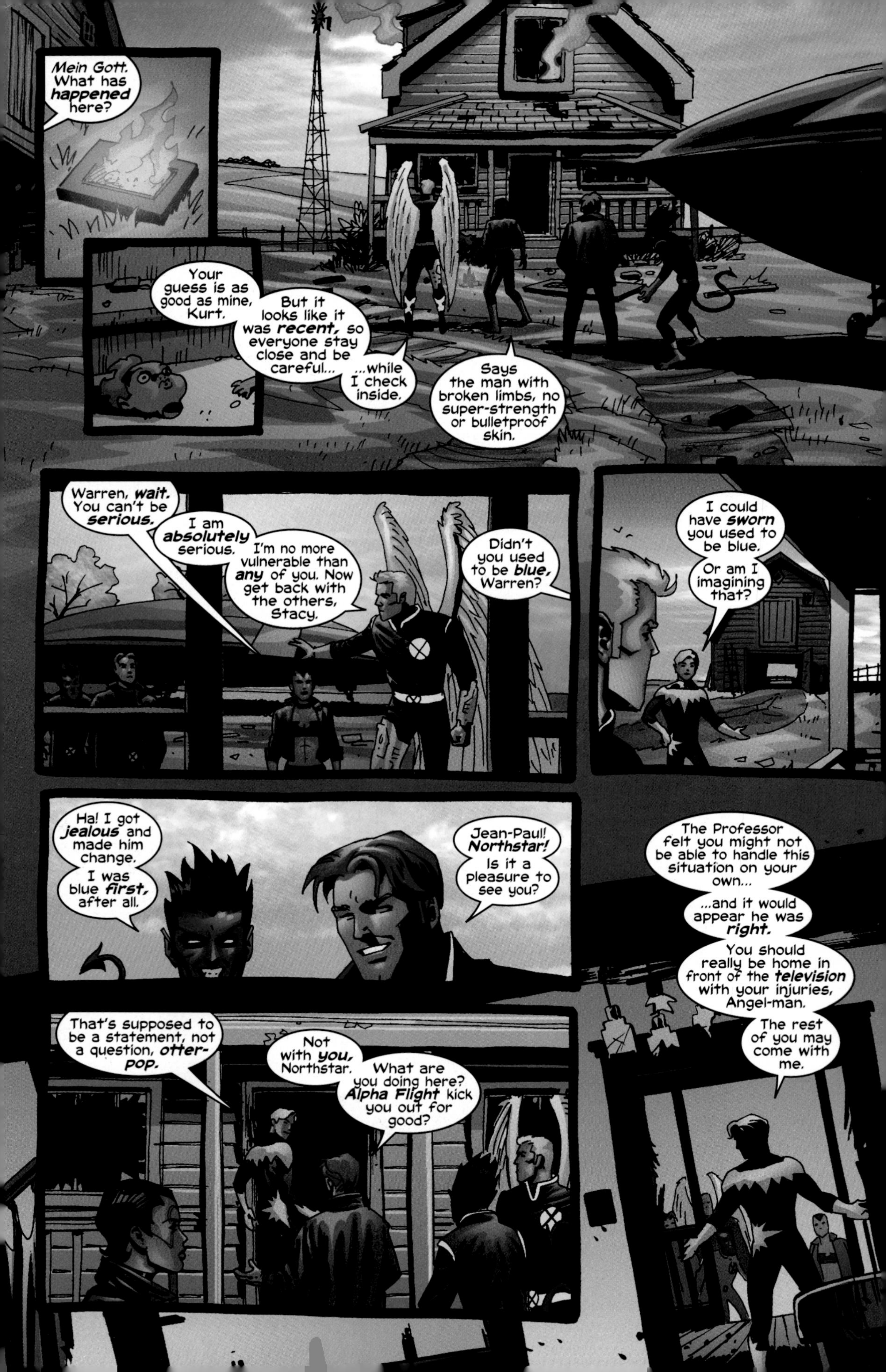
Mein Gott. What has happened here?
Your guess is as good as mine, Kurt.
But it looks like it was recent, so everyone stay close and be careful...
...while I check inside.
Says the man with broken limbs, no super-strength or bulletproof skin.
Warren, wait. You can't be serious.
I am absolutely serious.
I'm no more vulnerable than any of you. Now get back with the others, Stacy.
Didn't you used to be blue, Warren?
I could have sworn you used to be blue.
Or am I imagining that?
Ha! I got jealous and made him change.
I was blue first, after all.
Jean-Paul! Northstar!
Is it a pleasure to see you?
The Professor felt you might not be able to handle this situation on your own...
...and it would appear he was right.
You should really be home in front of the television with your injuries, Angel-man.
The rest of you may come with me.
That's supposed to be a statement, not a question, otter-pop.
Not with you, Northstar.
What are you doing here? Alpha Flight kick you out for good?

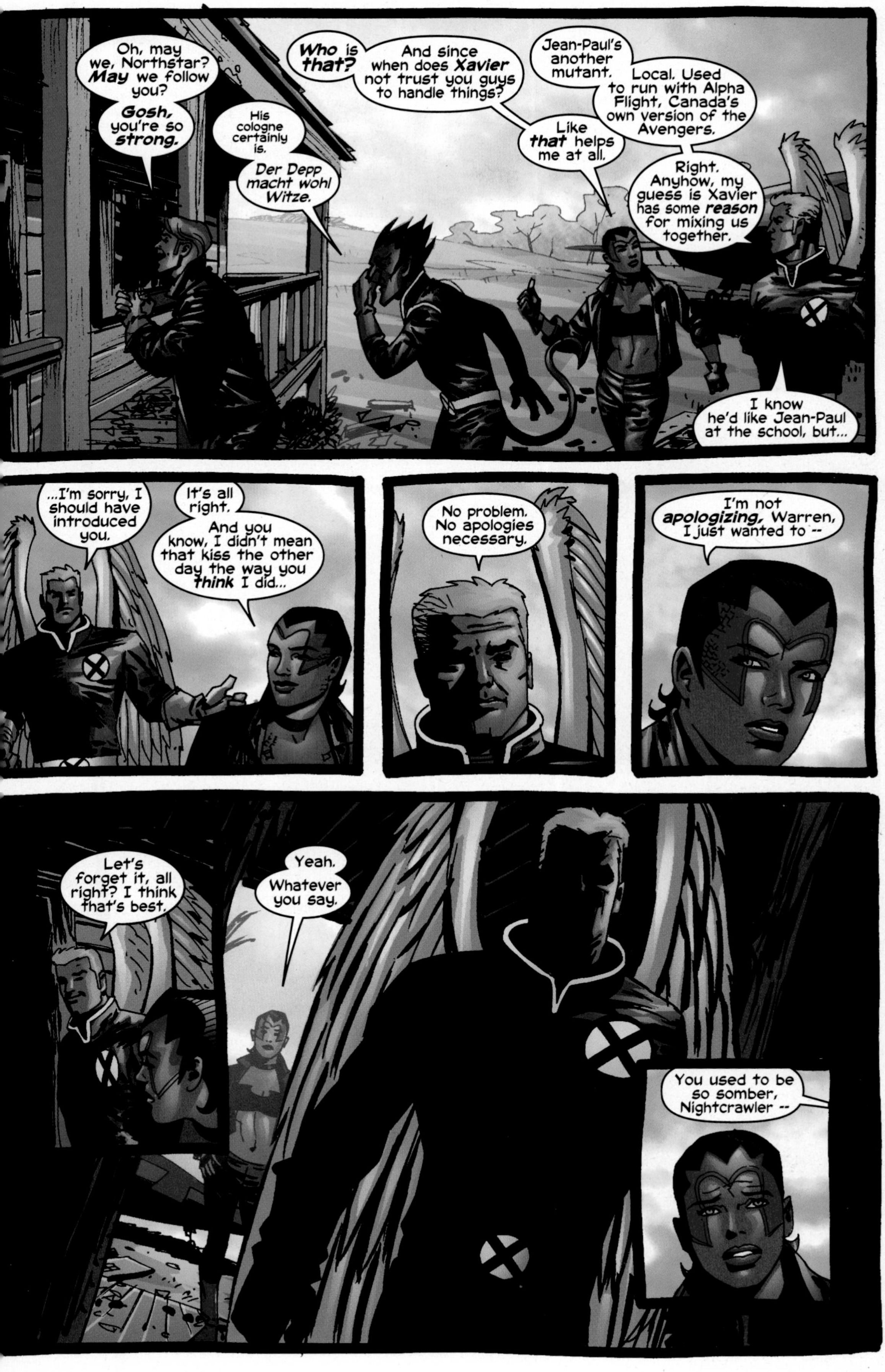
Oh, may we, Northstar? May we follow you?
Gosh, you're so strong.
His cologne certainly is.
Der Depp macht wohl Witze.
Who is that?
And since when does Xavier not trust you guys to handle things?
Like that helps me at all.
Jean-Paul's another mutant.
Local. Used to run with Alpha Flight, Canada's own version of the Avengers.
Right. Anyhow, my guess is Xavier has some reason for mixing us together.
I know he'd like Jean-Paul at the school, but...
...I'm sorry, I should have introduced you.
It's all right.
And you know, I didn't mean that kiss the other day the way you think I did...
No problem. No apologies necessary.
I'm not apologizing, Warren, I just wanted to --
Let's forget it, all right? I think that's best.
Yeah. Whatever you say.
You used to be so somber, Nightcrawler --

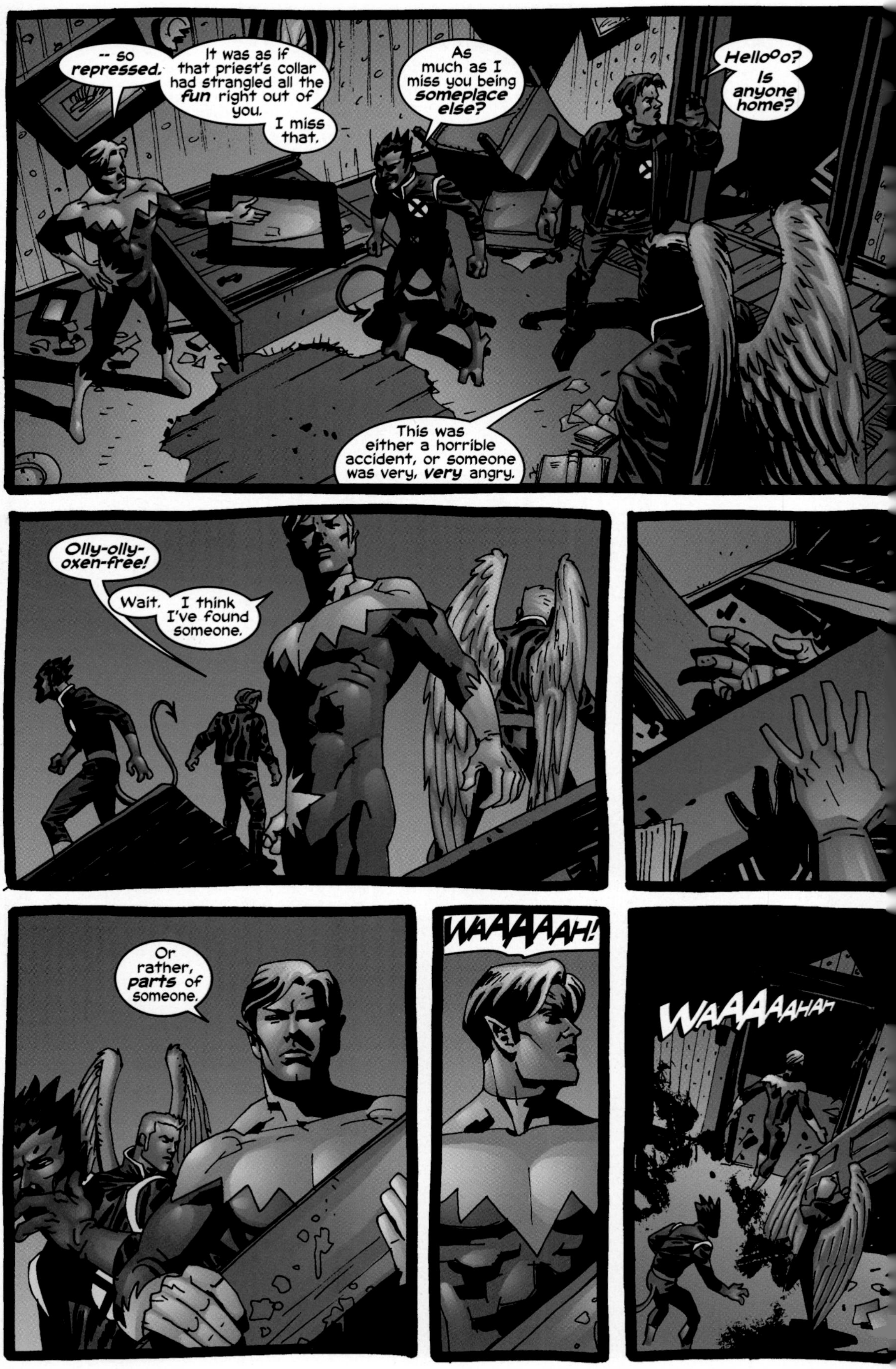
-- so *repressed.*
It was as if that priest's collar had strangled all the *fun* right out of you.
I miss that.
As much as I miss you being *someplace else?*
Hello°o? Is anyone home?
This was either a horrible accident, or someone was very, *very* angry.
Olly-olly-oxen-free!
Wait.
I think I've found someone.
Or rather, *parts* of someone.
WAAAAAH!
WAAAAAHAH

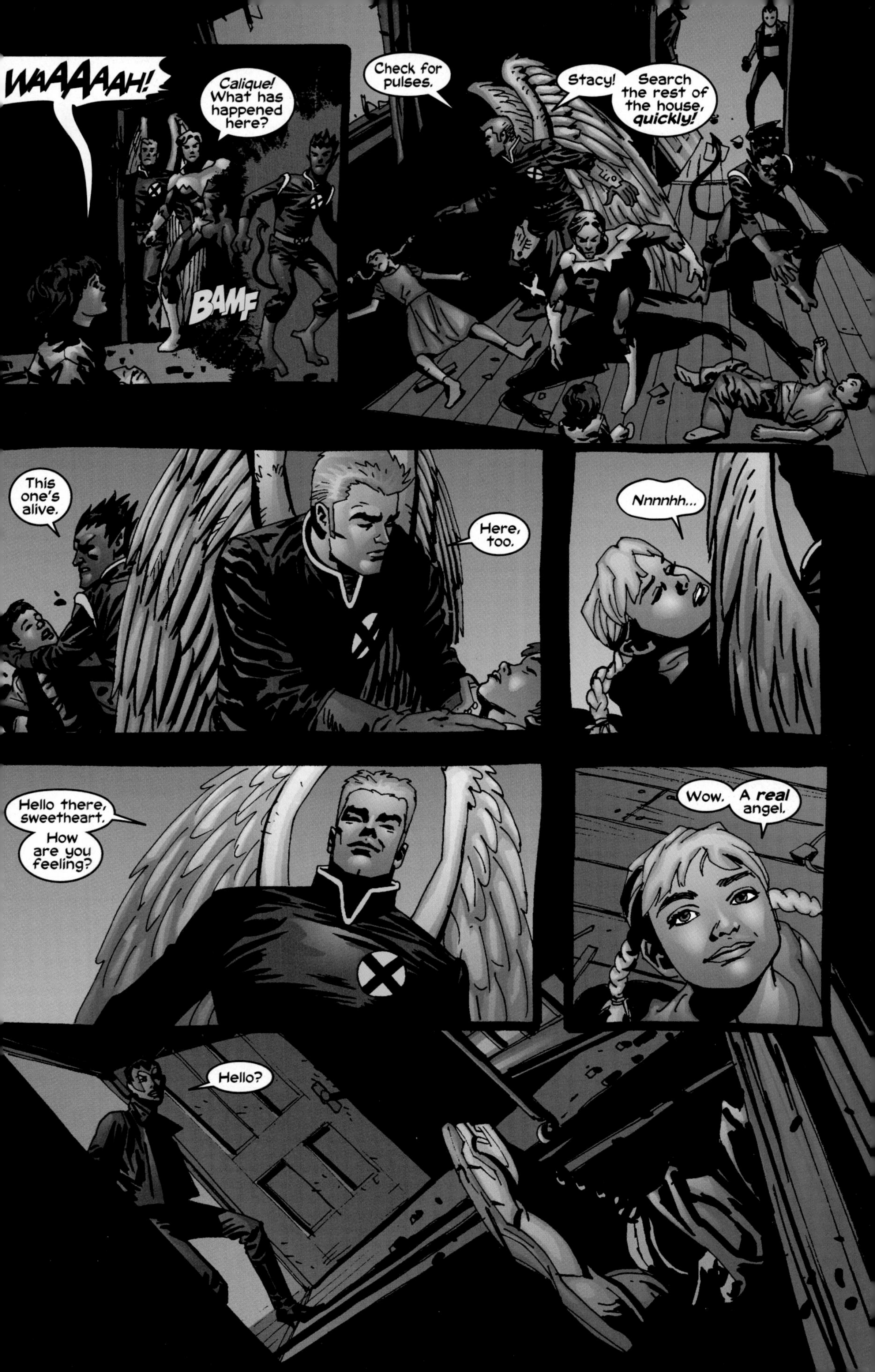
WAAAAAH!
Calique! What has happened here?
BAMF
Check for pulses.
Stacy!
Search the rest of the house, *quickly!*
This one's alive.
Here, too.
Nnnnhh...
Hello there, sweetheart.
How are you feeling?
Wow.
A *real* angel.
Hello?

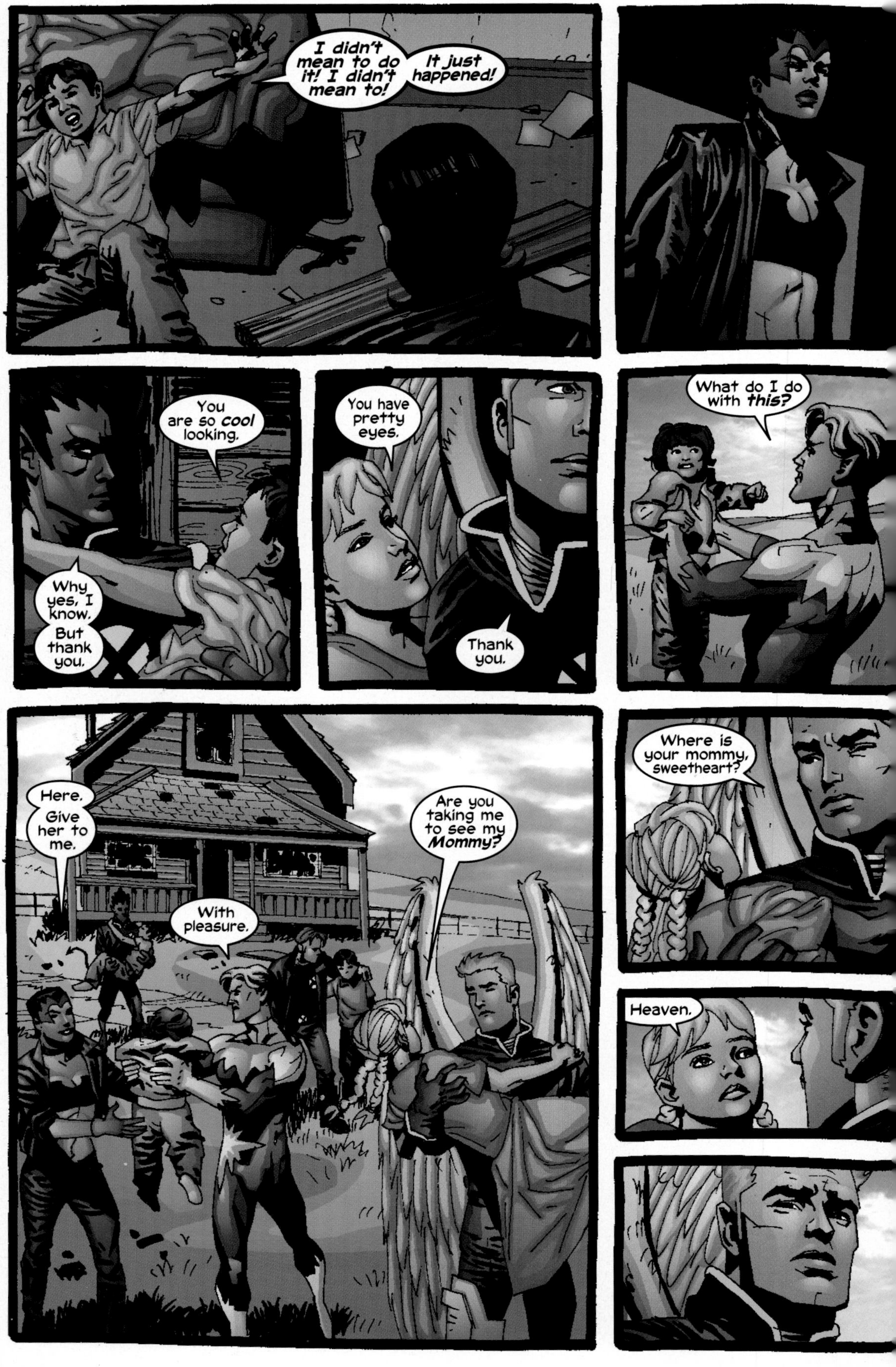
I didn't mean to do it! I didn't mean to!
It just happened!
You are so cool looking.
Why yes, I know.
But thank you.
You have pretty eyes.
Thank you.
What do I do with this?
Here. Give her to me.
With pleasure.
Are you taking me to see my Mommy?
Where is your mommy, sweetheart?
Heaven.

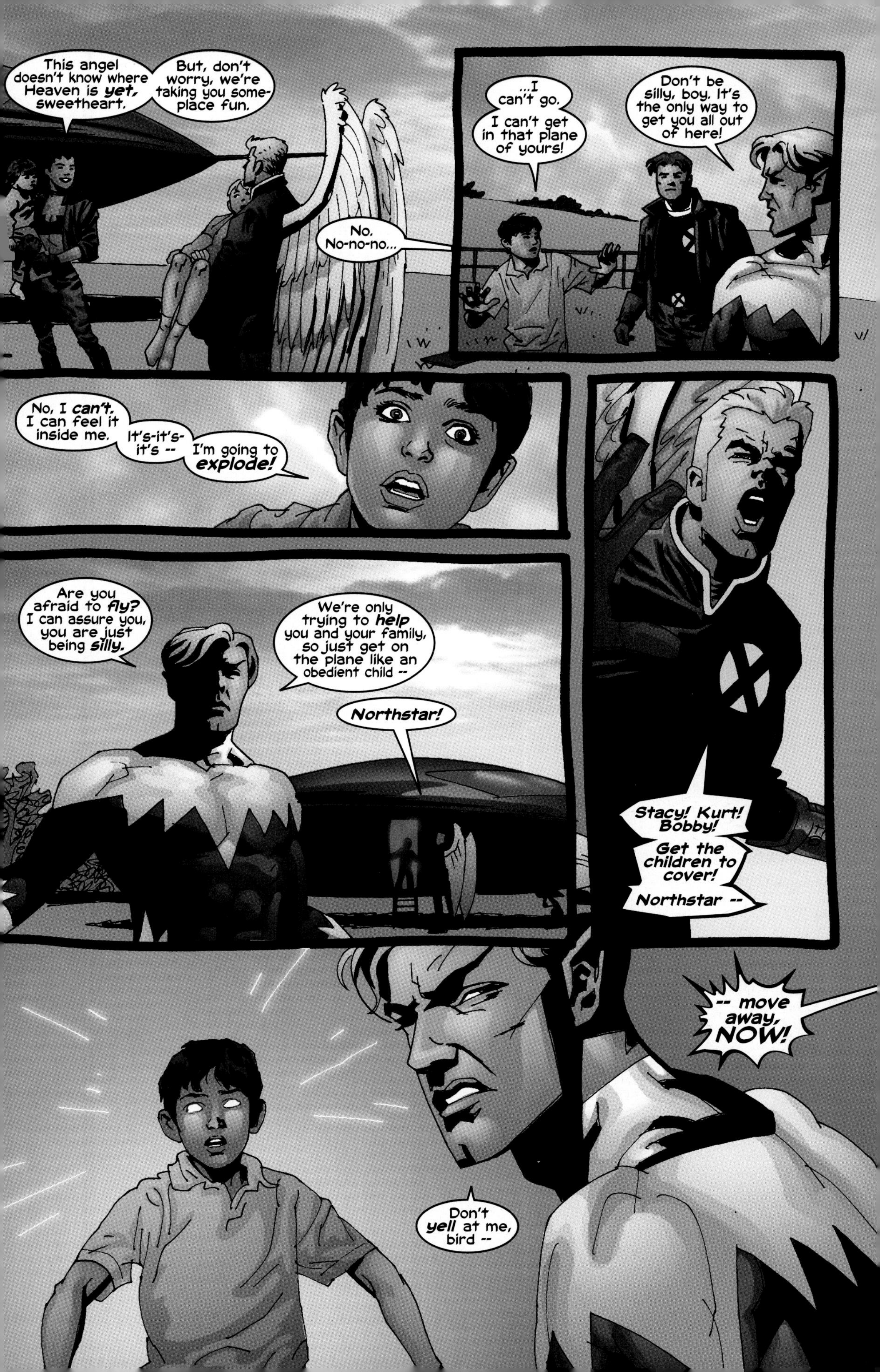

This angel doesn't know where Heaven is yet, sweetheart.
But, don't worry, we're taking you someplace fun.
No. No-no-no...
...I can't go.
I can't get in that plane of yours!
Don't be silly, boy. It's the only way to get you all out of here!
No, I can't. I can feel it inside me.
It's-it's-it's --
I'm going to explode!
Are you afraid to fly? I can assure you, you are just being silly.
We're only trying to help you and your family, so just get on the plane like an obedient child --
Northstar!
Stacy! Kurt! Bobby!
Get the children to cover!
Northstar --
-- move away, NOW!
Don't yell at me, bird --

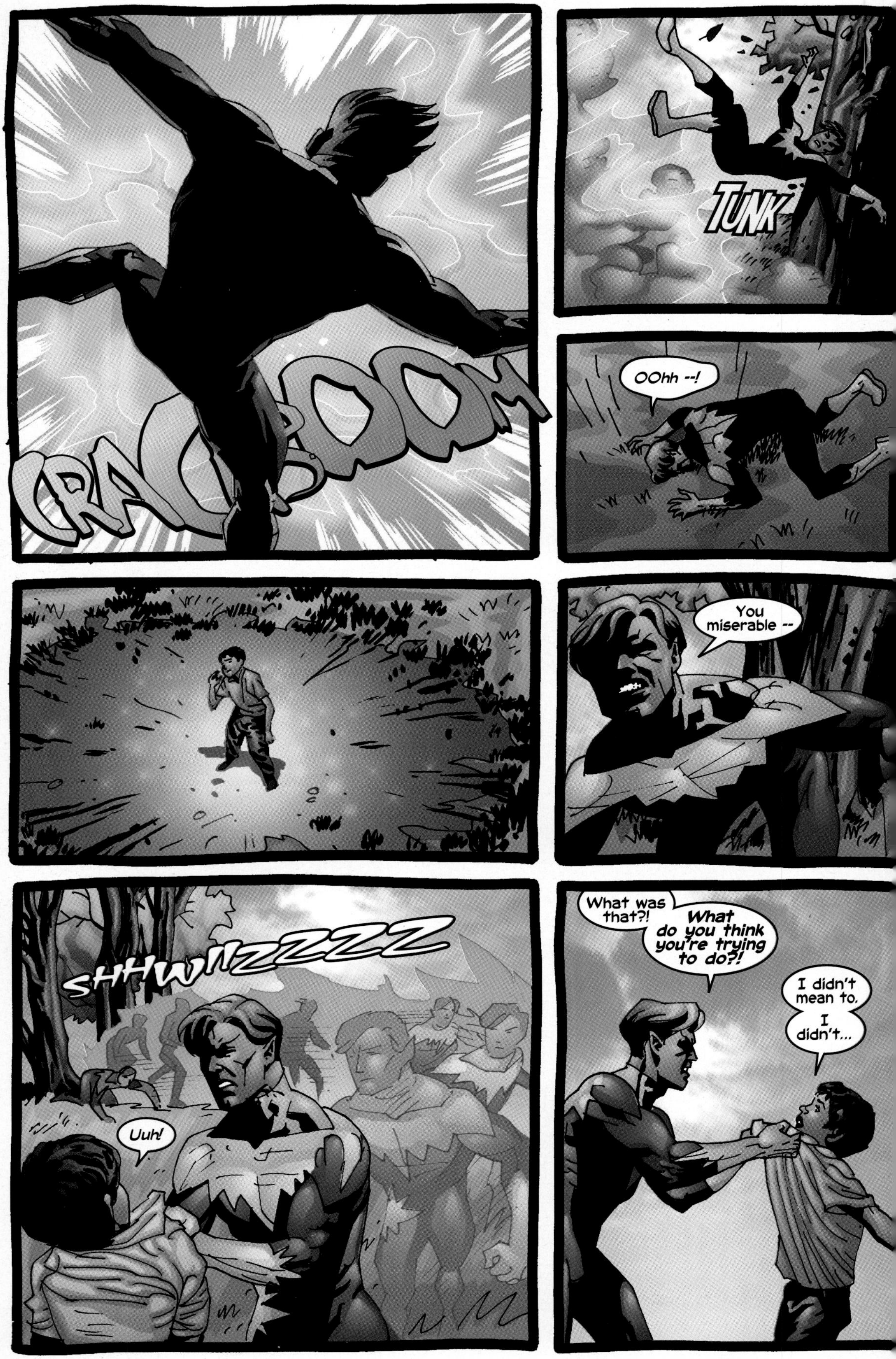
CRACKBOOM
TUNK
OOhh --!
You miserable --
SHHWIIZZZZZ
Uuh!
What was that?!
What do you think you're trying to do?!
I didn't mean to.
I didn't...

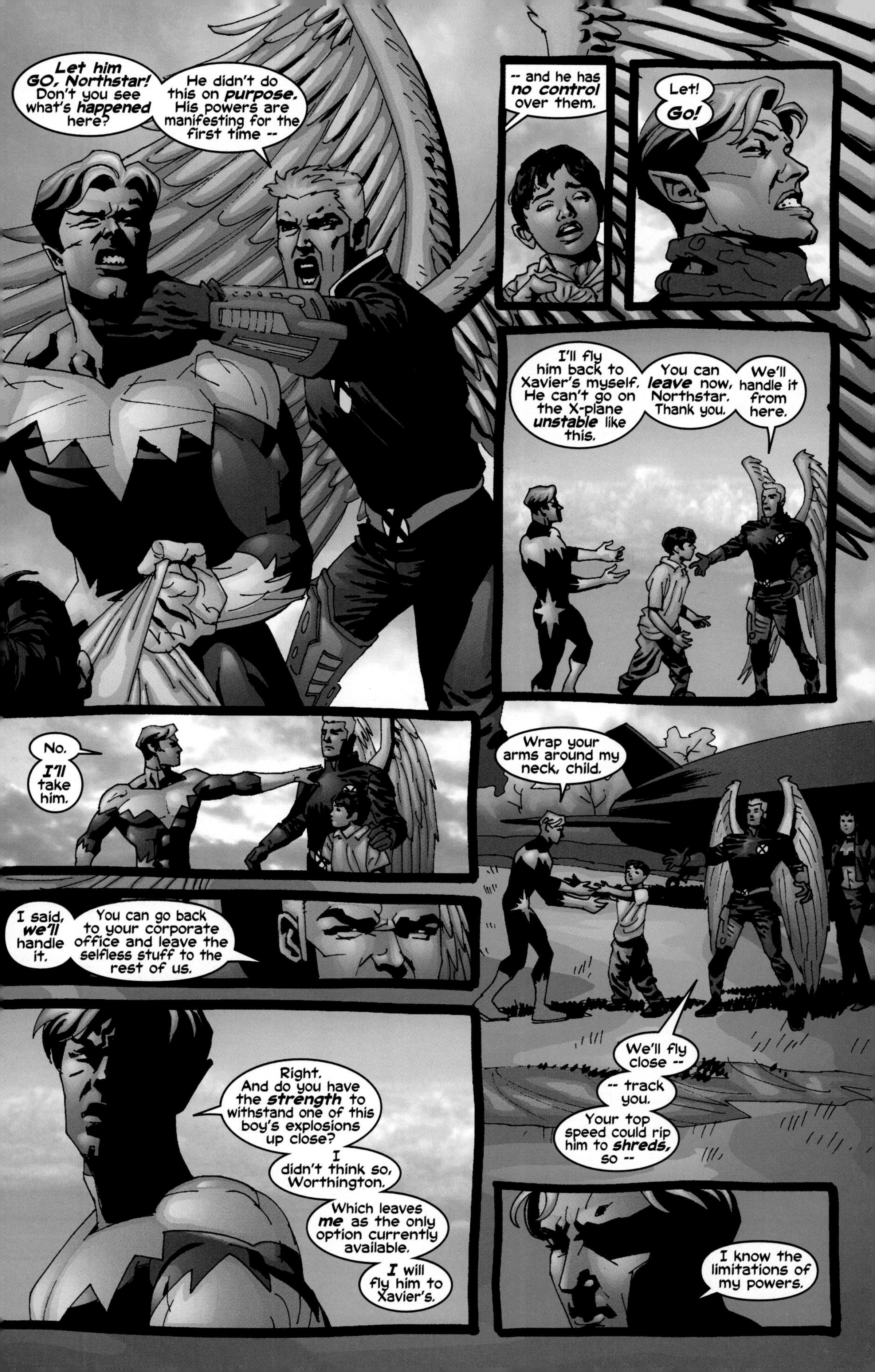
Let him GO, Northstar! Don't you see what's happened here?
He didn't do this on purpose. His powers are manifesting for the first time --
-- and he has no control over them.
Let! Go!
I'll fly him back to Xavier's myself. He can't go on the X-plane unstable like this.
You can leave now, Northstar. Thank you.
We'll handle it from here.
No. I'll take him.
I said, we'll handle it.
You can go back to your corporate office and leave the selfless stuff to the rest of us.
Right. And do you have the strength to withstand one of this boy's explosions up close?
I didn't think so, Worthington.
Which leaves me as the only option currently available.
I will fly him to Xavier's.
Wrap your arms around my neck, child.
We'll fly close --
-- track you.
Your top speed could rip him to shreds, so --
I know the limitations of my powers.

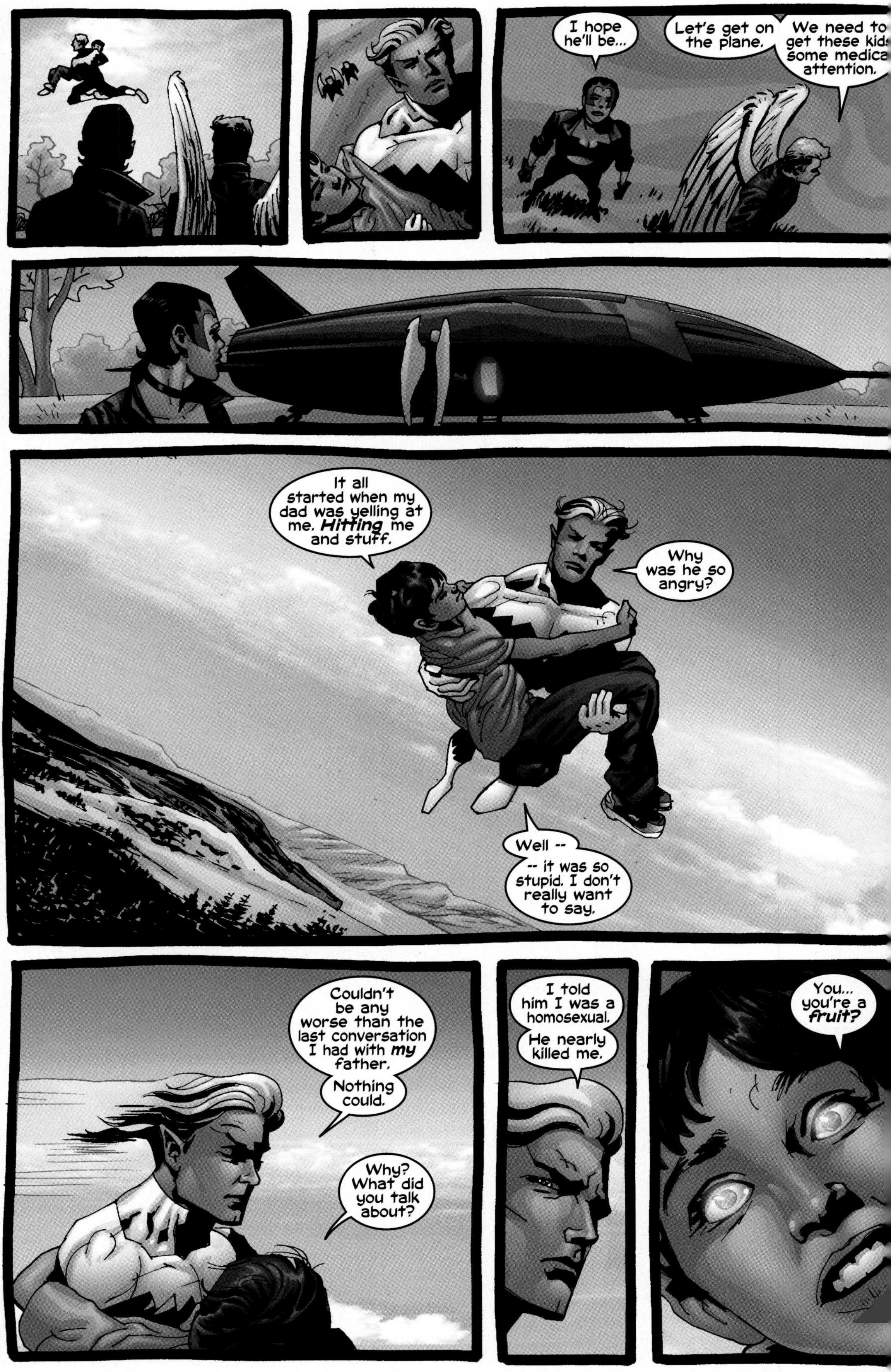
I hope he'll be...
Let's get on the plane.
We need to get these kids some medica attention.
It all started when my dad was yelling at me. *Hitting* me and stuff.
Why was he so angry?
Well --
-- it was so stupid. I don't really want to say.
Couldn't be any worse than the last conversation I had with *my* father.
Nothing could.
Why? What did you talk about?
I told him I was a homosexual.
He nearly killed me.
You... you're a *fruit?*

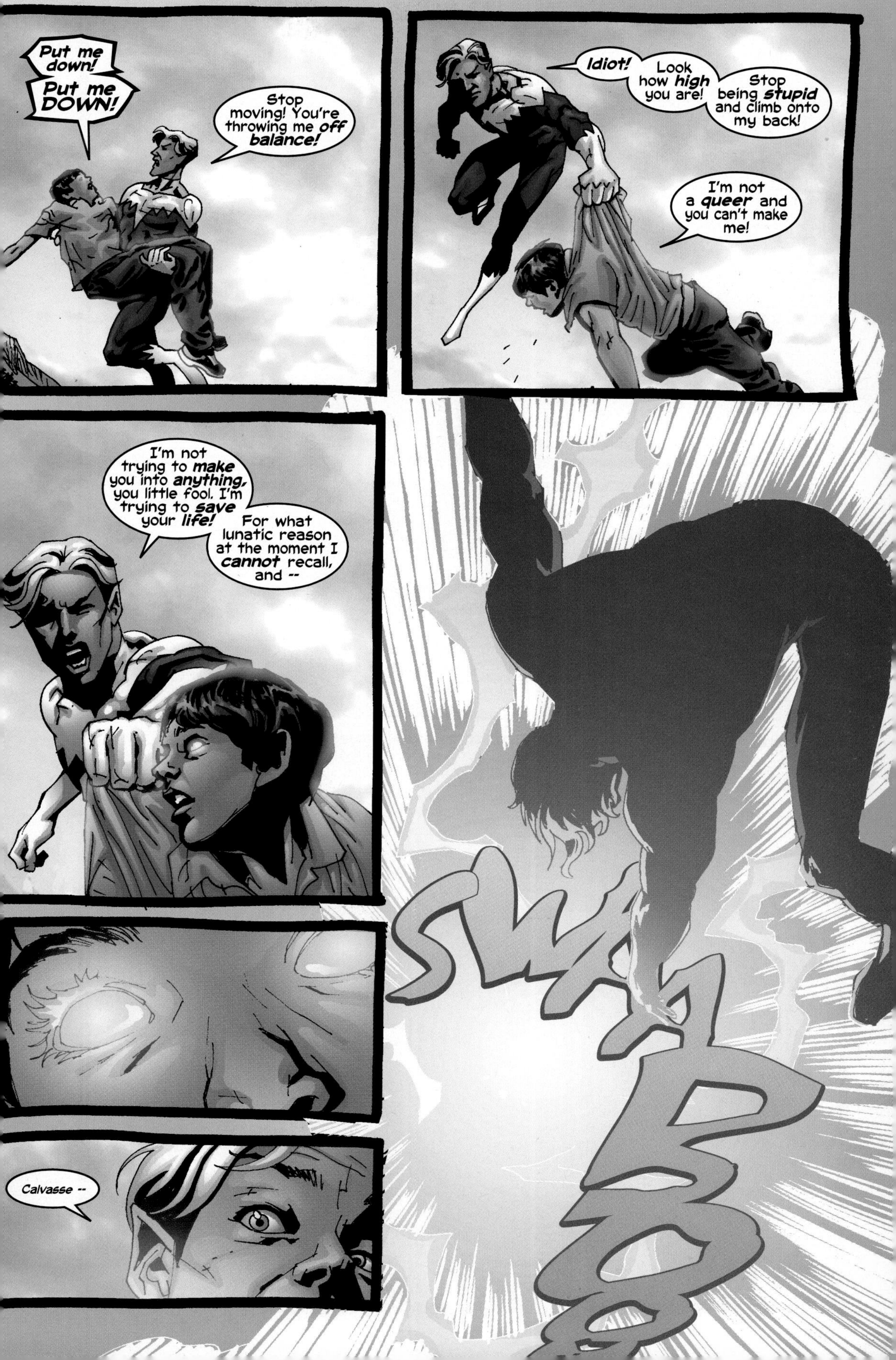
Put me down!
Put me DOWN!
Stop moving! You're throwing me off balance!
Idiot!
Look how high you are!
Stop being stupid and climb onto my back!
I'm not a queer and you can't make me!
I'm not trying to make you into anything, you little fool. I'm trying to save your life!
For what lunatic reason at the moment I cannot recall, and --
Calvasse --

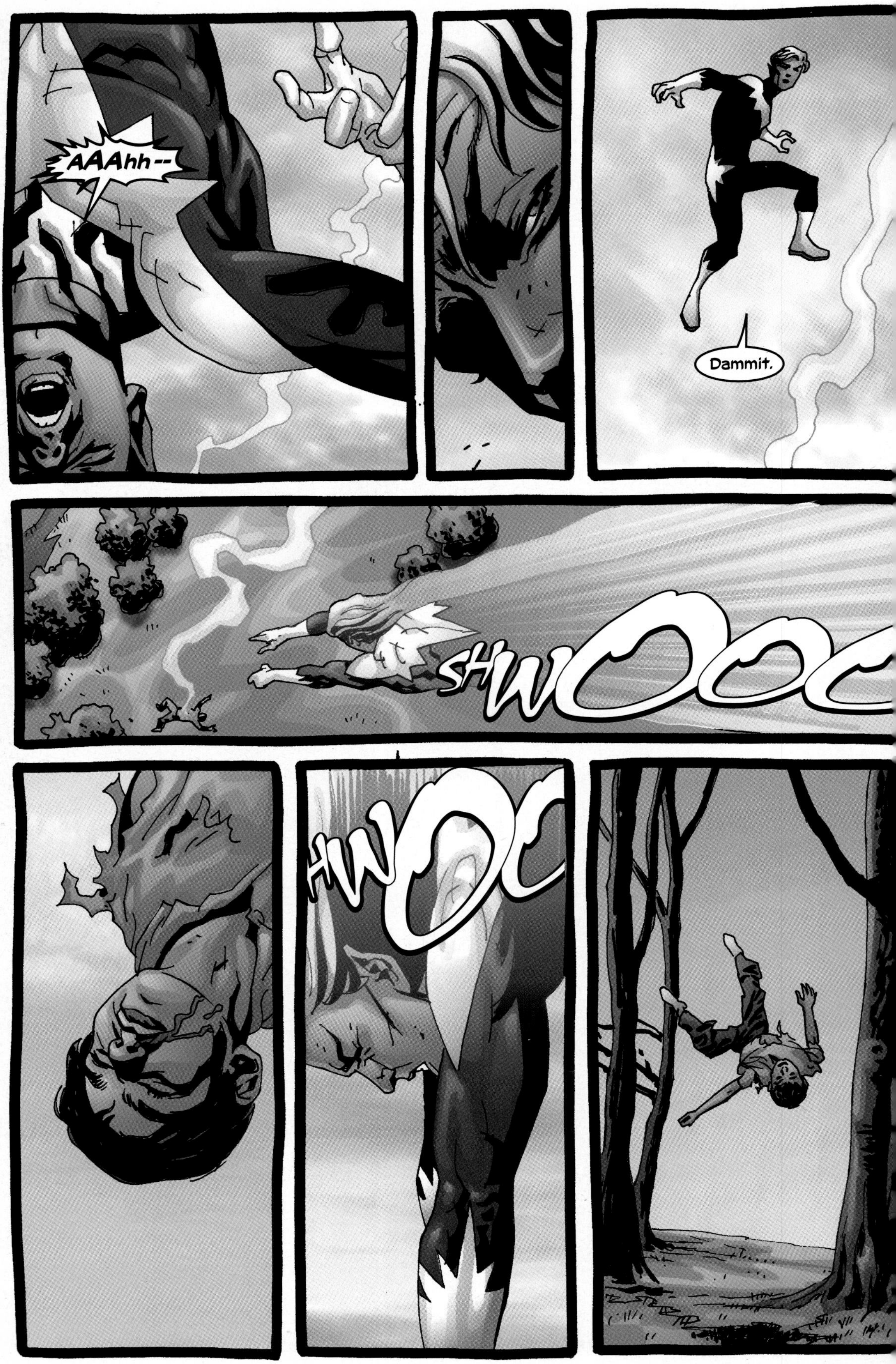
AAAhh--
Dammit.
SHWOOO
SHWOO

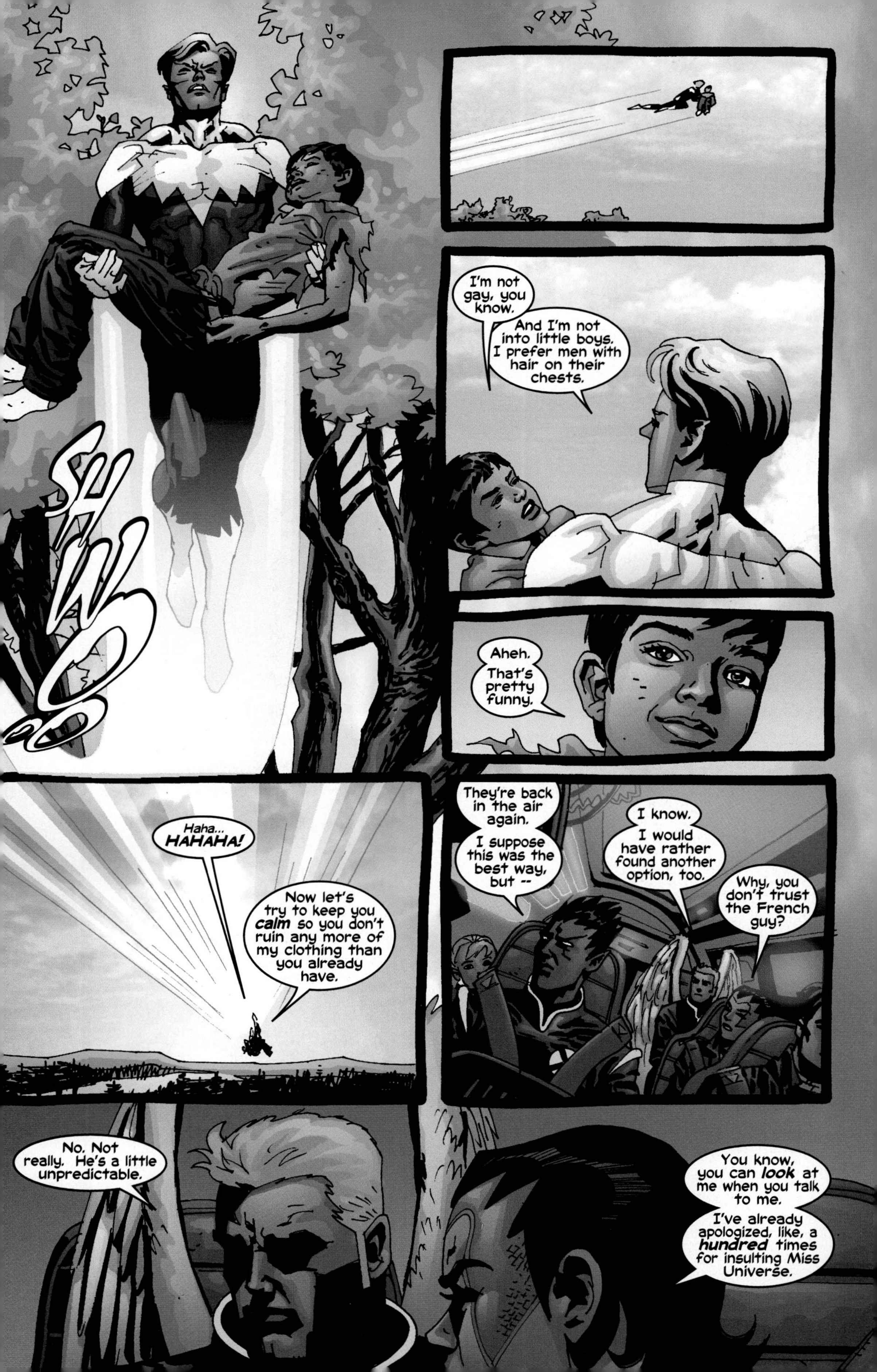
SHWOOO
I'm not gay, you know.
And I'm not into little boys. I prefer men with hair on their chests.
Aheh. That's pretty funny.
Haha... HAHAHA!
Now let's try to keep you calm so you don't ruin any more of my clothing than you already have.
They're back in the air again.
I suppose this was the best way, but --
I know.
I would have rather found another option, too.
Why, you don't trust the French guy?
No. Not really. He's a little unpredictable.
You know, you can look at me when you talk to me.
I've already apologized, like, a hundred times for insulting Miss Universe.

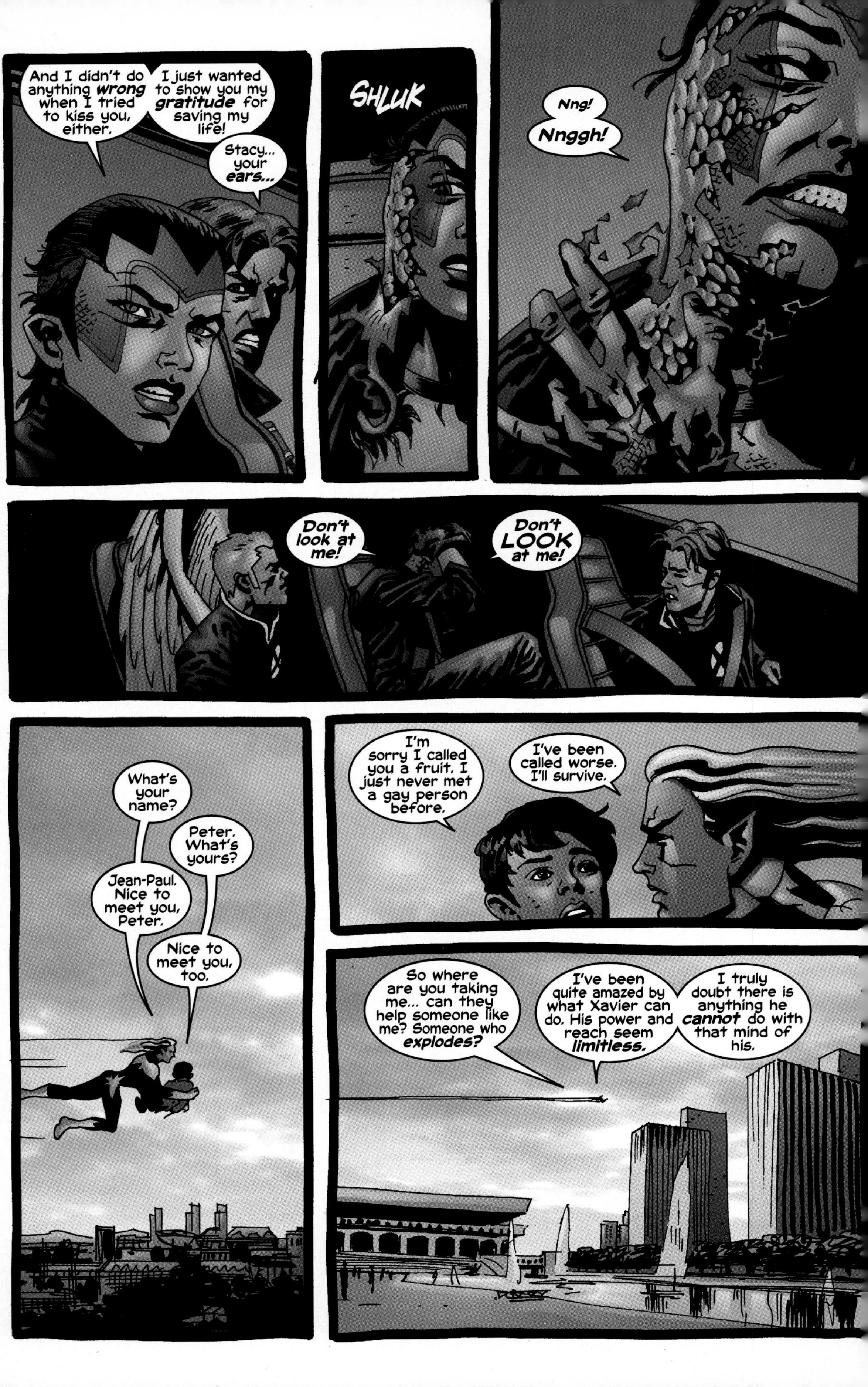
And I didn't do anything wrong when I tried to kiss you, either.
I just wanted to show you my gratitude for saving my life!
Stacy... your ears...
SHLUK
Nng!
Nnggh!
Don't look at me!
Don't LOOK at me!
What's your name?
Peter. What's yours?
Jean-Paul. Nice to meet you, Peter.
Nice to meet you, too.
I'm sorry I called you a fruit. I just never met a gay person before.
I've been called worse. I'll survive.
So where are you taking me... can they help someone like me? Someone who explodes?
I've been quite amazed by what Xavier can do. His power and reach seem limitless.
I truly doubt there is anything he cannot do with that mind of his.

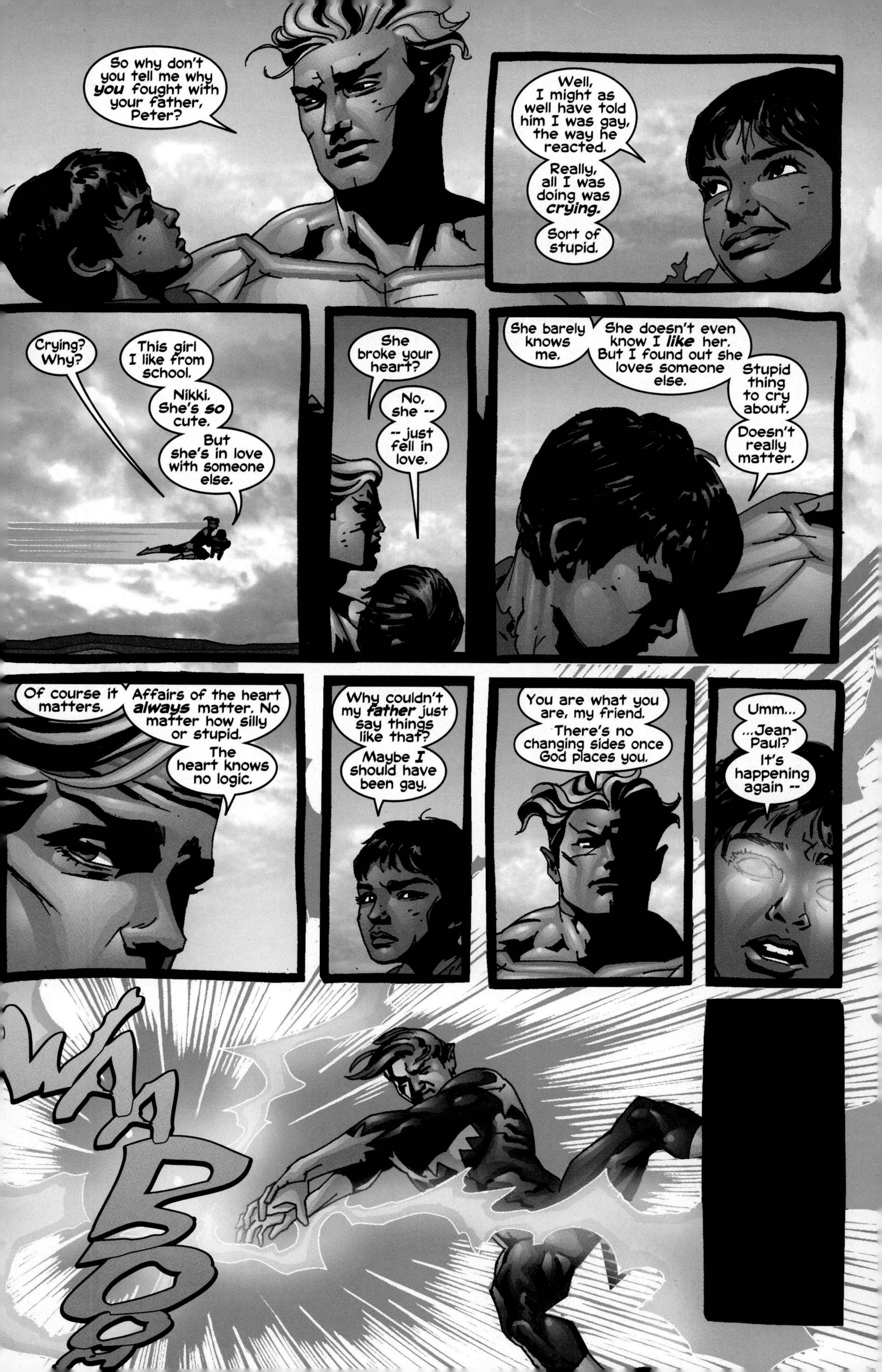
So why don't you tell me why *you* fought with your father, Peter?
Well, I might as well have told him I was gay, the way he reacted.
Really, all I was doing was *crying.*
Sort of stupid.
Crying? Why?
This girl I like from school.
Nikki. She's *so* cute.
But she's in love with someone else.
She broke your heart?
No, she --
-- just fell in love.
She barely knows me.
She doesn't even know I *like* her. But I found out she loves someone else.
Stupid thing to cry about.
Doesn't really matter.
Of course it matters.
Affairs of the heart *always* matter. No matter how silly or stupid.
The heart knows no logic.
Why couldn't my *father* just say things like that?
Maybe *I* should have been gay.
You are what you are, my friend.
There's no changing sides once God places you.
Umm...
...Jean-Paul?
It's happening again --

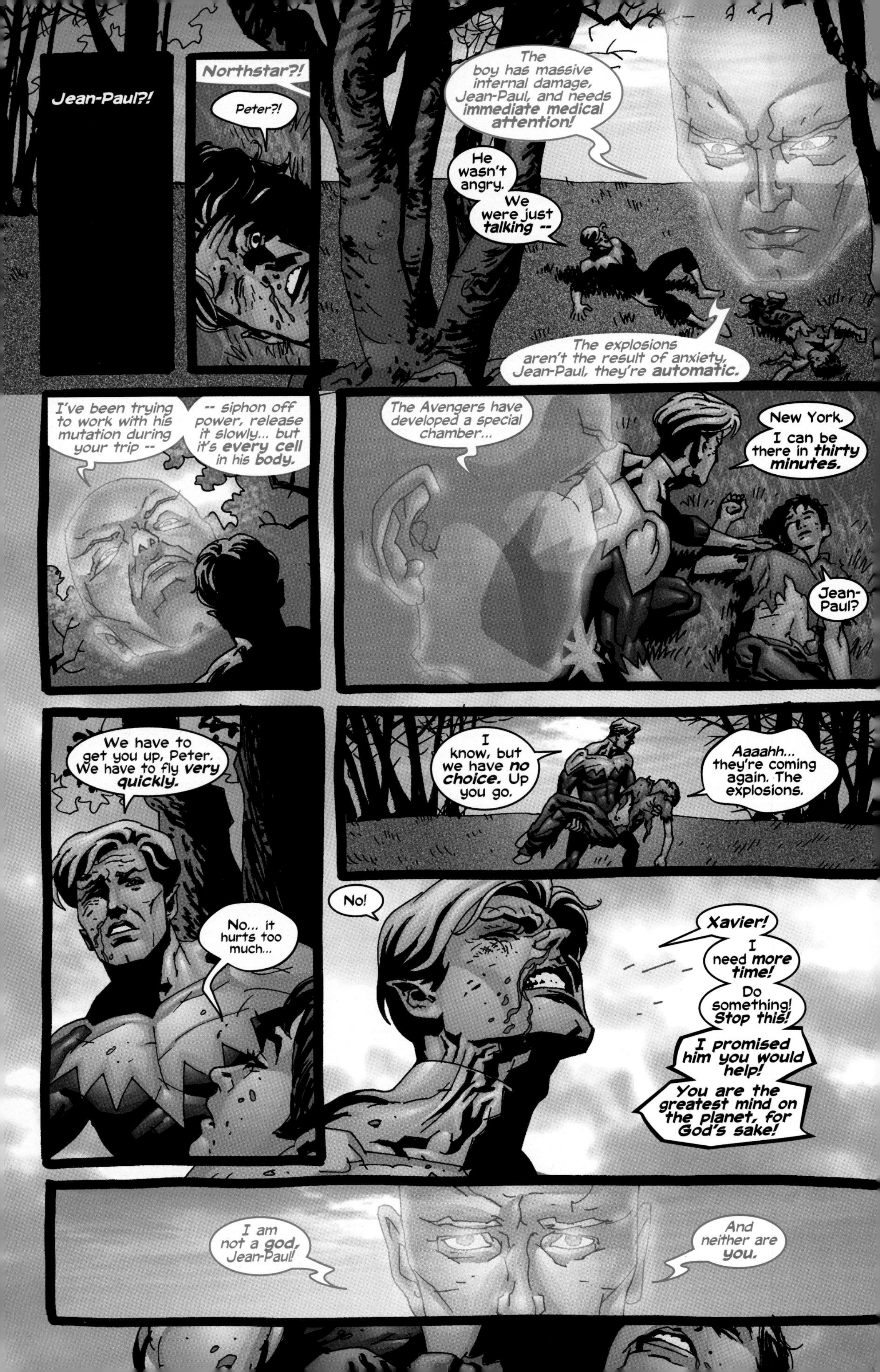
Jean-Paul?!
Northstar?!
Peter?!
The boy has massive internal damage, Jean-Paul, and needs immediate medical attention!
He wasn't angry.
We were just talking --
The explosions aren't the result of anxiety, Jean-Paul, they're automatic.
I've been trying to work with his mutation during your trip --
-- siphon off power, release it slowly... but it's every cell in his body.
The Avengers have developed a special chamber...
New York.
I can be there in thirty minutes.
Jean-Paul?
We have to get you up, Peter. We have to fly very quickly.
No... it hurts too much...
I know, but we have no choice. Up you go.
Aaaahh... they're coming again. The explosions.
No!
Xavier!
I need more time!
Do something! Stop this!
I promised him you would help!
You are the greatest mind on the planet, for God's sake!
I am not a god, Jean-Paul!
And neither are you.

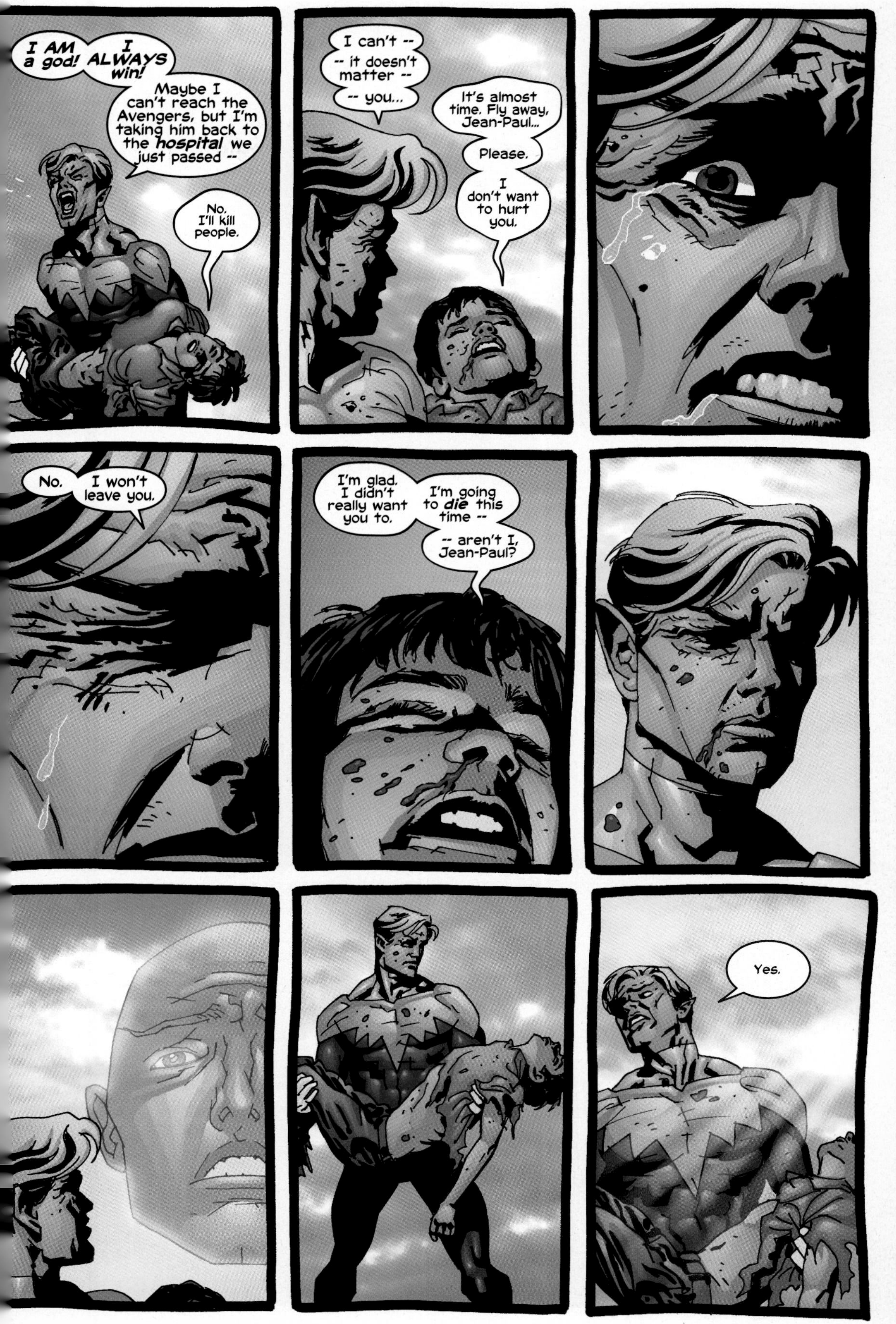
I AM a god!
I ALWAYS win!
Maybe I can't reach the Avengers, but I'm taking him back to the *hospital* we just passed --
No. I'll kill people.
I can't --
-- it doesn't matter --
-- you...
It's almost time. Fly away, Jean-Paul...
Please.
I don't want to hurt you.
No.
I won't leave you.
I'm glad. I didn't really want you to.
I'm going to *die* this time --
-- aren't I, Jean-Paul?
Yes.

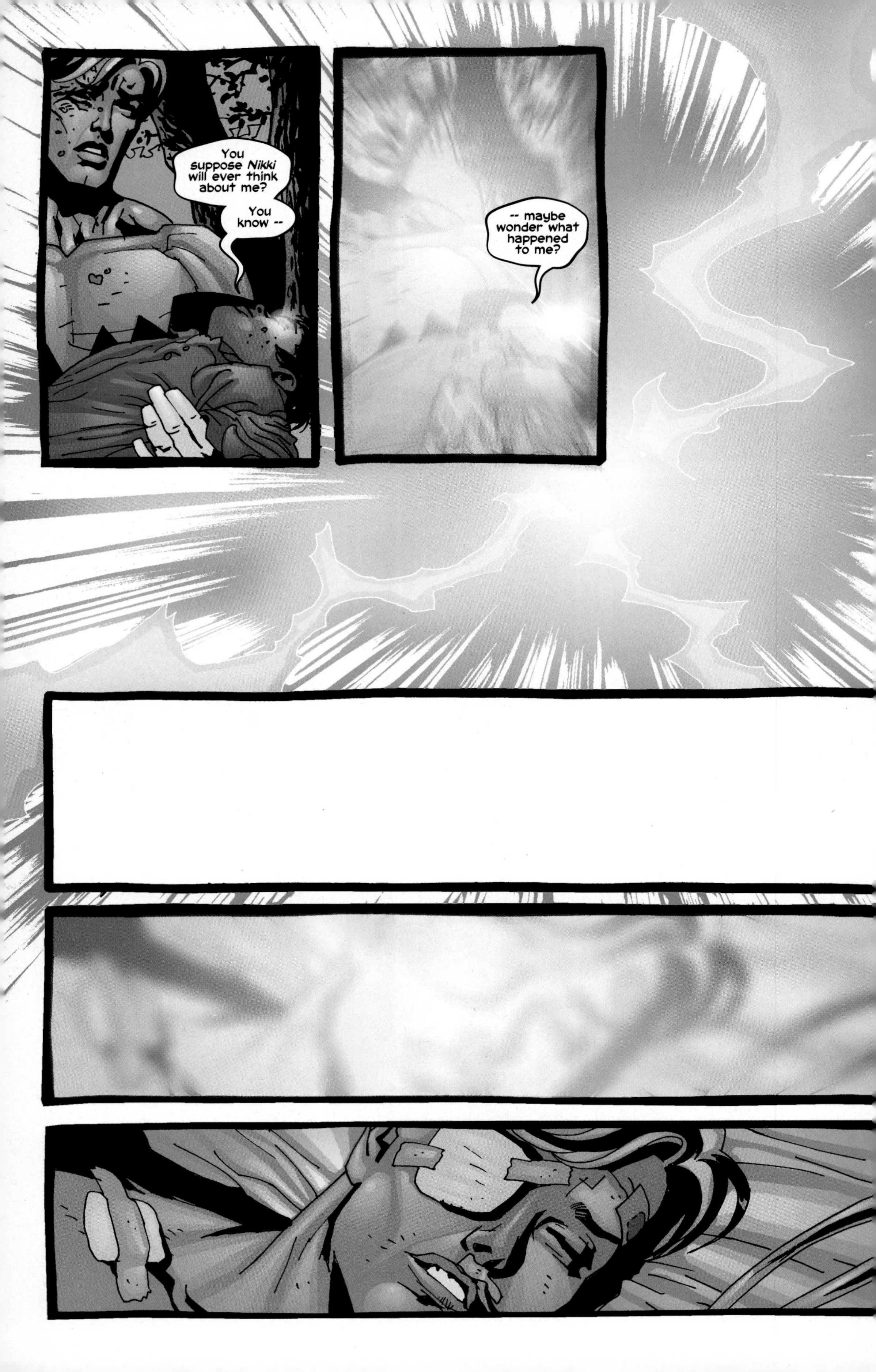
You suppose Nikki will ever think about me?
You know --
-- maybe wonder what happened to me?

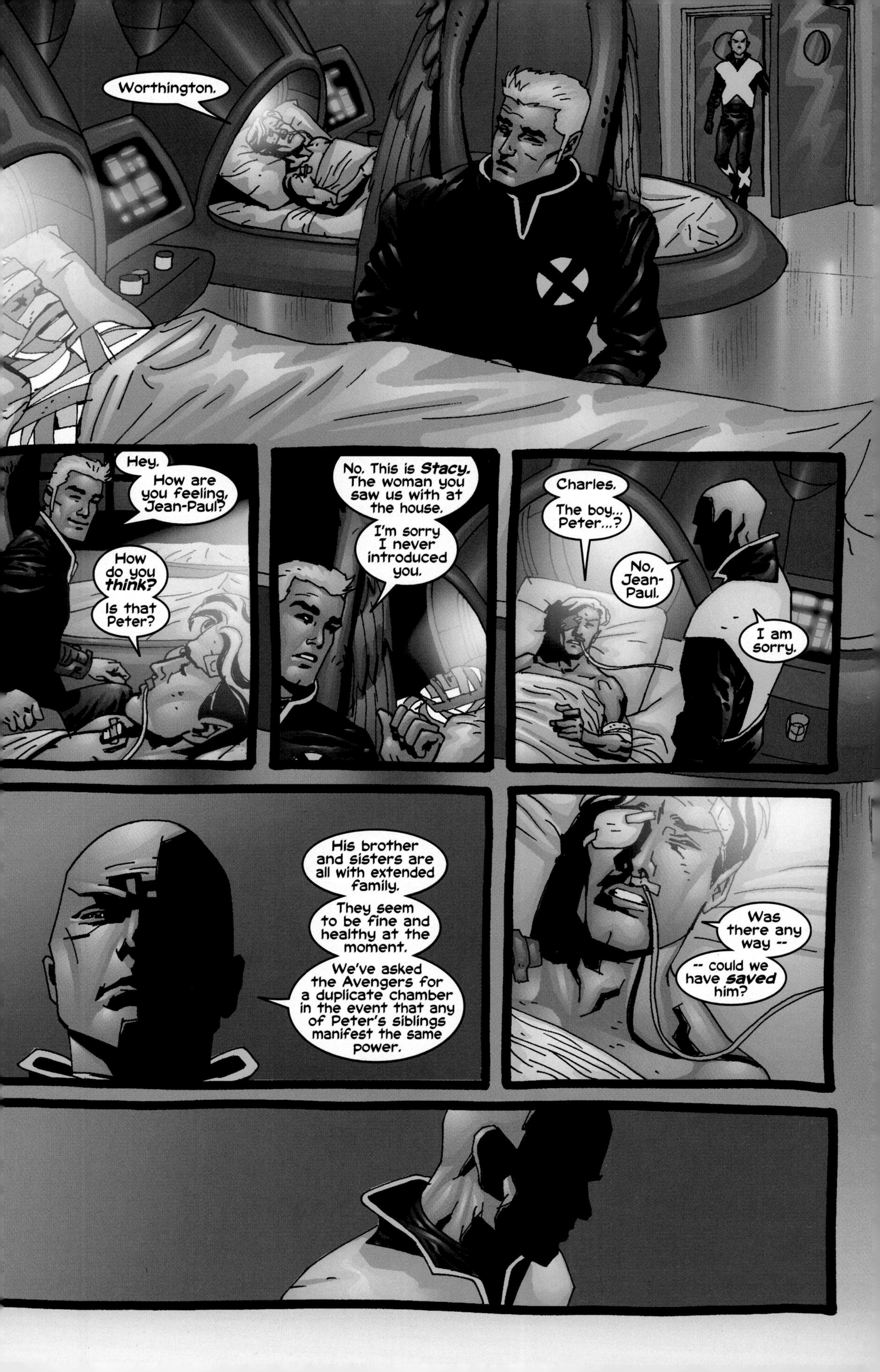
Worthington.
Hey.
How are you feeling, Jean-Paul?
How do you *think?*
Is that Peter?
No. This is *Stacy.* The woman you saw us with at the house.
I'm sorry I never introduced you.
Charles.
The boy... Peter...?
No, Jean-Paul.
I am sorry.
His brother and sisters are all with extended family.
They seem to be fine and healthy at the moment.
We've asked the Avengers for a duplicate chamber in the event that any of Peter's siblings manifest the same power.
Was there any way --
-- could we have *saved* him?

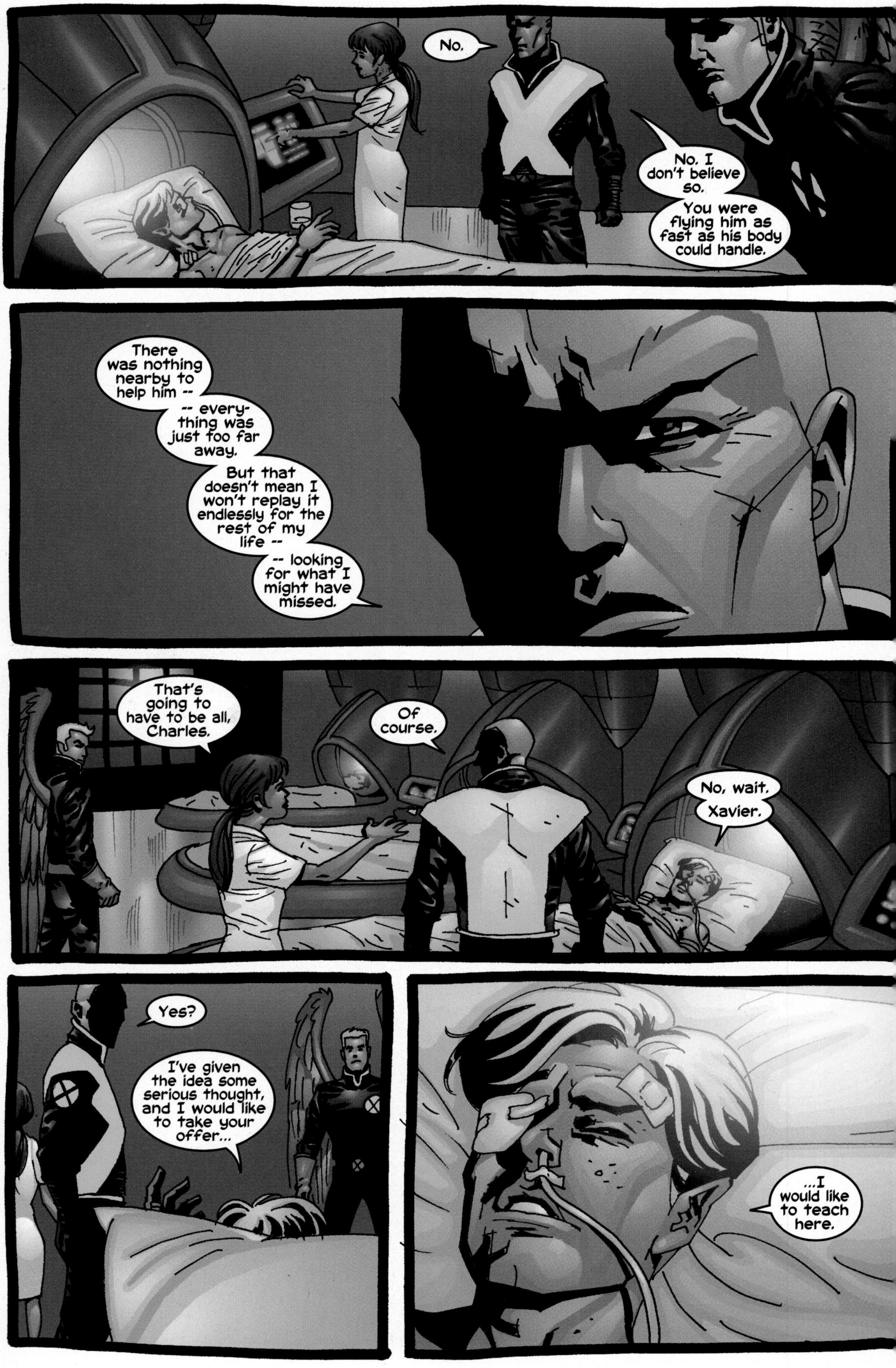
No.
No. I don't believe so.
You were flying him as fast as his body could handle.
There was nothing nearby to help him --
-- every-thing was just too far away.
But that doesn't mean I won't replay it endlessly for the rest of my life --
-- looking for what I might have missed.
That's going to have to be all, Charles.
Of course.
No, wait, Xavier.
Yes?
I've given the idea some serious thought, and I would like to take your offer...
...I would like to teach here.

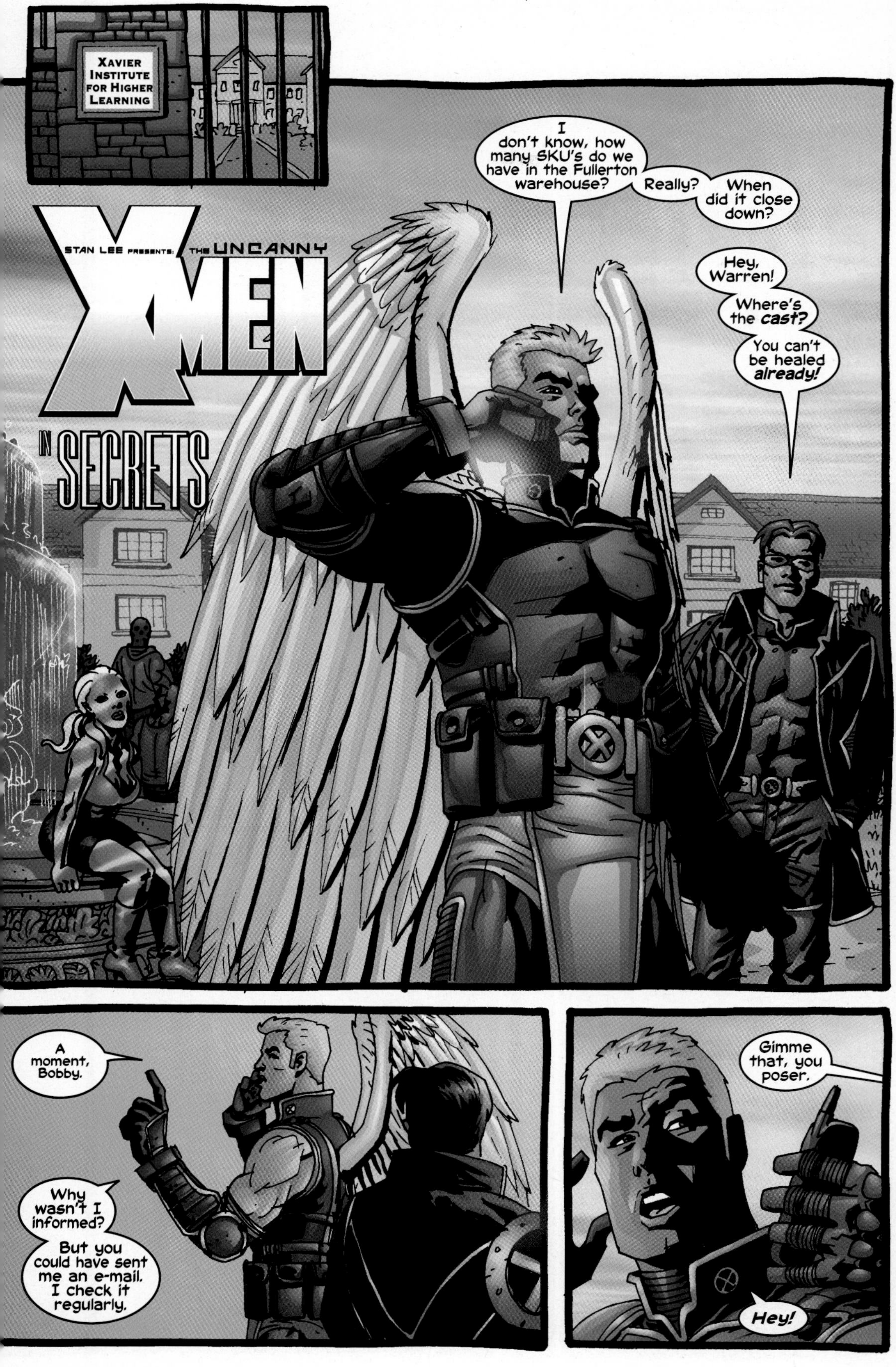
XAVIER INSTITUTE FOR HIGHER LEARNING
STAN LEE PRESENTS: THE UNCANNY X-MEN
IN SECRETS
I don't know, how many SKU's do we have in the Fullerton warehouse?
Really?
When did it close down?
Hey, Warren!
Where's the cast?
You can't be healed already!
A moment, Bobby.
Why wasn't I informed?
But you could have sent me an e-mail. I check it regularly.
Gimme that, you poser.
Hey!

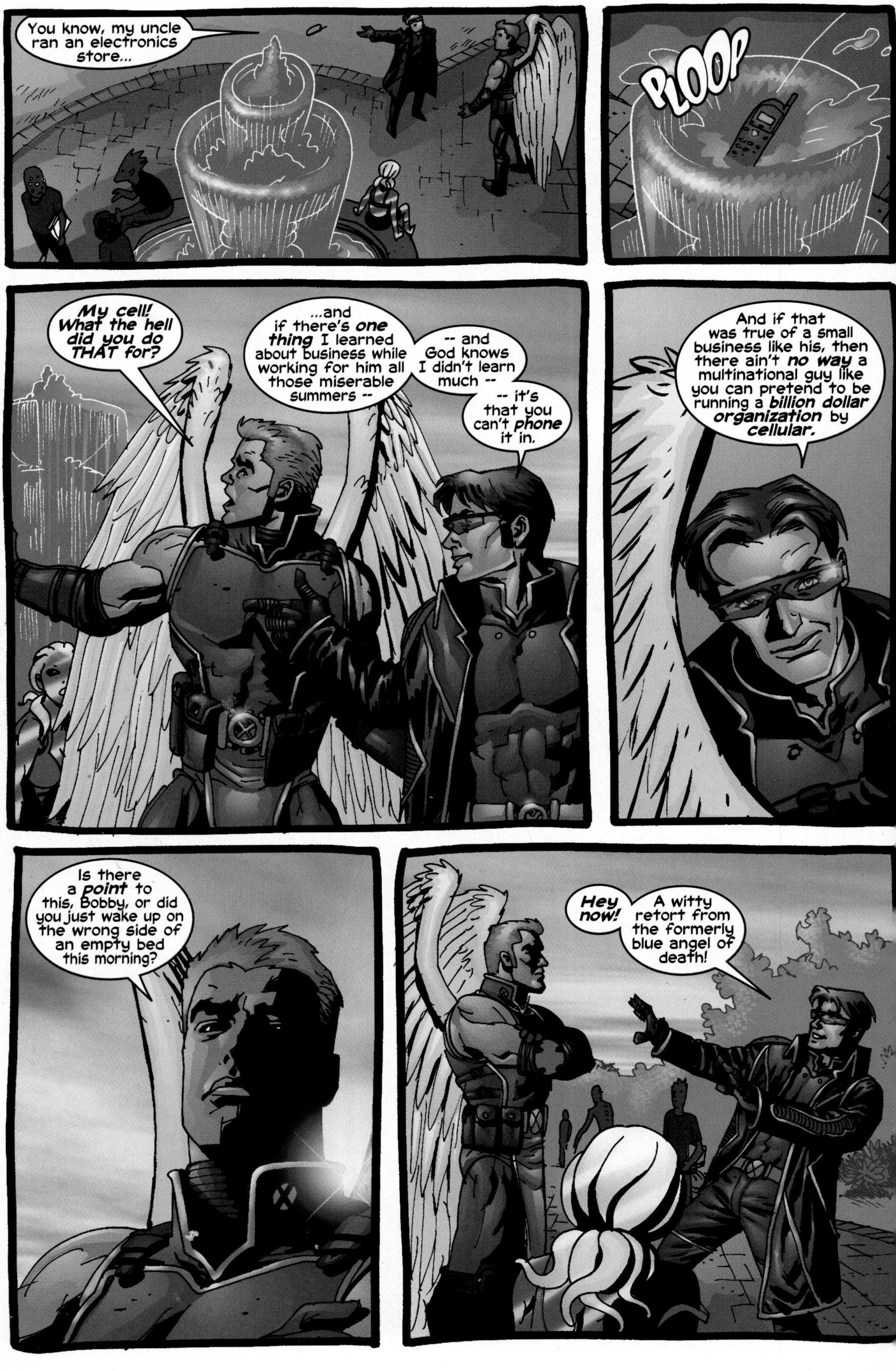

You know, my uncle ran an electronics store...
PLOOP
My cell! What the hell did you do THAT for?
...and if there's one thing I learned about business while working for him all those miserable summers --
-- and God knows I didn't learn much --
-- it's that you can't phone it in.
And if that was true of a small business like his, then there ain't no way a multinational guy like you can pretend to be running a billion dollar organization by cellular.
Is there a point to this, Bobby, or did you just wake up on the wrong side of an empty bed this morning?
Hey now!
A witty retort from the formerly blue angel of death!

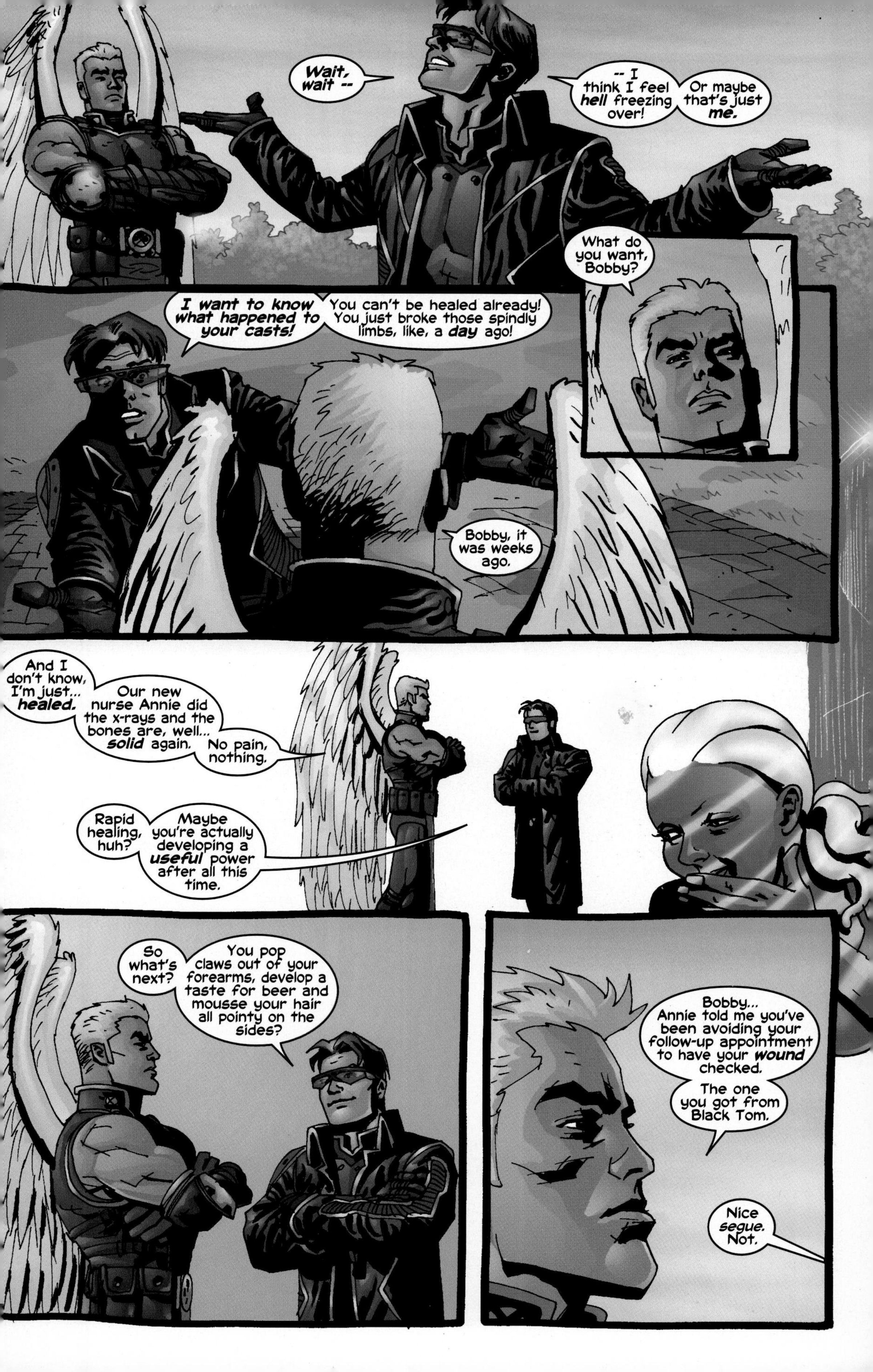

Wait, wait --
-- I think I feel hell freezing over!
Or maybe that's just me.
What do you want, Bobby?
I want to know what happened to your casts!
You can't be healed already! You just broke those spindly limbs, like, a day ago!
Bobby, it was weeks ago.
And I don't know, I'm just... healed.
Our new nurse Annie did the x-rays and the bones are, well... solid again.
No pain, nothing.
Rapid healing, huh?
Maybe you're actually developing a useful power after all this time.
So what's next?
You pop claws out of your forearms, develop a taste for beer and mousse your hair all pointy on the sides?
Bobby... Annie told me you've been avoiding your follow-up appointment to have your wound checked.
The one you got from Black Tom.
Nice segue. Not.

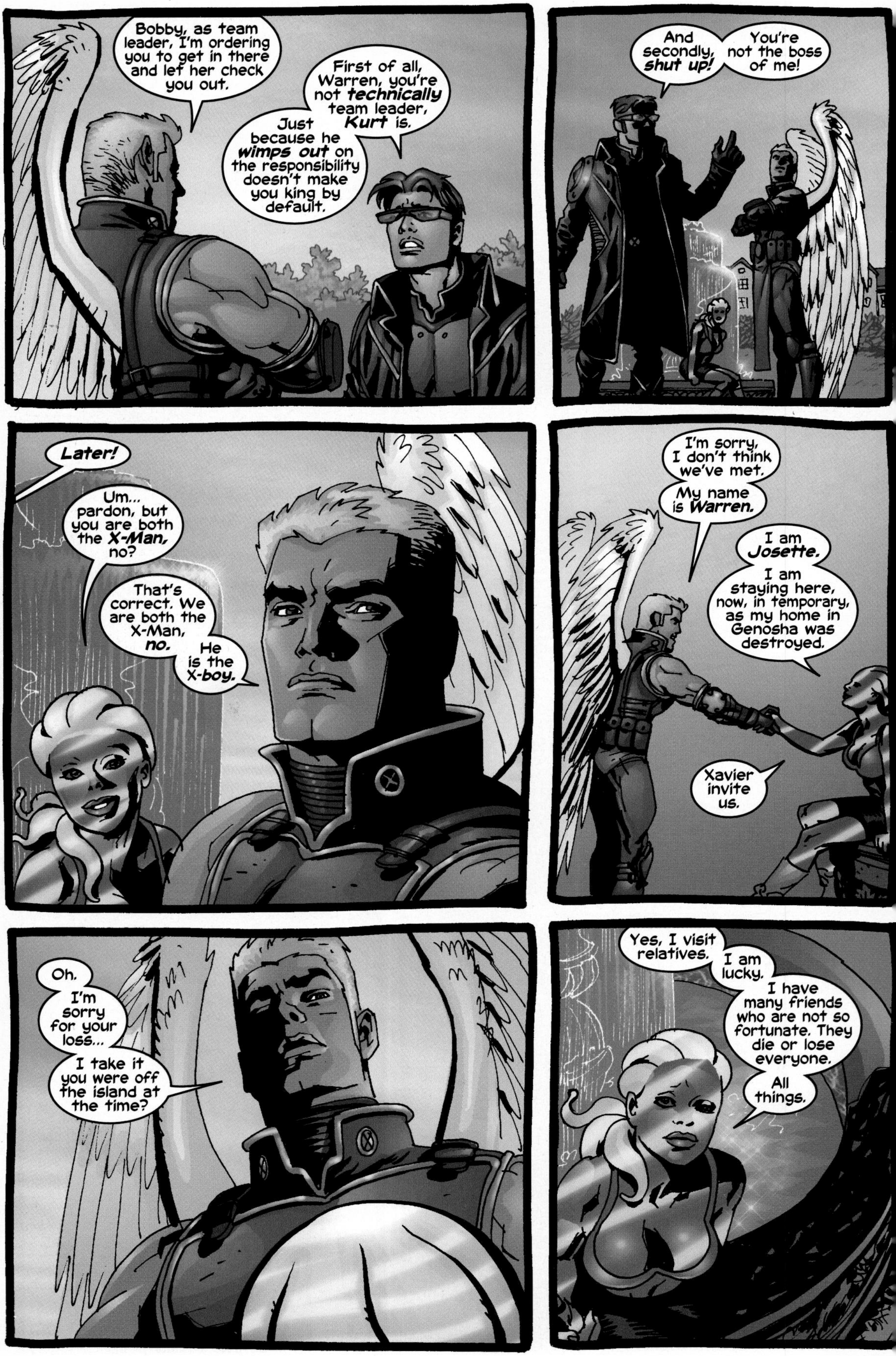

Bobby, as team leader, I'm ordering you to get in there and let her check you out.
First of all, Warren, you're not technically team leader, Kurt is.
Just because he wimps out on the responsibility doesn't make you king by default.
And secondly, shut up!
You're not the boss of me!
Later!
Um... pardon, but you are both the X-Man, no?
That's correct. We are both the X-Man, no.
He is the X-boy.
I'm sorry, I don't think we've met.
My name is Warren.
I am Josette.
I am staying here, now, in temporary, as my home in Genosha was destroyed.
Xavier invite us.
Oh.
I'm sorry for your loss...
I take it you were off the island at the time?
Yes, I visit relatives.
I am lucky.
I have many friends who are not so fortunate. They die or lose everyone.
All things.

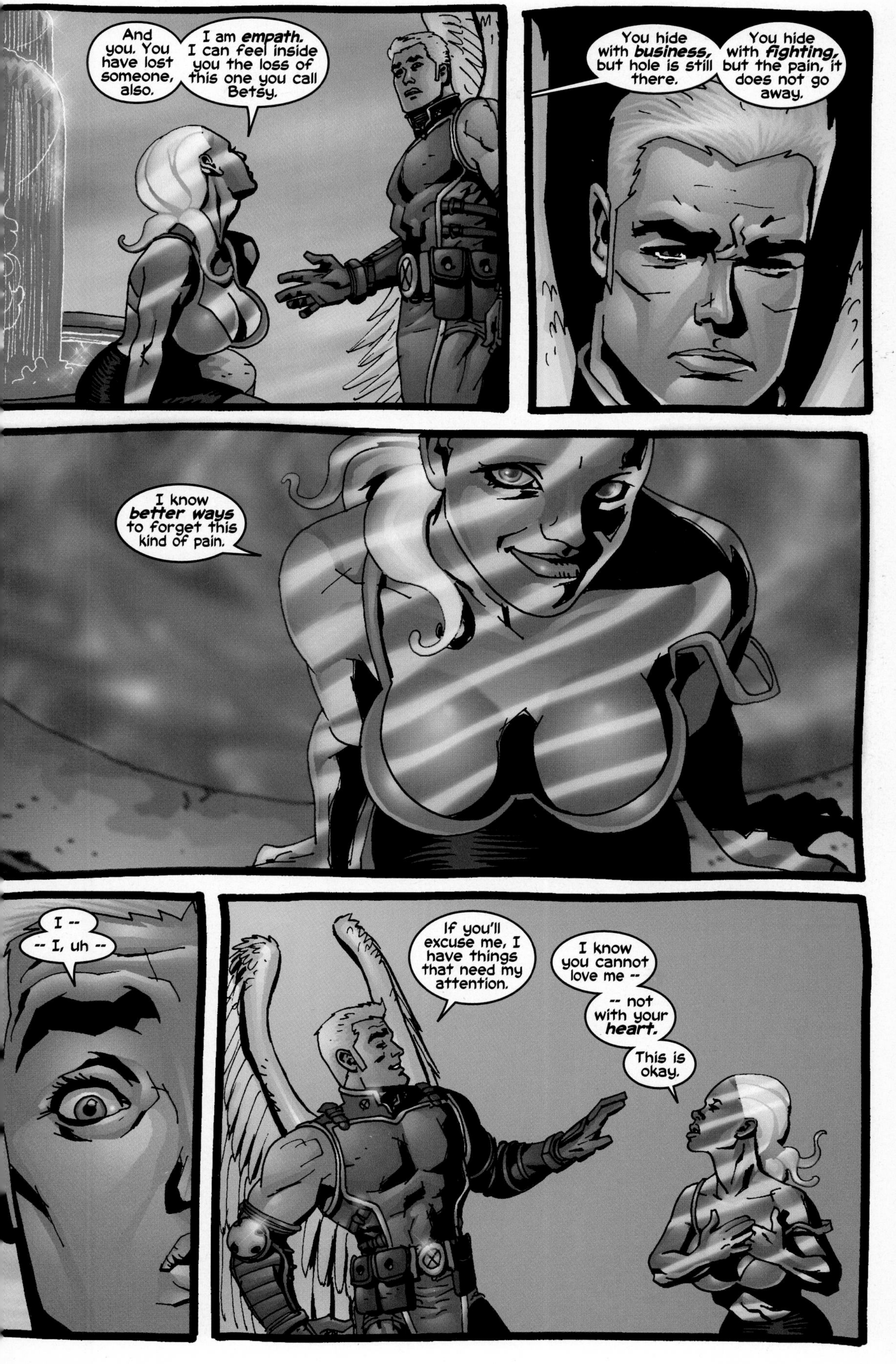
And you. You have lost someone, also.
I am *empath.* I can feel inside you the loss of this one you call Betsy.
You hide with *business,* but hole is still there.
You hide with *fighting,* but the pain, it does not go away.
I know *better ways* to forget this kind of pain.
I --
-- I, uh --
If you'll excuse me, I have things that need my attention.
I know you cannot love me --
-- not with your *heart.*
This is okay.

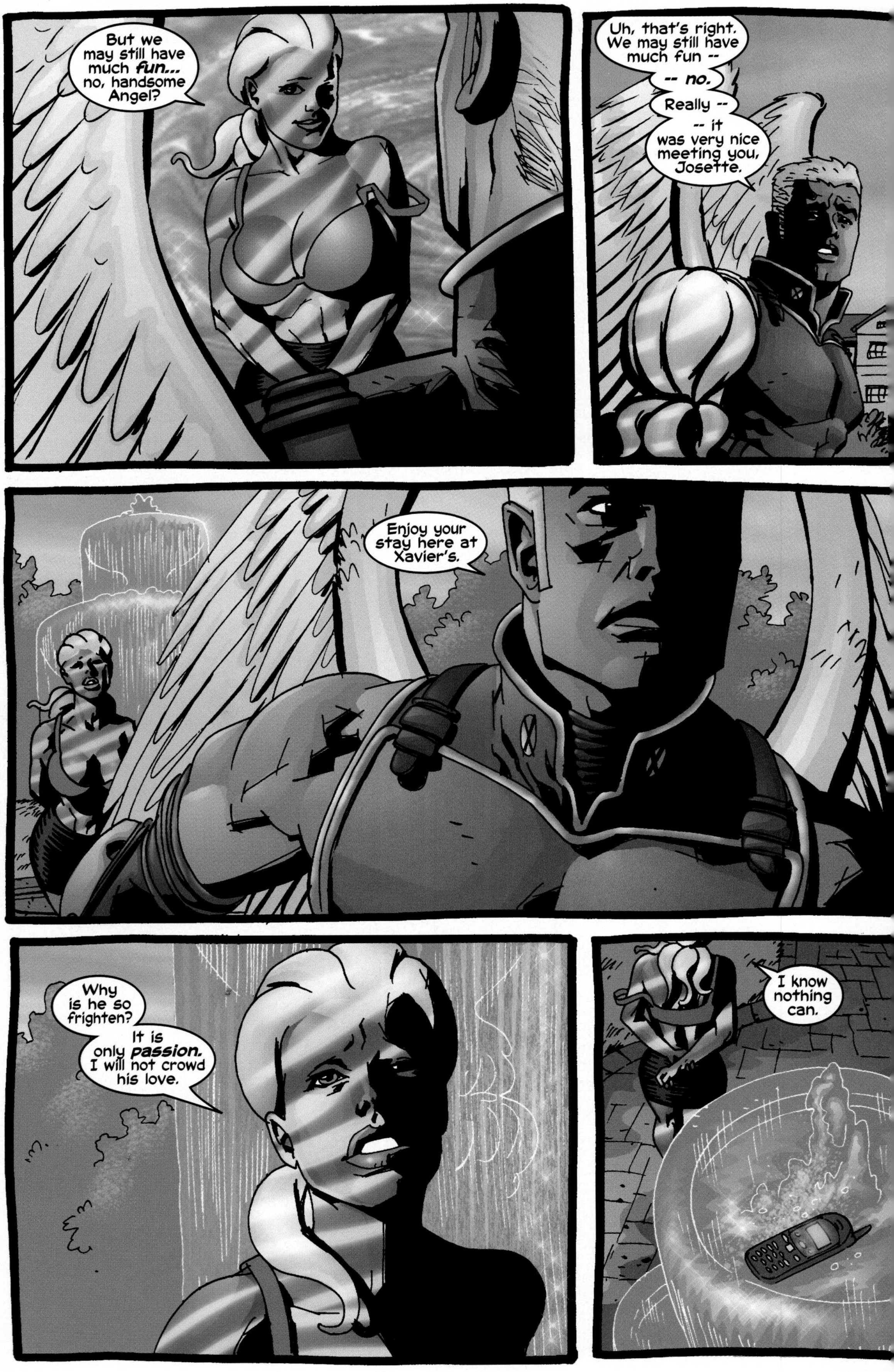
But we may still have much *fun...* no, handsome Angel?
Uh, that's right. We may still have much fun --
-- no.
Really --
-- it was very nice meeting you, Josette.
Enjoy your stay here at Xavier's.
Why is he so frighten?
It is only *passion.* I will not crowd his love.
I know nothing can.

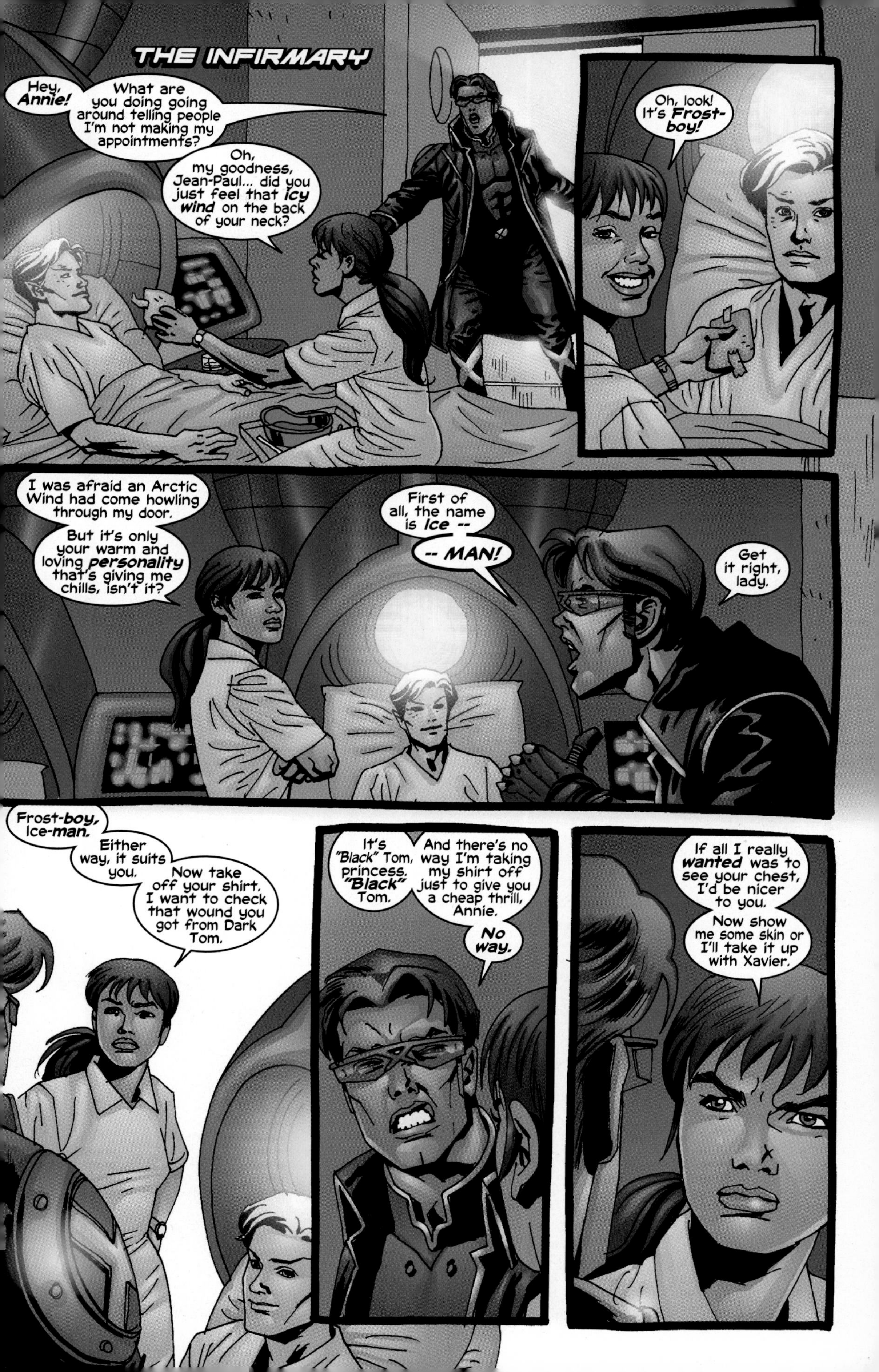
THE INFIRMARY
Hey, Annie!
What are you doing going around telling people I'm not making my appointments?
Oh, my goodness, Jean-Paul... did you just feel that icy wind on the back of your neck?
Oh, look! It's Frost-boy!
I was afraid an Arctic Wind had come howling through my door.
But it's only your warm and loving personality that's giving me chills, isn't it?
First of all, the name is Ice --
-- MAN!
Get it right, lady.
Frost-boy, Ice-man.
Either way, it suits you.
Now take off your shirt. I want to check that wound you got from Dark Tom.
It's "Black" Tom, princess. "Black" Tom.
And there's no way I'm taking my shirt off just to give you a cheap thrill, Annie.
No way.
If all I really wanted was to see your chest, I'd be nicer to you.
Now show me some skin or I'll take it up with Xavier.

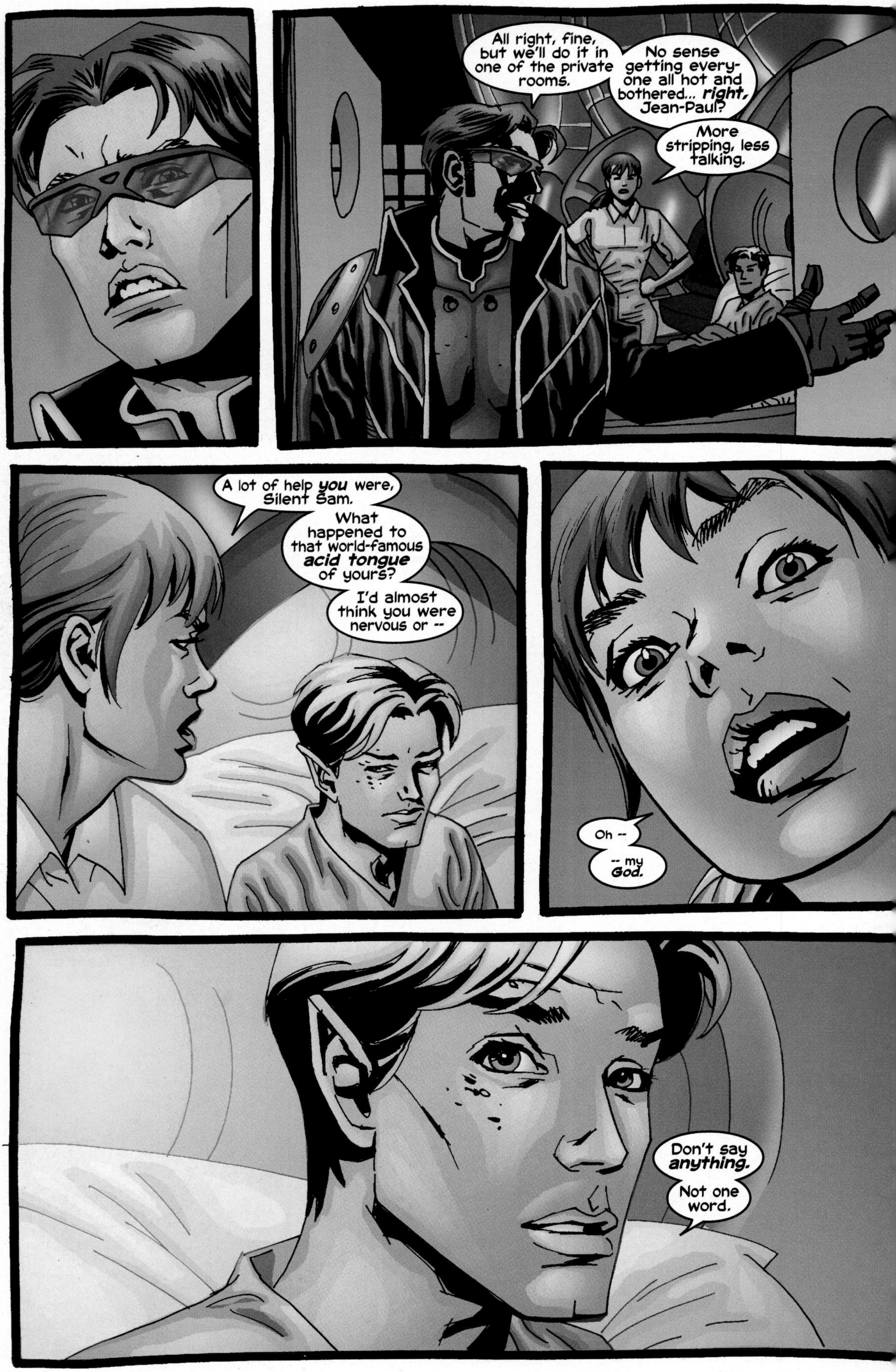
All right, fine, but we'll do it in one of the private rooms.
No sense getting every-one all hot and bothered... right, Jean-Paul?
More stripping, less talking.
A lot of help you were, Silent Sam.
What happened to that world-famous acid tongue of yours?
I'd almost think you were nervous or --
Oh --
-- my God.
Don't say anything.
Not one word.

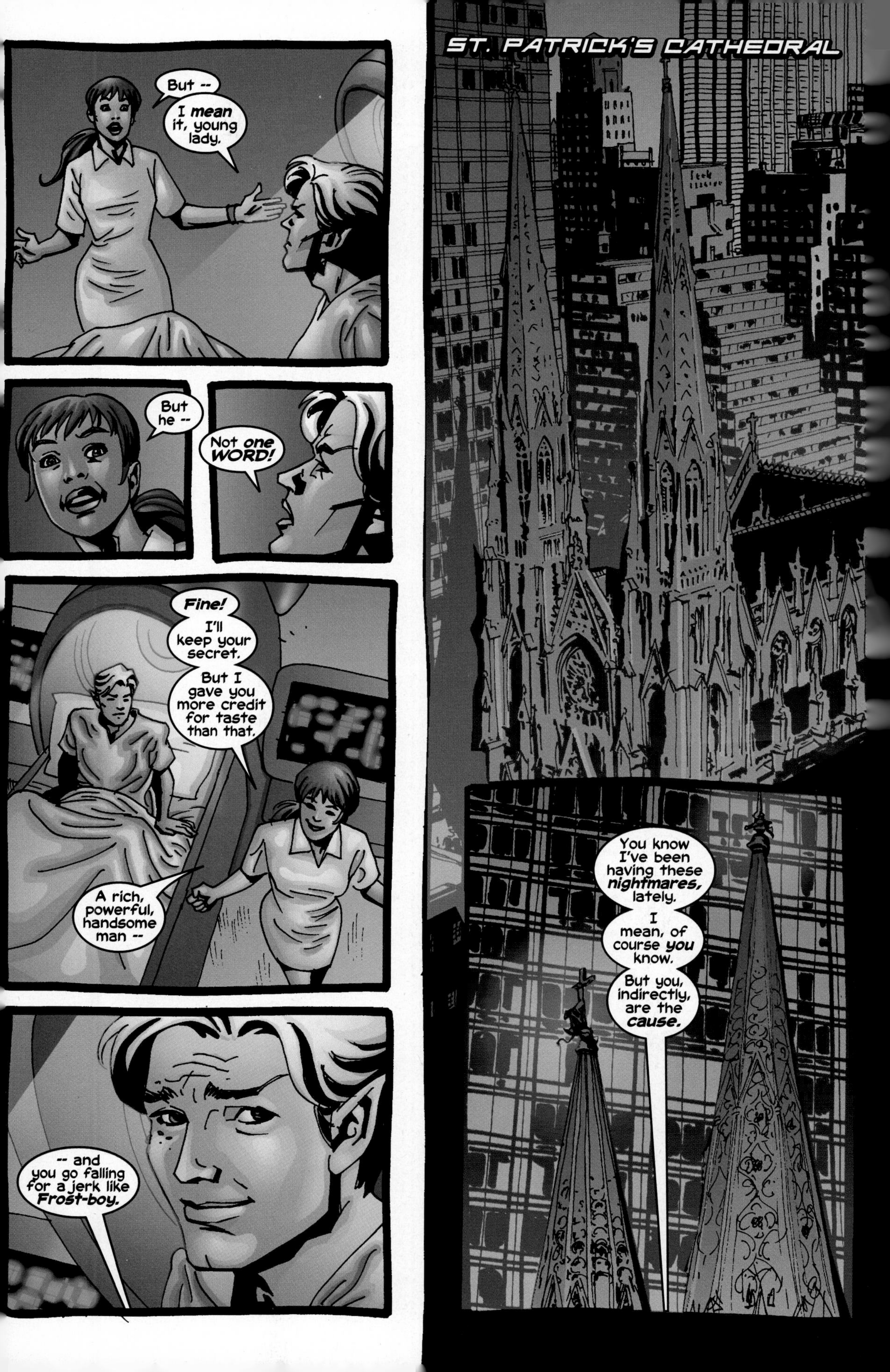
But --
I mean it, young lady.
But he --
Not one WORD!
Fine!
I'll keep your secret.
But I gave you more credit for taste than that.
A rich, powerful, handsome man --
-- and you go falling for a jerk like Frost-boy.
ST. PATRICK'S CATHEDRAL
You know I've been having these nightmares, lately.
I mean, of course you know.
But you, indirectly, are the cause.

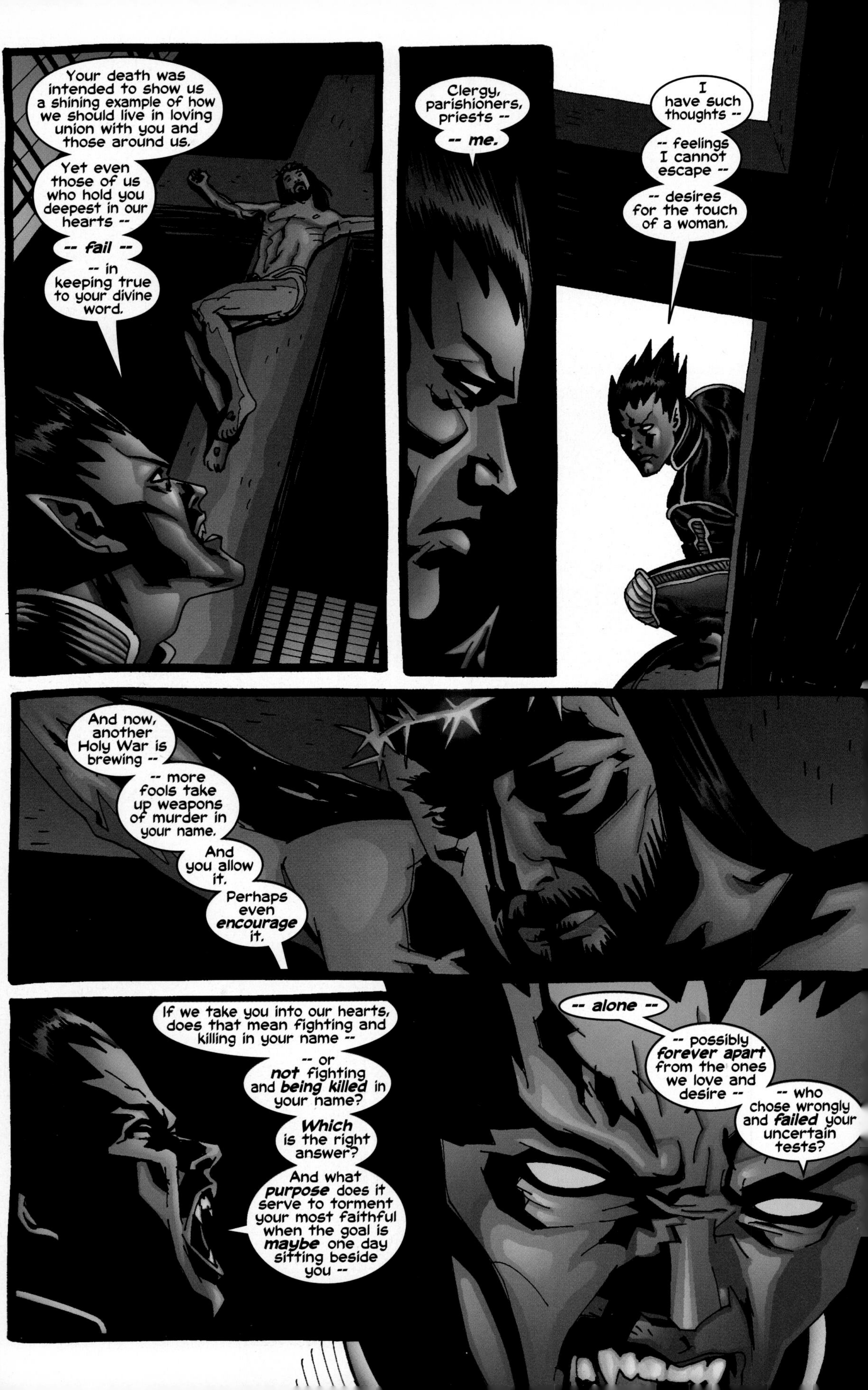
Your death was intended to show us a shining example of how we should live in loving union with you and those around us.
Yet even those of us who hold you deepest in our hearts --
-- fail --
-- in keeping true to your divine word.
Clergy, parishioners, priests --
-- me.
I have such thoughts --
-- feelings I cannot escape --
-- desires for the touch of a woman.
And now, another Holy War is brewing --
-- more fools take up weapons of murder in your name.
And you allow it.
Perhaps even encourage it.
If we take you into our hearts, does that mean fighting and killing in your name --
-- or not fighting and being killed in your name?
Which is the right answer?
And what purpose does it serve to torment your most faithful when the goal is maybe one day sitting beside you --
-- alone --
-- possibly forever apart from the ones we love and desire --
-- who chose wrongly and failed your uncertain tests?

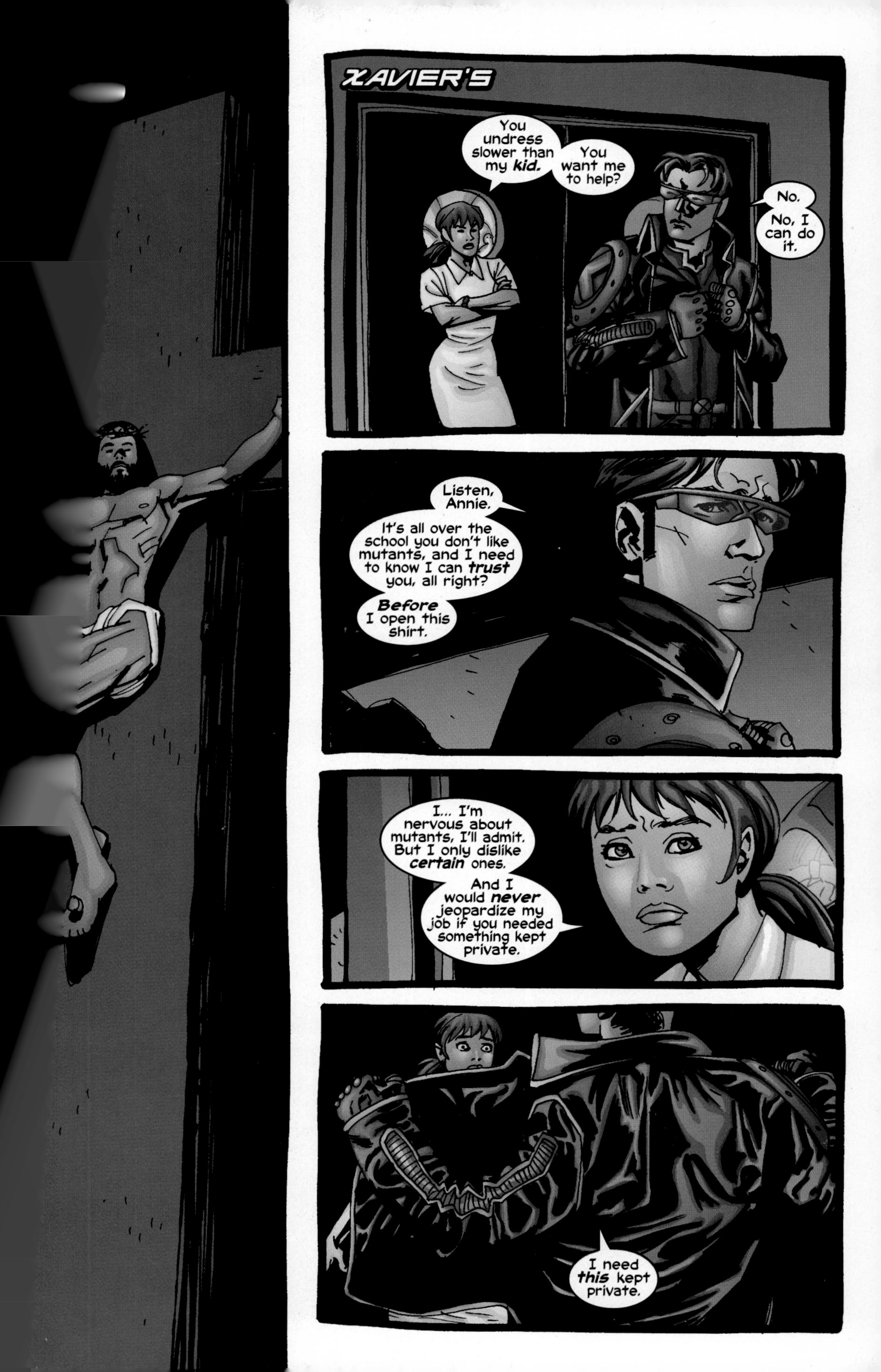
XAVIER'S
You undress slower than my kid.
You want me to help?
No.
No, I can do it.
Listen, Annie.
It's all over the school you don't like mutants, and I need to know I can trust you, all right?
Before I open this shirt.
I... I'm nervous about mutants, I'll admit. But I only dislike certain ones.
And I would never jeopardize my job if you needed something kept private.
I need this kept private.

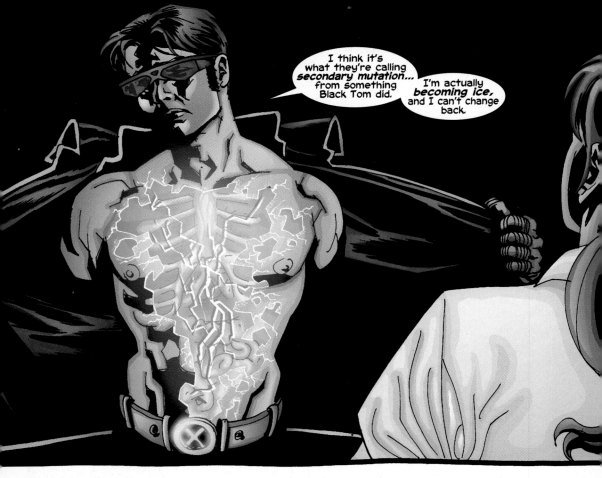

I think it's what they're calling *secondary mutation*... from something Black Tom did.

I'm actually *becoming ice*, and I can't change back.

LATER...

Thanks for the check-up, Annie.

So... when you gonna get up off your lazy butt and start doing some *work* around this place, Northstar?

He can actually leave the infirmary now, for walks and meals, as long as it's not too strenuous.

If he wants.

Why don't you two go get something to eat?

Grab some *dinner* together?

Well, I --

-- uh --

Yeah, come on. The Dining Commons is still open.

I'll buy.

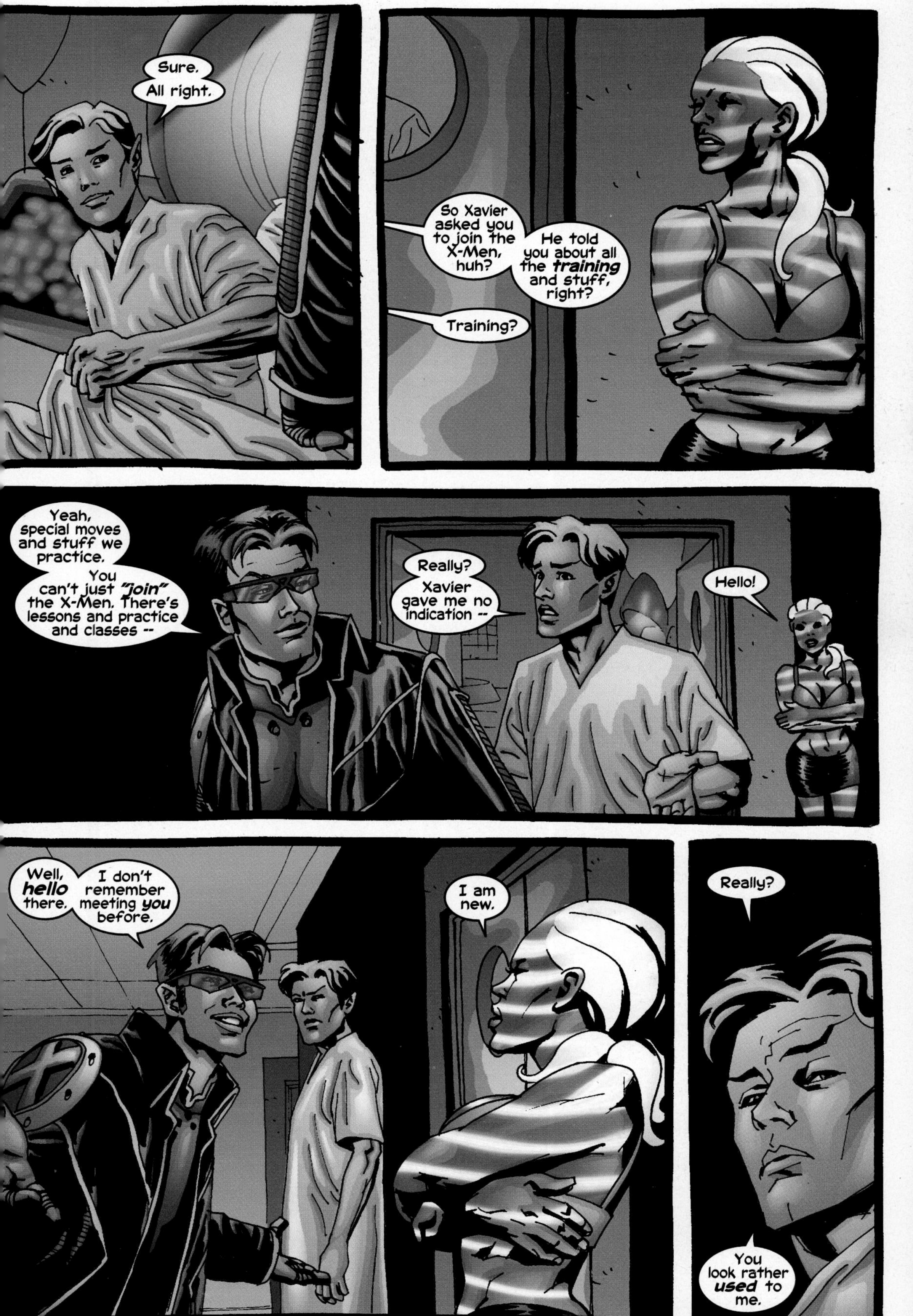
Sure.
All right.
So Xavier asked you to join the X-Men, huh?
He told you about all the *training* and stuff, right?
Training?
Yeah, special moves and stuff we practice.
You can't just *"join"* the X-Men. There's lessons and practice and classes --
Really?
Xavier gave me no indication --
Hello!
Well, *hello* there.
I don't remember meeting *you* before.
I am new.
Really?
You look rather *used* to me.

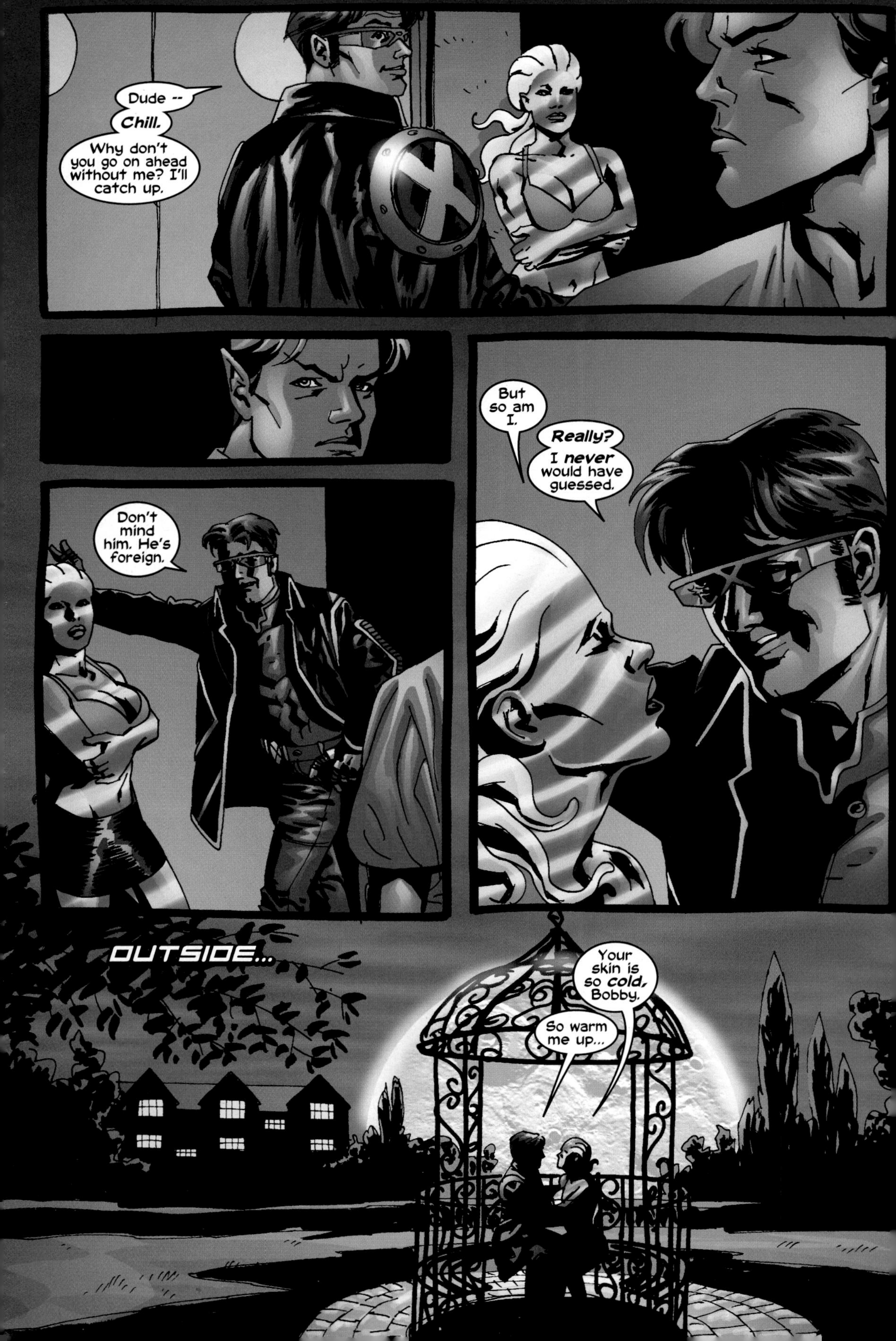

Dude --
Chill.
Why don't you go on ahead without me? I'll catch up.
Don't mind him. He's foreign.
But so am I.
Really? I never would have guessed.
OUTSIDE...
Your skin is so cold, Bobby.
So warm me up...

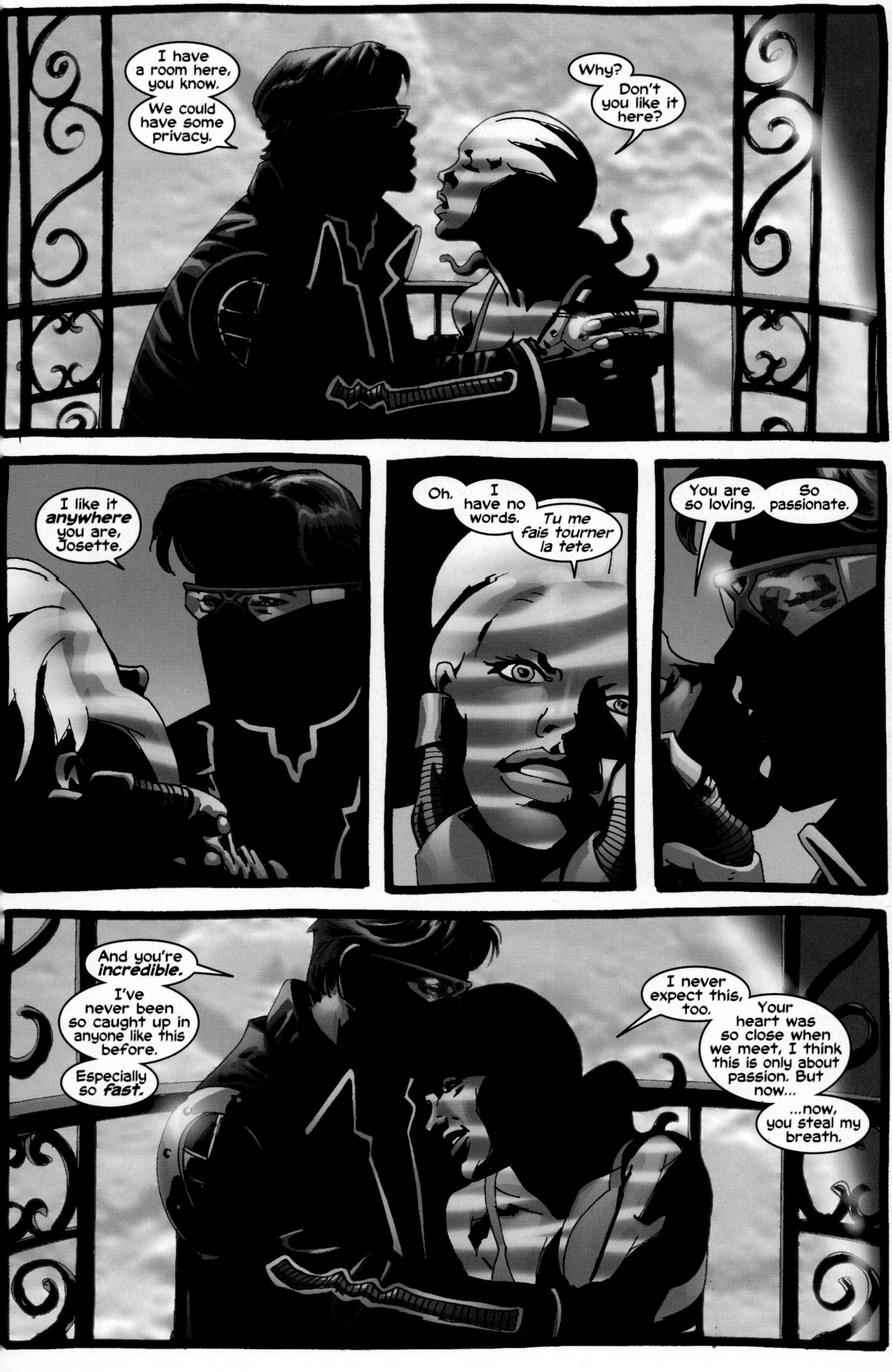

I have a room here, you know.
We could have some privacy.
Why? Don't you like it here?
I like it *anywhere* you are, Josette.
Oh,
I have no words.
Tu me fais tourner la tete.
You are so loving.
So passionate.
And you're *incredible.*
I've never been so caught up in anyone like this before.
Especially so *fast.*
I never expect this, too.
Your heart was so close when we meet, I think this is only about passion. But now...
...now, you steal my breath.

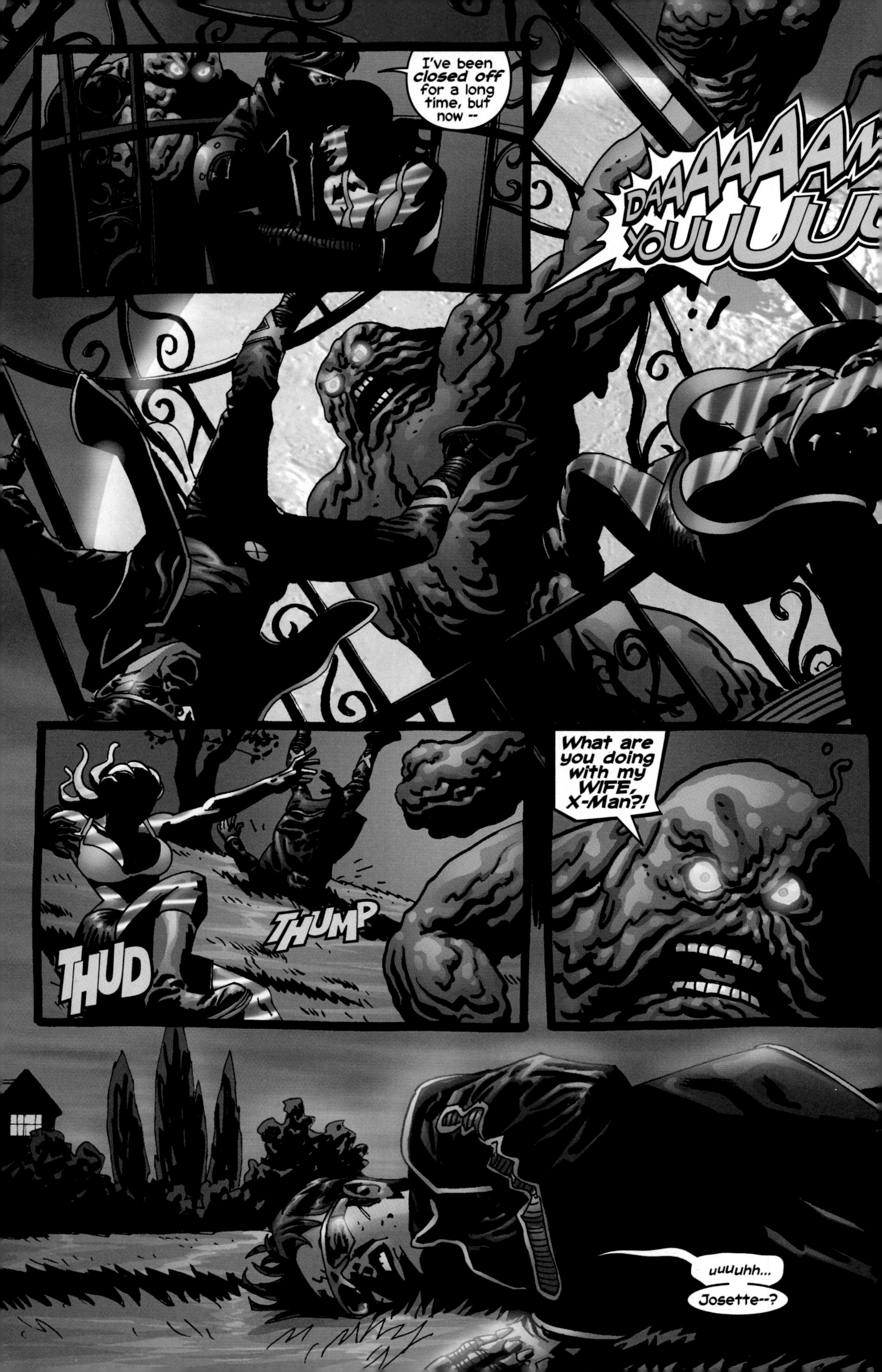
I've been closed off for a long time, but now --
DAAAAAAM
YOUUUUU
THUD
THUMP
What are you doing with my WIFE, X-Man?!
uuuuhh...
Josette--?

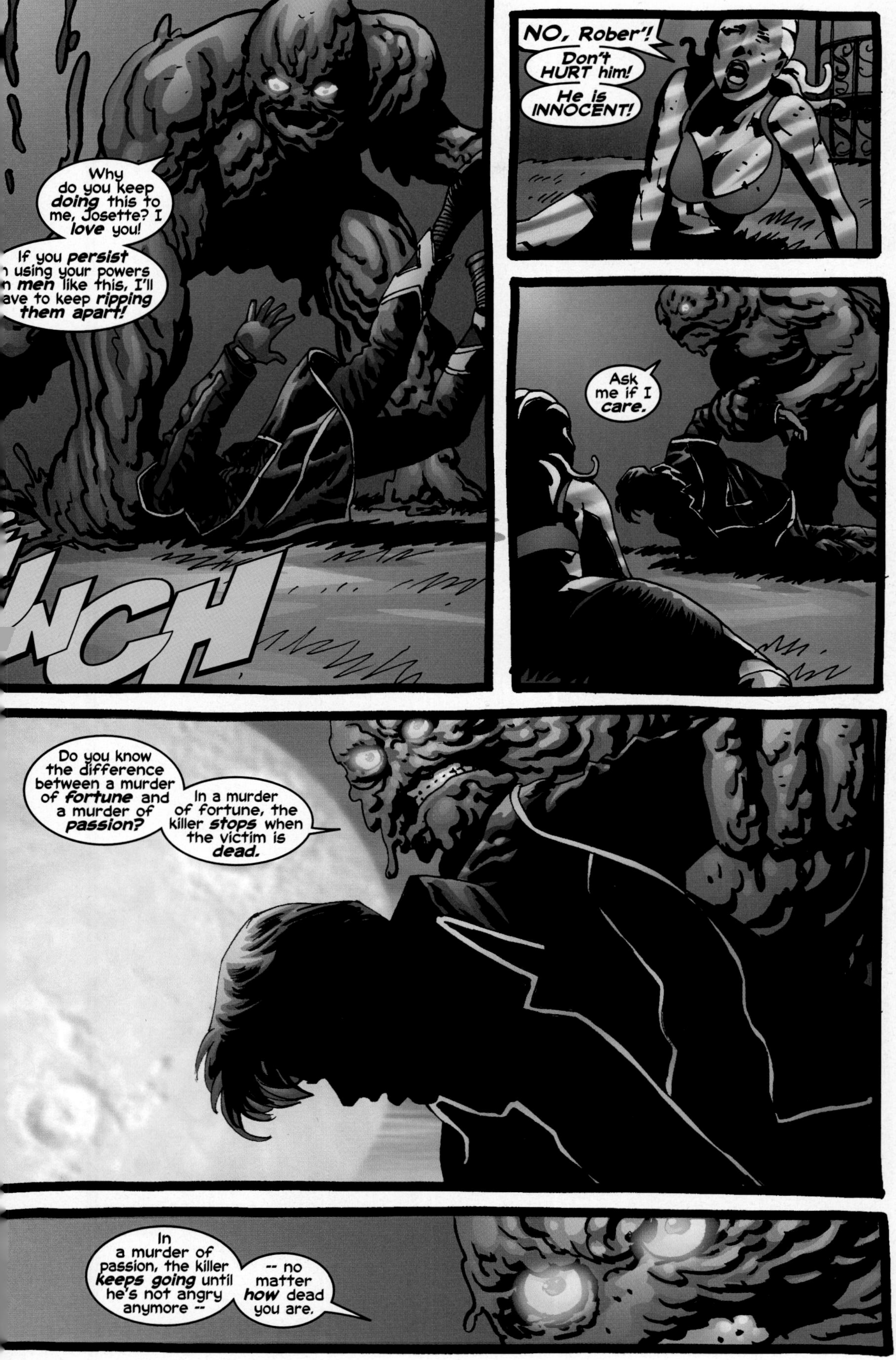
Why do you keep *doing* this to me, Josette? I *love* you!
If you *persist* in using your powers on *men* like this, I'll have to keep *ripping them apart!*
NCH
NO, Rober'!
Don't HURT him!
He is INNOCENT!
Ask me if I *care.*
Do you know the difference between a murder of *fortune* and a murder of *passion?*
In a murder of fortune, the killer *stops* when the victim is *dead.*
In a murder of passion, the killer *keeps going* until he's not angry anymore --
-- no matter *how* dead you are.

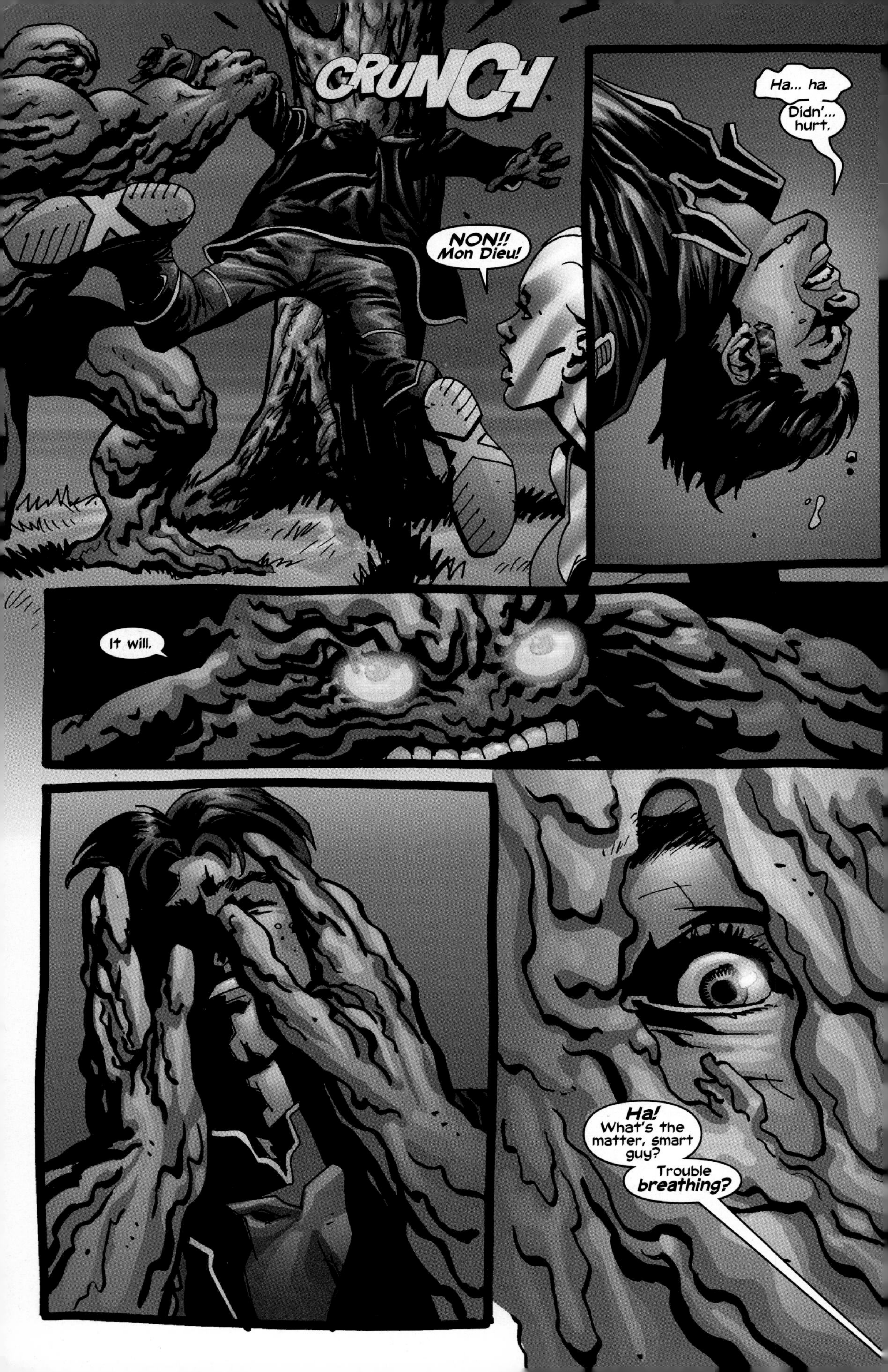
CRUNCH
Ha... ha.
Didn'... hurt.
NON!! Mon Dieu!
It will.
Ha! What's the matter, smart guy?
Trouble breathing?

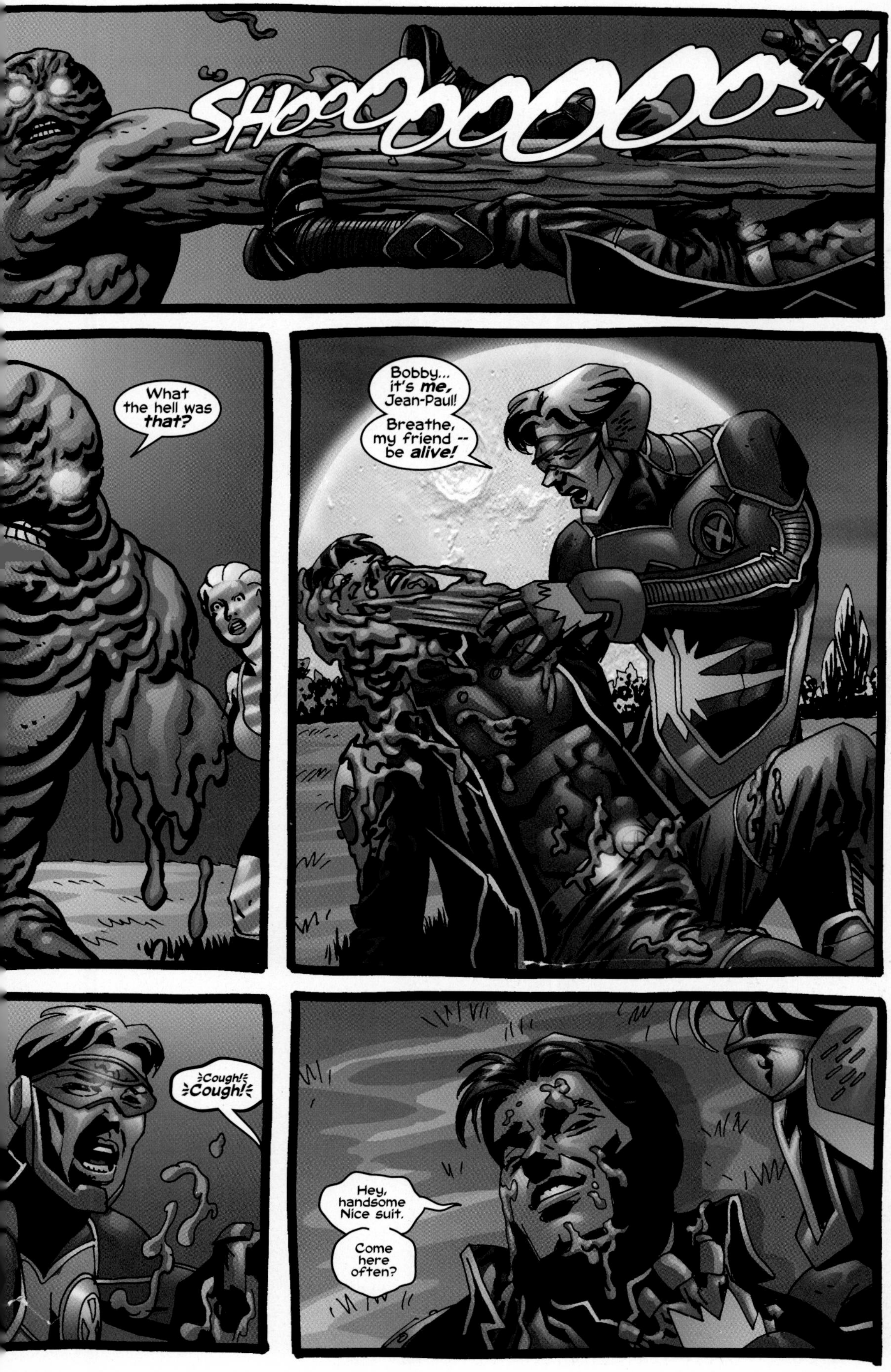
SHOOOOOOOOOOSH
What the hell was that?
Bobby... it's me, Jean-Paul!
Breathe, my friend -- be alive!
Cough! Cough!
Hey, handsome Nice suit.
Come here often?

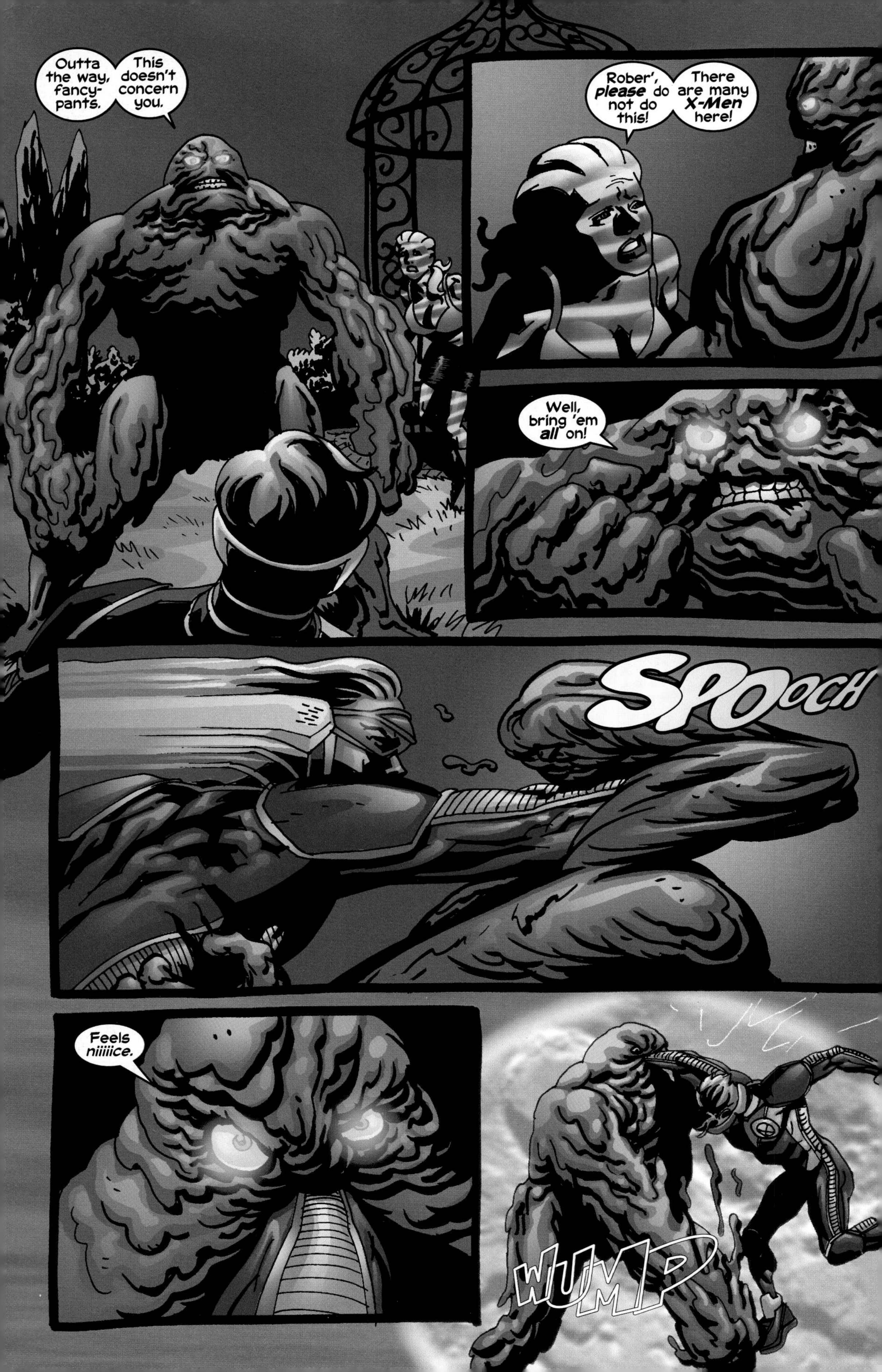
Outta the way, fancy-pants.
This doesn't concern you.
Rober', please do not do this!
There are many X-Men here!
Well, bring 'em all on!
SPOOCH
Feels niiiiice.
WUMP

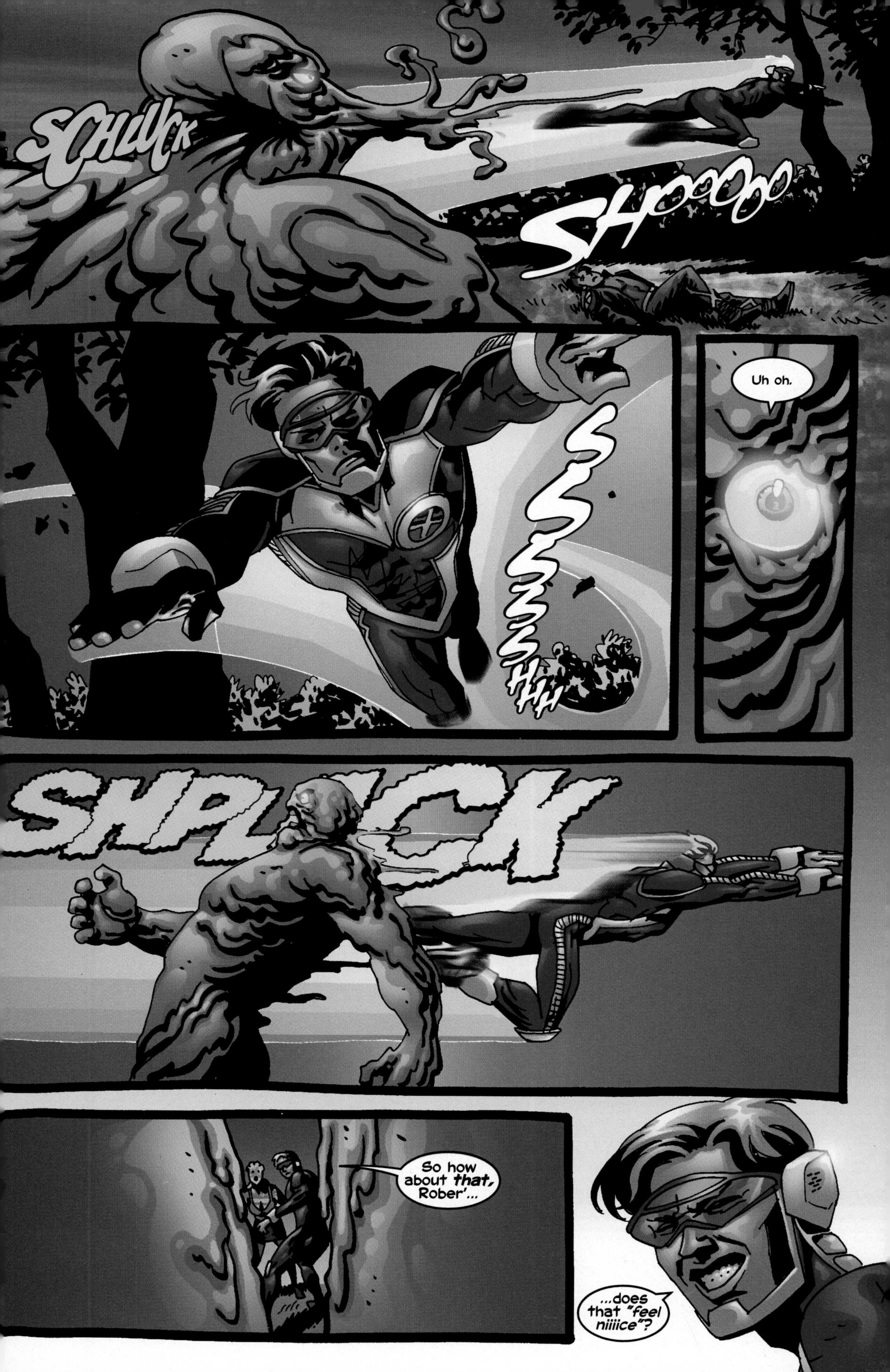
SCHLUCK
SHOOOOOO
SSSSSSHHH
Uh oh.
SHPLACK
So how about *that,* Rober'...
...does that "feel niiiice"?

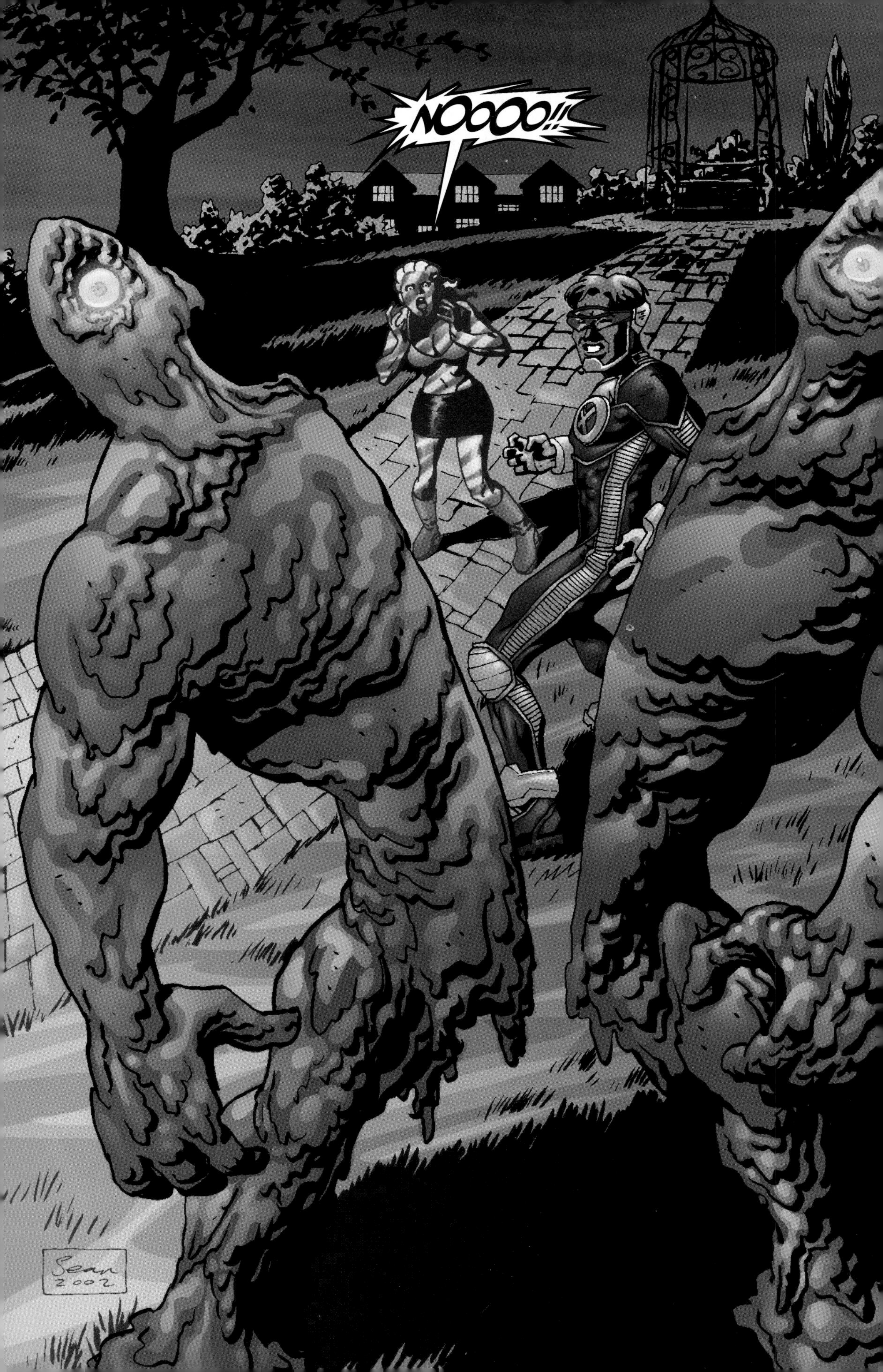
NOOOO!!
Sean 2002

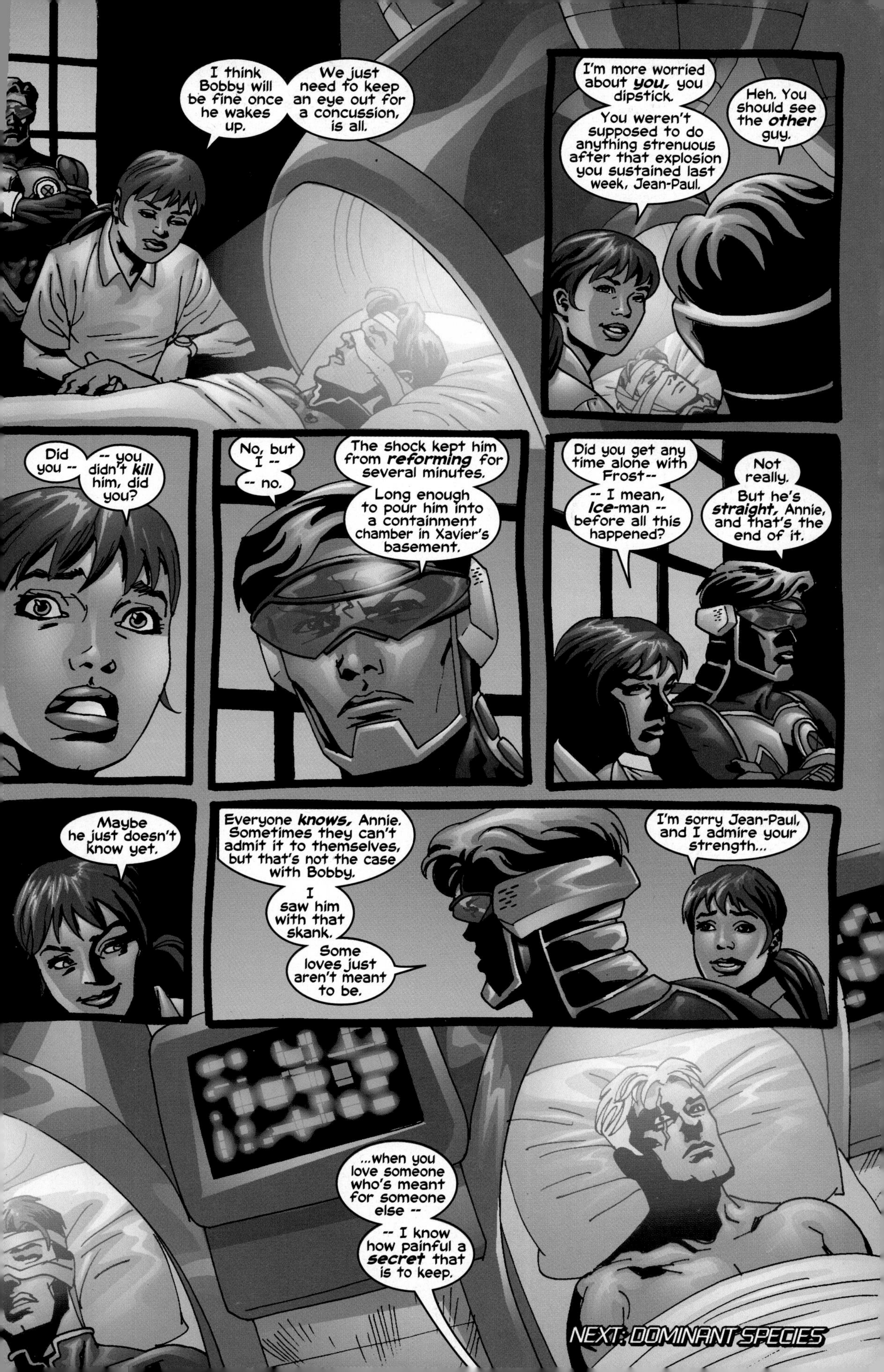
I think Bobby will be fine once he wakes up.
We just need to keep an eye out for a concussion, is all.
I'm more worried about ***you,*** you dipstick.
You weren't supposed to do anything strenuous after that explosion you sustained last week, Jean-Paul.
Heh. You should see the ***other*** guy.
Did you --
-- you didn't ***kill*** him, did you?
No, but I --
-- no.
The shock kept him from ***reforming*** for several minutes.
Long enough to pour him into a containment chamber in Xavier's basement.
Did you get any time alone with Frost--
-- I mean, ***Ice***-man -- before all this happened?
Not really.
But he's ***straight,*** Annie, and that's the end of it.
Maybe he just doesn't know yet.
Everyone ***knows,*** Annie. Sometimes they can't admit it to themselves, but that's not the case with Bobby.
I saw him with that skank.
Some loves just aren't meant to be.
I'm sorry Jean-Paul, and I admire your strength...
...when you love someone who's meant for someone else --
-- I know how painful a ***secret*** that is to keep.
NEXT: DOMINANT SPECIES